A Rhino Through the Looking Glass

© William Etheridge

Published in 2024 by The Bruges Group

ISBN: 978-1-7393152-6-9

The Bruges Group Publications Office
246 Linen Hall, 162-168 Regent Street, London W1B 5TB
www.brugesgroup.com

Bruges Group publications are not intended to represent a corporate view of European and international developments. Contributions are chosen on the basis of their intellectual rigour and their ability to open up new avenues for debate.

Scan me for Bruges Group

Twitter @brugesgroup, LinkedIn @brugesgroup
GETTR @brugesgroup, Telegram t.me/brugesgroup, Facebook @brugesgroup
Instagram @brugesgroup, YouTube @brugesgroup

A Rhino Through the Looking Glass

"Why, sometimes I've believed as many as six impossible things before breakfast".
Through the Looking Glass, Lewis Carroll.

"The Rhino" is a nickname given to me by my ex-wife.

William Etheridge

www.brugesgroup.com

Summary

Sex, booze, politics, intrigue, betrayal, danger... now I've got your attention, I would like to tell you *my* story.

This is the autobiographical story of how a man born to a relatively normal family from a modest background in the West Midlands managed to achieve national prominence through a series of often hilarious and always honestly recounted exploits and misadventures.

Dealing with the reality of the issues behind the headlines, *A Rhino Through the Looking Glass* is a brutally honest story of the highs and lows of a life led with the motto that there are always possibilities.

From depictions of life growing up in Wolverhampton in the 1970s to depictions and anecdotes about encounters with huge names in politics, sports and entertainment, this book is a unique journal of a life that has, at times, stretched the boundaries of credulity in its levels of drama.

Featuring encounters with three different British Prime Ministers, World Champion sportsmen and international pop stars, as well as a very long working relationship with Nigel Farage, the book is packed with fascinating stories.

Contents

List of Illustrations

In the Beginning

I like to watch programmes about true crime, particularly psychopaths and serial killers. Indeed, on one occasion, I was fortunate enough to spend some time with TV psychologist Emma Kenny, who has made a career of specialising in these people who embark on strange misadventures with very little grasp of reality.

Usually, you tend to find that these notorious characters have had some kind of awful experience in childhood that has traumatised them and allowed their particular strand of insanity to come flying to the forefront, enabling them to suspend the standard belief systems and limitations that most of us live by. Having done the research and begun writing this book, it struck me that the reader, at a casual glance, might suppose that my life has been a much less violent but no less peculiar version of these strange characters with their lack of a grasp on reality and their unrealistic aims and ideas.

Let me set your mind at rest. Despite having spent some time tracing my ancestry and finding a reasonable number of my forefathers had either spent time in lunatic asylums or been deported for some form of criminality, which could have been anything from stealing an apple to something much more sinister, my childhood and upbringing was blissful. No, there are no horrifying moments in my childhood that could account for what I concede to be somewhat odd behaviour during my life; in fact, quite the opposite.

My parents were and always have been my life's most supportive and loving people. Married in 1966, thereby having the event somewhat overshadowed by Messrs Moore, Charlton, and Hurst, they have enjoyed the kind of loving marriage many of us can only dream of. As regards their parenting, they were always kind and loving whilst establishing ground rules and ensuring that I had to work to earn pocket money and praise. So basically, it's all as it should be.

My dad taught me how to play football, cricket, tennis, badminton, and table tennis from a very early age. He made a point of always making time for me even though he worked many long hours as an accountant and even more hours passing further exams and doing coursework at home. He had a few strict rules, which stood me in good stead in later years. He never let me win at anything; I had to always fight for victory, and he would not accept my demands or even use the words "I want" when it came to toys. I was allowed to write what I wanted in a letter to Santa, but there was absolutely no guarantee it would come to pass. My mom was the perfect foil for this, always showing a deeply loving feeling towards me, spending time helping me learn how to read before I even started school and regaling me with tales of King Arthur and other magical figures of folklore. She also introduced me to a love of psychedelic heavy rock, with her favourite band being Eric Clapton's 60s supergroup "Cream."

I spent a lot of time with my Grandparents, who were just as much the ideal version as my parents are. One set of grandparents were from deep in the Black Country, speaking in a very rich local dialect that anyone from more than three or four miles away would never have understood. Nan, with her fussy but always loving approach, usually wearing a hairnet and smoking a cigarette, and Grandad, the strong, quiet ex-foundry worker who spent many comfortable hours smoking his pipe in his armchair and passing the occasional word about football with me, were very good to me, and I always felt cared for in their company.

My other Grandparents on the Etheridge side were a very strong influence on me growing up. Grandad was very much the man of the house but always had time for his grandson. He still had a lot of the army about him, having served in a tank during World War 2, but he was also great fun. I vividly remember him coming to my room one evening at the age of four years old to wish me goodnight on one of my many weekend stays. Seeing my light on, he actually uttered the following words, and from his strong but kind Lancastrian accent, it didn't sound ridiculous: "Are you a man or a mouse?" He then retired to bed only for his macho grandparenting to be undone some ten minutes later as Grandma crept into my room, put her finger to her lips, and switched the light back on. I spent many wonderful times with my grandparents, playing endless games of cards and eating tonnes of homemade cakes. Grandma outlived Grandad by many years, and even into young adulthood and my twenties, I spent a lot of time with her, often taking her out to eat the kind of exotic foods that Grandad's puritanical tastes would not have allowed, such luxuries as curry and Chinese food were real eye-openers to her and we thoroughly enjoyed our adventures together.

We were not a wealthy family by any means. Both of my parents had hailed from council estates and a line of people as working class as you can imagine. My dad worked very long and extremely stressful hours as an accountant before coming home and continuing to study to get better qualifications in his chosen field. For the first few years of my life, my mom still worked part-time. It was a family that used to be classed as aspirational working class.

Despite his long hours, Dad always found time to play sports or a board game with me. As I grew older, he would tie the playing of games to how much homework I had successfully completed. I didn't get a set amount of pocket money; the amount was limited to how well I had done at school or in a sporting activity. I received a cash bonanza of nearly £1 when I learned to swim, and both dad and grandad chipped in.

Despite our limited funds, my childhood, excluding the time I spent at school, which was the closest I hope to come to Hell, was a wonderfully happy time. Each Christmas was truly magical, with mom going out of her way to decorate the house to perfection, presents wrapped with bows, and Christmas dinner always a feast that seemed sprinkled with magic. Dad had the tradition of reading A Christmas Carol initially to me and eventually with me, starting on the first of December and perfectly timed to end on Christmas Eve. He would attempt to do all of the voices of the different characters, which, whilst not particularly effective, was definitely funny.

I always had gifts to open on Christmas morning, which I was absolutely convinced had been delivered by Father Christmas, although now I'm in my fifties, I have a sneaking suspicion that may have been stealthily placed there in a sack by my mother displaying Ninja-like agility and silent movement. I did not know at the time that those gifts were mainly bought second-hand after Dad had placed an advert in the post office window, but it would not have mattered anyhow. Action Man, Toy Soldiers, model ships, and spacecraft were things of wonder to me, and I didn't care where they had come from or how much they had cost.

Being short of money, we did not have foreign holidays; indeed, any holiday at all was quite the occasion. We spent time in dark and rainy Welsh coastal resorts, with the occasional stay in Devon if we were lucky.

My happiest recollections of holidays include memories of walking across windswept shingle beaches in Wales wrapped up in my parka with Mom bravely leading the way through the pouring rain. Another memory is of the dreaded moments when Dad declared that my Dad and I were "going on an adventure." This effectively meant that we would walk for miles fairly aimlessly, with a highlight being an occasional fossil or ruined castle. On one occasion, we got hopelessly lost in Devon and were still walking late into the night in the dark. It was not all bad, though, as we had company from bats that appeared determined to dive bomb us as we sought to navigate the country lanes.

I did have another version of a holiday, though. My Nan and Grandad took me on a coach trip to Blackpool to see the illuminations for several years. I was invariably travel sick to Blackpool, using up several plastic bags to catch the vomit, much to the displeasure of my fellow travellers. Then, when we arrived in Blackpool, it was compulsory that we visited the arcades to see if Grandad could win on the "penny falls" machines. Despite hours of dropping in one and two-pence pieces with great concentration, I do not believe he ever did win anything. After that, we had to get the tram to Fleetwood to savour what were the best fish and chips in the world, as I was reliably and very seriously informed by my Nan. After that, it was back to Blackpool to join the coach and marvel at the illuminations as it slowly drove through them, then a journey back to Wolverhampton, during which I would vomit up everything I had eaten and drunk all day, sadly including the world's most excellent fish and chips.

On one memorable occasion, I managed to change the order of things. I noticed a sign saying "Doctor Who Exhibition" This was a marvellous thing to see. I had grown up watching John Pertwee as the flamboyant Time Lord bravely leading his team of Sarah Jane Smith, Brigadier Lethbridge Stewart, and the troops of UNIT into battle against Daleks, The Master, and, of course, Sea Devils, amongst other monsters.

I begged my grandparents to take me to the exhibition. Nan finally gave way and agreed to accompany me, with Grandad declaring he would stay outside to smoke his pipe as the whole thing was "Saftness." We entered the exhibition, and it was beautiful. The theme music was blasting out as we entered and walked past glass display cases containing recreations of various enemies of humanity. It then culminated in a perfectly laid-out room as the TARDIS's control room. This was almost more exciting than I could stand, but it was unexpectedly becoming even more exciting.

My Nan was a tiny woman but extremely forthright and not shy about expressing an opinion. She was standing with me fairly disinterestedly as I played with various nobs and levers on the TARDIS control panel when, out of the corner of my eye, I saw a rather prominent figure shambling towards her. One of the Doctor's most fearsome opponents was the Sea Devils. Dressed in rags, they had heads resembling a very large Amphibian and were not the prettiest-looking creatures in the universe. Someone in the management team of the exhibition had decided it would be good fun to get someone to dress as a Sea Devil and shamble around, giving people a humorous moment and a bit of fun. Sure enough, the man in the Sea Devil outfit approached my nan and put his hand on her shoulder; he couldn't possibly have anticipated the reaction. She screamed, slapped his hand away and very loudly, in a broad Black Country accent, shouted, "What the bloody hell do you think you're doing, you bloody fool." She then grabbed my hand and dragged me out. Obviously concerned that he had caused some offence, the man chased after us, seeking to apologise, but unfortunately, he forgot to take his Sea Devil head off. As we were in the doorway, Nan turned round and launched another volley of abuse. "You nearly gave me a bloody heart attack, you daft bugger" Realising he should assure the elderly lady that he wasn't a monster that had dragged itself out of the sea to attack us, the gentleman removed his headpiece and followed us out of the exhibition only to be confronted by my grandad, who was a rather large tough-looking foundry worker, pipe firmly clenched between his teeth staring directly at him as my breathless nan was looking in her handbag for a heart tablet. There followed a brief moment when the ex-Sea Devil deliberated, trying to appease us further, then decided It may be a little too dangerous, and he vanished into the exhibition. Grandad looked down at me to see I was OK, then took Nan's hand and led us away, simply saying, "Come on, wench, no more saftness."

It was a wonderful childhood, and I could write a whole book about it, but I'm pretty sure that's not what people are reading this book for, so I will leave it there.

So, there is no real explanation for the madness that follows, so embrace it and hopefully enjoy the exploits I have to recount with laughter and perhaps a slight bemusement; I know I did!

Education

Unlike the majority of people I would encounter later in life, I attended a state school. More specifically, an inner-city comprehensive in Wolverhampton.

Educationally, it was not great. The main focus of my day-to-day schooling was to try and get through the day without being beaten up or to have some strange and exciting new torture inflicted on me.

As a youngster, I was pretty tall but skinny and, most importantly of all, something of a nerd in the eyes of my fellow pupils. I was the kid who always attended with the correct school uniform, a new satchel, and my own stationery set. I was the weirdo who tried to engage in the lessons and follow the teachers' instructions. I was the "Posh boy" who didn't have a strong accent or speak in slang, and I was the kid who had been told that fighting was wrong by his parents. In short, I had a huge target painted on me from day one.

As well as regular beatings at the hands of the other kids, I was also subjected to some extra special treatment like being stabbed with multiple drawing pins, having pennies thrown at me, and everyone's favourite party treat being held down and forced to swallow "Daddy Long Legs" by the dozen when the season was right. I also had my belongings regularly stolen and my satchels slashed by pen knives on more than one occasion.

Yes, those were happy days. It seemed I was continually bullied and targeted until reaching the age of fifteen; I had something of a change of heart and started being moderately violent back. On one occasion, a kid spat in my face; I saw red, chased him around the playground and beat him until he fell to the floor before finishing the event with a swift, well-directed kick. A few minutes later, I had calmed down and walked away from the scene, not feeling particularly proud of myself and dreading what my parents would say if they found out. I was rather surprised to find the flood of new friends whom I gained when the word got out that I had performed an act of violence. I began to be accepted or at least tolerated.

When I entered the sixth form at the school, I was of sufficient size and reputation not to be the butt of bullies anymore. I began to enjoy my education a little more and learn things. It helped that most of the vicious kids from my year didn't carry on to the sixth form. Briefly thinking back, I can tally several armed robbers, a kidnapper, and a murderer amongst those who mercifully left the school before we witnessed them achieve their full potential. One of them had publicly beaten the headmaster in what was known as "The quad" space between our multi-story blocks of classrooms. I vividly recall the headmaster on his knees with blood streaming down his head as the fifteen-year-old future murderer beat him viciously with a bicycle chain whilst kids were leaning out of the class windows chanting, "Kill, Kill" Ah yes, those were the days.

In the sixth form, I had the great privilege of being taught by one of those teachers who changed my life through their general approach and attitude. Chris Withey was head of sixth form and our History A level teacher. He looked quite like Jermy Corbyn, and his politics were very similar to comrade Corbyn's, but he believed in stimulating debate as a method of teaching. We would always begin lessons with a brief debate about the news of the day, where I would inevitably be drawn into a Thatcherite diatribe in response to his deliberately provocative Marxist openings to the lesson. We would then move on to the actual lessons, and rather than just learning history, we discussed it and tried to understand the reasons why certain events had happened, and people had behaved in the ways they had. There was another great advantage to Chris. He would allow a few of us to load into his car at lunchtime, and we would all go for a pint just far enough away from the school so that we would not be noticed. He was a great guy, and we kept in touch for many years after I left school, enjoying some uproarious pub crawls around his home town of Shrewsbury, debating and bantering as we went. It was thanks to Chris Withey that I became seriously interested in the effect of politics on modern history and how what had happened in the past inevitably comes back in a slightly different form to happen in the future.

After leaving the sixth form, I was unsure what to do, so I entered into further education. I attended Wolverhampton Polytechnic and was enlisted on a new course called Business Information Technology, which, broadly translated, meant it was a cross between Business Studies and Information Technology. The most notable thing about my time at the polytechnic was that I shared a class for a while with Suzie Perry, who would later become a moderately famous TV presenter hosting "The Gadget Show" and working on Motor racing coverage. She was very beautiful, very intelligent, very nice and very much out of my league despite a few utterly pathetic and somewhat embarrassed efforts to strike up conversations.

I learned the importance of teamwork at the Polytechnic. It was soon very apparent that I was utterly useless at the "IT" part of the course but reasonably adequate at Business Studies. I teamed up with a couple of lads, Lawrence and Dave, and we basically took turns doing each other's assignments. The only issue arose when we were supposed to write a computer programme and then had to demonstrate it. These moments were among the first times that I learned the importance of being able to think on my feet and bluff my way through a situation in which I knew nothing at all about what I was doing. It is a skill that stood me in good stead for many years to come.

We did enjoy a couple of great nights out at the Student Union. It was split into two parts. Upstairs was the Mandela bar, and downstairs, which was bigger with a stage, was called the Biko bar. Names that really sum up the times we were living through. They also had savagely subsidised beer prices, meaning that even skint students could get very drunk on cheap Ruddles Bitter on draft.

I saw two very notable bands perform at the Biko bar. One was The Quire Boys, who I believe are still going strong some thirty-plus years later. They performed a great set of pure Rock and Roll music, which featured a drunken guitarist falling off the stage but continuing to play. Then they joined a few of us at the bar for even more beer with the whole sum of their conversation and answer to every question seeming to be, "Look, man, it's rock and roll, dude." As general and repeated answers go, it's a pretty strong one. The other notable performer was "the Rebel MC", who, according to the lyrics of his most popular song, was all about being "Fresh like a Ninja, stinging like a Bee." He proved this by punching the head of the student union to remove him from the stage to great applause from the assembled crowd.

It was at one of these events that I witnessed my first-ever police raid. I noticed a commotion at the door, and then someone grabbed the microphone and shouted that the police were there. I can honestly say I have never seen so many people move so quickly towards the toilets. The sound of the band had been suspended as the police went about their business, and the only sound you could actually hear was the constant flushing of toilets. If the old Urban Myth about Alligators living in the sewers is true, the ones living in Wolverhampton certainly got extremely high that night.

I also learned a little about computers and business studies during my time at the Polytechnic. I also learned the wonders of a drink called Green Damage. This was the staple of most of the students there at my time. A mixture of Cider, Lager, Orange Juice, and Blue Bols liquor, if exposed to the right kind of light in an otherwise dimly lit bar, glowed green. It was also extremely potent and certainly made the days fly by quite quickly, as well as ensuring a very solid eight hours of sleep literally anywhere you laid your head.

Sport

Sport is a metaphor for life. I firmly believe you can tell more about a person and their character from playing sports with them than you can from hours of conversation or researching them on the internet.

Bill on the cricket pitch

As a young man, I was able to play most sports thanks to my dad teaching me almost as soon as I could walk. Being able to play is, however, not the same as being any good. I was able to hold a game and compete at most things, but Cricket was the one and only sport I have ever excelled at. Now, anyone reading this who has played cricket with me over the last few years has probably just collapsed in hysterical laughter as they read the fat, bald, slow old guy who can't score any runs when batting due to not being able to properly see the ball and bowls a selection of extremely slow spinners in a style which has been compared to "Chucking pies" and was once referred to by former England Test Match player Neale Radford as looking like I was throwing "fucking grenades" but hold your laughter a moment chaps it wasn't always this way.

Back in 1981, my parents decided to take me to my first international cricket match. I had already attended a few football matches at the Wolves, with my debut being as a fan there in 1974, but this was my first cricket match. As it turned out, it was to be the last day of an England versus Australia Ashes Test match. The ground was not full, as it seemed almost certain that the Australians were going to win and win easily. As we settled into our seats that day, we had no idea we were about to see something magical that would change my life forever. England was bowling, and from one end, the huge figure of local hero Bob Willis was charging in as if his life depended, with his mop of fuzzy hair flying behind him as he flew to the wicket. At the other end, the bowler was a young, powerful-looking man by the name of Ian Botham. We witnessed an absolute cricket miracle that day. Botham took 5 Australian wickets, conceding only one run. The atmosphere was beyond electric, the intensity was overwhelming, and the sheer force of nature that Botham became that day was as spectacular to watch as if the ground had been overwhelmed by a violent thunderstorm with lightning striking Australian wickets at incredibly regular intervals. On taking the final wicket, the entity named Botham ran down to the stumps and held the middle stump aloft above his head like King Kong bellowing atop the Empire State Building, holding a captured aircraft in his giant hands. It was a moment that will never leave me as long as I live. From that moment, I was determined to be the next Ian Botham.

Strange to say it now, but as a young man, I was pencil-thin and could run fast. As a teenager, I grew my hair to shoulder-length partly in homage to my heavy rock heroes in bands like Whitesnake and Deep Purple, but also because that's how Ian Beefy Botham had his. I was a quick bowler, and I could bat a bit as well, mainly dealing in boundaries and shots, which were at the time considered wild, but in the modern era of T20, Cricket probably wouldn't raise an eyelid.

I actually got to the point where I was selected to play for the Shropshire Under 16s side against Somerset, but as with the vast majority of youngsters who want to make a career out of sport, I was good but not good enough. I have played cricket my whole life, it seems, with a few gaps for having to be involved in piffling matters like campaigning for Brexit and seemingly endless elections. I played for Claverley in Shropshire from 1984 to 2022 and have played for Springhill in Wolverhampton since then.

During that time, my cricketing claims to fame have been to have bowled against South African Test Match player Claude Henderson, who scored a century against my bowling, and an eleven-year-old playing for Wolverhampton called Vikram Solanki, who later went on to have a very good career playing for Worcester and England. He scored a hundred against my bowling as well.

Now, I know you non-cricketers will probably be yawning at this point, but let me tell you, cricket isn't all about what takes place on the pitch. In fact, when you play at the level I've played at, it has almost nothing to do with what happens on the pitch; it has everything to do with the drunken antics that take place afterwards. Many of our away games for Claverley were in the Worcester area, so what a great excuse for us all to hit Worcester city centre after the match. We all behaved outrageously, but our skipper at the time, "Gaz", was particularly prolific with the ladies. On one occasion, we were all back in the vehicles waiting to go home, with many of us very much the worse for wear, but we couldn't leave until Gaz had finished saying his goodbyes to a local lady he had met that evening underneath a bridge near the carpark. It was taking a while, so we all decided to hit the scene with headlights on full beam in the hope of speeding things up or bringing them to a conclusion. How wrong we were as Gaz took this as a spotlight to perform to, and we were treated to another five minutes of his naked backside thrusting into his more than willing and not at all shy new friend. He even paused to wave and hurl abuse at us. Oh, how the camera phone has changed things; if only that piece of technology had been available, we would have had a very spectacular video to add to the club's end-of-season presentation.

The absolute highlight of my time playing cricket came in 2015 when I was invited to play in a Rest of the World XI against the British Judiciary XI at the famous New Road cricket ground home of Worcester Cricket Club. Our side was Captained by Neale Radford, who I had spent much of my younger years watching perform heroics for Worcester, and he had a surprisingly brief career playing Test and One Day Cricket for England. Amongst other notable former top-quality players was cricket legend Collis King. Collis had been an all-rounder playing for the West Indies, and his most famous moment was partnering the "Master Blaster" himself, Sir Vivian Richards, to victory in the World Cup final of 1979. Despite being over sixty, Collis still played at a decent club level in the North of England and, as he showed during the game, could still hit a cricket ball a very long way. During one drinks break, Collis beckoned me to join him, and as the other players drank water and juice on the pitch, we nipped into the club bar and quickly put away a couple of Bacardi and Cokes. It just doesn't get better than that, in my opinion.

My performance in the game was understandably not exactly up to the standard of the other players, but I managed to bowl a few overs and actually took a wicket. Ever direct, when it was the end of my spell Captain Radford patted me on the shoulder and said, "Good spell, take a break", following it up with a cheeky grin and saying, "thank Fuck, that's over."

Seeking to make up for my shoddy bowling, I tried to field up to a decent standard, on one occasion diving full length to stop a ball. I was used to playing in village cricket grounds with very lush outfields where you can dive, and it's like landing on a mattress. I can testify that the outfield at New Road was nothing like that; I felt like I had landed on granite, and every bone in my body jangled on impact as the ball whizzed past me for a boundary.

As we left the pitch, I chatted with Collis. A young boy ran onto the pitch with a printed scorecard the club had distributed to the fans turning up for the day and asked for autographs. So there you have it, I have signed an autograph as a cricketer whilst walking off the pitch with a World Cup winner. If I live to be a hundred, I doubt many things will make me feel quite as good as that moment.

I played a lot of pub football from the age of eighteen to thirty-six when my knees, ankles, and general inability to move for the best part of a week after a game made it clear that it was time to stop. I was never very good, but I was notable for being a very heavy tackler and quite a vicious fouler. Indeed, my only sporting trophy is "Bulls Head Most Red Cards 1997."

When playing in the Sandwell league which is basically full of West Bromwich Albion fans, I used to wear the top of whatever pub I was representing at the time over a Wolves top which I would flash as brazenly as possible once I was on the pitch. Just in case anyone is in any doubt, West Brom and Wolves fans do not get along particularly well, and most of my football matches had more to do with elbows and fists than passes and goals.

Anyway, the point is I absolutely love sport. I even engaged in a ridiculously hard and dangerous sport for the first time when I was in my mid-forties. I took up boxing. Now, by any standards, that wasn't a very bright idea, but let me explain.

I was going through a very difficult time in my political life. I had been subjected to a concerted attack and a very unpleasant betrayal by a series of women who seemed determined to outdo each other to see just how much they could publicly humiliate me, and there was literally no space on my body for metaphorical daggers from people who were supposed to be on my side in my own party. I felt down, and I was drinking and eating to huge excess. I became ridiculously overweight rather than my normal "Morbidly obese". In despair, I asked a mate what he thought I should do to get myself together. His words have stayed with me to this day "I have got a mate called Richie, he's a boxing coach. He trains me sometimes and afterwards I'm trembling like a shitting dog." Well, who could resist that kind of recommendation and thus I began being trained by and ultimately developing a friendship with Richie Ghent.

Richie Ghent is a phenomenal bloke. In fact, he is exactly the kind of man who I would normally really be pissed off by. Over twenty years younger than me, ridiculously good looking and hard as nails, he is also blessed with extraordinary talent as a small businessman and, most of all, a fantastic boxing coach. To top it all off, he is an Albion fan, but despite all of that, we hit it off straight away. He listened to my tale of woe about how frankly horrific my life was at that stage and then trained me as he puts it "to destruction" regularly over a period of many months. I combined the world-class coaching I was getting from Richie with regular hypnotherapy sessions to get my mind clear and focussed, as well as tips from a UKIP supporter based in the North who was an excellent nutritionist and health expert and within seven months, I was down six stone, feeling great and if I say so myself looking pretty good.

Richie believes in setting tough targets, and it works. He currently has a growing stable of professional boxers who appear bound for glory and a huge number of male and female amateur fighters, all doing well. He achieves his results partly by a range of excellent techniques mixed with the hectoring style of a Sergeant Major, which he combines with a cheeky glint in his eye so that you want to do well so as not to let him down and partly by setting challenging targets that he instils the confidence in you to believe you can achieve. My target was a simple one: he was preparing me for an exhibition fight against a man fifteen years younger than me who had not only had over a hundred bouts but was an ex-Para! This was compounded by the fact that it was going to be in front of a paying crowd of three hundred and the cameras of the local newspaper. Believe me, this was excellent motivation to get myself into the best possible shape. I basically trained on physical fitness every day and lived on a diet of Tuna and boiled eggs in preparation for the fight.

My fellow MEPs in Brussels found this all extremely funny. In fact, Paul Nuttall offered to sponsor the bottom of my shoes as that was all he expected anyone to be able to see after I had suffered a first-round knockout. Unperturbed, I donned my running gear every lunchtime and ran to the park near the royal palace in Brussels, did a couple of circuits, and ran back each day.

On the night of the fight my dad and my uncle came to cheer me on along with a few friends and colleagues from the UK MEP office. My mother refused to come as she could not cope with seeing me knocked out as everyone had expected.

I walked to the ring with cameras flashing and my chosen walk-on music blaring. I had chosen "Still Unbroken" by American rock group Lynyrd Skynyrd as the words resonated with me with their focus on being old and having been through a lot but still standing and fighting. By the time I got to the ring, I felt pretty good and was ready to perform as a gladiator and give it my all. Then the lights dipped before dramatically coming on full, and my opponent walked to the ring swinging his hugely muscled arms as he moved to the ominous sound of "Enter Sandman" by Metallica. I must admit at that moment I had a feeling beyond panic or fear it was a feeling of resignation that I was about to be battered senseless in front of hundreds of people with detailed photos of it appearing on the front page of tomorrows newspaper.

Now, I'll let you in on a secret that I didn't know before the bout. Richie had told my opponent not to hit me in the face as I may have to appear on TV, and my opponent was happy to oblige as he was actually a UKIP supporter. I truly wish I had known this before the fight, as it may have diminished the feeling of impending doom.

The bell for the first round rang and I have never felt such adrenalin in my life, it was a rush beyond anything I have ever experienced and probably never will again. I started moving around and employing the techniques Richie had so meticulously taught me, extending a long jab whenever possible and keeping my form behind a tight guard. I managed to get through the first round with nothing but a few sharp jabs to the ribs to worry about, and my confidence grew. The second round started and I continued with my studied technique and form, suddenly an opportunity came out of nowhere. My opponent was showboating, and his guard was down perfectly within range of my right hand. I breathed in deeply and threw a right hook with every ounce of power I possessed. It landed flush on the side of his face and ... and there was absolutely no reaction, nothing not even a blink. In fact, I'm sure he smiled. My confidence evaporated quickly and I kept a distance for the rest of the round. My fast-diminishing confidence totally vanished between rounds when my corner man told me that I had made a massive mistake by landing that punch and that in the third and final round, my opponent was likely to try to floor me to restore his pride. Their instructions were simple "Stay the fuck away from him." The bell rang for the third and final round, and I can honestly say I spent the whole round trying everything short of literally sprinting to get away from him. I could hear the crowd baying for blood, my blood and I could hear my corner shouting in a frantic voice "Move, move, bloody get out of his way, move." It was the longest three minutes of my life but miraculously I avoided being demolished. With the beauty of respect that only boxing can instil between two contestants we embraced on the final bell and a friendship was forged.

My adrenalin was still pumping around me, at least at the speed of a comet hurtling through space after the bout. I downed three pints of lager without them touching the sides and would have had a fourth, but the bar had closed, and my uncle had decided to down my remaining pint for me. I got showered and changed and decided to head into Wolverhampton accompanied by a few friends. I ended up in the famous Giffard Arms rock bar, dancing wildly to heavy metal and drinking gallons of beer. For that brief period of about an hour or so, I felt that I was master of the world, totally invulnerable to harm and capable of seducing any woman that came my way. The adrenaline decided it had had enough and stopped pumping and I slumped to a chair struggling to breathe. In his efforts to avoid damaging my pretty face my opponent had managed to crack and bruise my ribs an injury which if you have not had it is let me tell you not very comfortable at all. The onset of reality continued with a stinking hangover the next day, but I still felt particularly proud of myself. My first boxing match had taken place in my late forties, and I had managed to survive largely intact.

Rhino in the ring

There would be two more visits to the ring in my brief sojourn into the world of exhibition and white-collar boxing. The first was a bout in Wolverhampton against a gentleman of a similar age and size to me called Billy. We trained long and hard for the fight sparring many rounds together and enduring plenty of banter from the lads at the gym with comments like "The bus from the old folks' home must have arrived" but we took it in good humour and were determined to put on a good show. We had every intention of displaying boxing skills in a calm and controlled exhibition of everything Richie had taught us. Unfortunately, on the night of the bout when we entered the ring the corner men forgot to give us the headguards we were supposed to wear and we both decided it was a golden opportunity to go for the knockout and all thoughts of a calm exhibition were abandoned. I dominated the first round coming out swinging with all I had and Billy was back on the ropes looking to survive by the end of the round. The second round was a more even affair as the two old timers took to the middle of the ring and a head-to-head slugging fest ensued. The third round was a nightmare for me I was literally punched out and could barely move my arms I had to spend much of it back on the ropes covering up as I could not muster the energy to swing. At the end the crowd gave us a huge cheer and despite there being no winner as it was officially an exhibition bout most people called it a draw and we were officially declared the fight of the night. At the end of the bout as I was still gasping for breath Richie came over and gave me an enormous bollocking pointing out that my exhaustion in the last round was a direct result of not training hard enough and he was right even though I could not get my breath enough at the time to say so.

My third and final fight was not an exhibition it was a win or lose bout as part of a charity event in Southampton. I had been challenged by a UKIP activist in the area by the name of Kim Rose. Although Kim was older and smaller than me, he was significantly fitter and put in several months of very hard training in preparation. I on the other hand was very slack and only started training properly a month or so before the fight. It was clear that I was going to go into the bout very overweight and not at all fit, so I needed to take drastic action.

I spoke to Dean Perks who was the guy who had originally introduced me and asked him to do some sparring with me. My logic was that sparring with Dean would toughen me up and prepare me for the fight, as it was highly unlikely Kim would be as good or strong as Dean. For context, Dean is a good friend and a nice guy. He is also six foot eight inches tall and a very good boxer with a professional fight in his history, as well as having been a good kickboxer in his day. Now my idea of sparring was clearly very different to Dean's I thought we would be going through the moves and hitting each other with the power taken out of the shots, just working on technique. It soon became very clear that was not Dean's impression of what we were there for. I had to work very hard over several rounds of sparring to stay alive, he was deceptively quick, working the angles jabbing me with his very long reach and throwing big right-handed bombs over the top of my guard. It was during this session that I was punched harder than I have ever been hit by anything in my life. I got my movement all wrong and walked onto a huge right hook unleashed by the very powerful Mr Perks. It landed flush on my temple, and for a moment, I felt like my soul had been punched clean out of my body; then I started seeing stars in a way very similar to the characters in the old Disney cartoons used to, but importantly I didn't go down, and Richie rang the bell for the end of the round. I had learned a lot from the sparring; most importantly, it would take something close to a sledgehammer to make me go down. Strangely enough, the beating boosted my confidence significantly as I was firmly of the opinion that nothing in the coming bout could possibly hurt me.

The bout in Southampton was quite an experience. I entered the ring acutely aware of having a very large gut, and with Richie's last words as I had set off ringing in my ears, "I'm confident you have the technique and durability to do well, and the only thing that can stop you is having a heart attack, you fat bastard."

I had spoken to Kim before the bout and said I thought we should keep it controlled, just moving around jabbing each other for a few rounds before ending the fight both standing and in good condition, having raised a few quid for charity. It did not turn out that way.

Maybe it was the chanting of his name by a crowd of over five hundred that motivated him but Kim came out swinging wildly pushing me onto the back foot and clearly trying to drop me. This in turn flicked a switch in my mind, I forgot all my good intentions and the red mist descended I fought like I was back in Wolverhampton as a youth fighting for my life against people who clearly wanted to damage me and hated me. I'm not proud to say it but I combined the techniques Richie taught me with some street fighting from my youth and went onto the offensive landing some fearsome shots on my opponent. At the end of the round, we both staggered back to our corners. I was exhausted and struggling to breathe, not from punches landed on me but from the number of punches I had thrown. Fortunately, I had an experienced corner man. He forced me to swallow ice cold water which opened my lungs and helped me to breathe then told me to cut down on the amount of work and focus on my technique. The second round started and a clearly wounded Kim came out bravely still swinging and on the front foot but this time I was prepared and I used my jab and footwork far better employing the high-quality techniques Richie had taught me. Towards the end of the round Kim slumped onto the ropes and I expected the Ref to give him a standing count instead of which he told me to go in and finish him off. Fortunately, by that point I was in a much calmer place and stood back until he had recovered much to the chagrin of the crowd who were baying for blood. As the third round started it was clear Kim was done and after a few more heavy shots his corner threw the towel in and I had won. Afterwards, I felt awful as it was clear that Kim was quite badly hurt in the head and ribs. When I realised how bad it felt to hurt someone, I decided that was my last boxing match. I had no animosity to and, in fact, felt nothing but warmth and respect for him. To his credit, Kim has repeatedly challenged me to a re-match. Still, I'm confident my time in the ring is over, and I remember my last fight with feelings of great admiration for my opponent's fighting spirit and a certainty that I do not want to do it again.

The Steel Industry

I worked in the Steel Stockholding industry for most of my working life. I got my first job in the trade in 1990, joining Simpson Stainless, a division of British Steel.

I joined the industry at the end of a golden era where fun had been as important as profit, and productivity was not a topic of interest. Yes, the Steel stockholding industry had at least as much to do with excess in alcohol, food, and sex as it did with transporting steel from manufacturer to end-user; at least it did wherever I worked.

The youngsters entering the trade were constantly subjected to a rough baptism into the ways of the stockholder, which took some survival, but once you came through the other side, you were part of the crew, and times were good. I vividly recall a young man of a similar age to me being called to the works office to be told there were some unidentified items in the steel racks in our vast warehouse, and he needed to check them out. He was handed a piece of paper with various locations on it, all on the top rack, which was some 20 feet up, and he had to be lifted to it by forklift. He was far from happy when he realised that the items he was looking for were, in fact, the pieces of the body kit off his car and even a couple of tyres that a joint effort between the lads in the works and sales had removed. The only thing that upset him more was when he was still up on the top rack at 5pm, the lights were turned off in the warehouse, and everyone went to leave. Fortunately for him, one kind-hearted soul stayed back to help him with the forklift, but nobody stayed to help him put the pieces back in his car. Legend has it he was still there trying to rebuild his car at midnight.

My baptism to the steel trade came through working in the purchasing department as an assistant or, as we were known in the trade, "sprogs." I shared a desk with the stock controller, who was a decade older than me and a famous veteran of the trade with an almost magical ability to make stock fit the often rather casual work instructions raised by salesmen who resented not being able to scribble them on the back of a cigarette packet. Martyn refused to speak to me or acknowledge my existence for at least six months. Then, one day, he turned up at work very angry about an issue with his car; he called me to one side and spent at least ten minutes screaming the most obscene abuse imaginable directly into my face. After he fully vented and saw I was still standing there, he told me I had passed the test, I was officially "alright", and I would do well. That was the start of a friendship that is still going strong thirty-five years later.

Martyn was quite a character and can be classed as a bona fide legend of the steel trade. On one infamous occasion, he was held hostage by a disgruntled customer. The customer had filed a complaint that a steel delivery had been made which contained significant errors in quality and quantity. The business representatives on both sides had failed to settle the issue, so it was agreed that Martyn was an acknowledged expert and that he would be sent over to the customer's warehouse to inspect the delivery. On his arrival, his reception was extremely hostile, with managers and staff of the customer involved hurling every shade of abuse possible in his direction. Martyn is a small man and nobody's idea of a tough guy, but he is also extremely bloody-minded and determined. He ignored the abuse and continued to make the inspection before flatly rejecting the claim. This was greeted with renewed rage and anger from the customer and culminated in them locking him in the warehouse, stating that he would not be released until the issue was resolved to their satisfaction. In the end, it took a convoy of cars from the company Martyn was working at to turn up at the customer's car park and engage in a Spaghetti Western-style face-off before he was freed from captivity.

On another occasion, Martyn had agreed to drive back a colleague from a training day, which had resulted in the typical all-night drinking session. When the colleague got into the car, there were warning signs that he had not at all recovered from the session, and as Martyn began to drive, it became clear that the journey was not going to go well. Sure enough, the colleague in question managed to vomit the previous night's alcohol and general excesses all over Martyn as he drove them to work. Unperturbed, he continued the journey and delivered his passenger to work, then calmly and deliberately recounted the story to everyone he could, much to the hungover salesman's embarrassment.

Martyn often had fitness drives, which would result in him cycling to work. On several occasions, he would get soaked with rain on the way. His solution to this was to strip down to his vest and underwear and hang his clothes to dry on the radiators near his desk. It was quite a bizarre sight, particularly as he would carry on with his working day acting as if nothing was amiss and directly challenging anyone who dared to question why he was barely clothed.

We had some extremely unpleasant diversions and distractions during our working days, but they were not only tolerated but encouraged and participated in by management. Some of the standard jests during a working day included offering to get someone a coffee but then handing it to them steeped full of teaspoons of salt. Another variation was to get a coffee from the vending machine and then place it on a tray in the microwave for a few seconds; this would ensure that when the recipient took the coffee, the plastic vending cup would melt and scalding hot water would go all over their fingers. As well as these japes, there was always the hotly contested crown of who could deliver the most well-timed and grotesque fart or belch. Extra kudos was awarded if you could launch the flatulence at someone who was mid-sandwich.

One of the strongest competitors in the office wars was a friend of mine called Wayne Fraser. We were similar ages, but in fairness to Wayne, as he had proved himself to be an excellent salesman and a prolific drinker, he was way ahead of me in the pecking order. We started going out drinking together in the evenings and working together. We raised the bar on excessive and outrageous behaviour to heady heights. When Wayne found out I was writing this book, he was kind enough to remind me of one evening when he absolutely got the better of me in the pranks department. Our standard evenings would normally hit the region of ten pints of beer, then completely spiral out of control, tending to end up in an Indian restaurant. On one such evening, Wayne massively got the better of me. We had been drinking hard for several hours, but to my surprise, he seemed quite sober while I was rapidly losing my mind; little did I know that every few drinks, he had been visiting the toilet and making himself sick, thus vastly reducing the amount of alcohol in his system. By the time we hit the curry house, I was steaming drunk and typically for an inebriated young man of about 21 claiming I could eat a hotter curry than anyone else. We ordered our food, and I left the table to go to the toilet. While I was away, Wayne told the waiter to replace my medium-strength curry with a phaal. Now, if you do not know what a Phaal is, imagine the strength and heat of a vindaloo, then multiply it by an almost infinite figure. On my return from the toilet, I downed another pint at the table and started tucking into my food. At first, I found the flavour absolutely delicious, but then, within seconds, I felt a burning sensation engulfing my lips, gums and throat. Then, shortly after that, I felt nothing but numbness and rivers of sweat pouring down my face as if someone had thrown a bucket of water over me. Apparently, my face was bright red, and the waiters became concerned. They quickly removed the curry and replaced it with yoghurt and pints of milk, which I downed one after the other. After a while, I looked over at Wayne; he was doubled over the table, his shoulders shaking and tears streaming down his eyes; no, it was not a concern for his friend; they were tears of hysterical laughter, and I found myself having to give him kudos he had well and truly stitched me up a job well done by a master of the art.

During my twenty years in the steel industry, it changed to the point of being totally unrecognisable. Wild times and inventive selling with salesmen and the lads from the works all pulling together to make things happen were replaced by number crunching, cold and rather tedious methods of working that I am not entirely convinced achieved better results but certainly made life more boring. I was lucky enough to work with legends of the trade like Dave "Dasher" Downing. Dasher was the first outside representative, or as we called them, "Sales Reptile", that I was allocated to work with when I moved to the sales department. I had secured my move by waiting until the West Midlands Sales manager was ragingly drunk at the Christmas party and then persuaded him, with more alcohol, that I would be a good man for his team. I was allocated to Dasher, and I learned a lot. The main thing I learned was that you do not need to work at a hundred miles per hour to make sales; instead, you need to know what makes the potential customer tick. Some customers were all business, but Dasher had spent many years finding a collection of buyers who were far more interested in being taken out for a nice meal or being delivered a very nice Christmas gift off work premises. He was the epitome of the old-fashioned salesman, always well dressed and seemingly always with time to lean on the filing cabinets drinking coffee and chain-smoking cigarettes when he was in the office. He also had a magic stash of orders that weren't essential or urgent in his desk drawer that he could produce at a moment's notice if our sales figures were questioned. There were times when he was an absolute nightmare to work under as he never appreciated that the orders that he casually threw onto my desk needed to be put into some form of legible and logical order before being passed to the works, but my abiding memory of him is of a fun and ultimately kind man who was very generous to me in terms of his time and support. His finest moment in my presence was when he phoned a customer from the office to try to prompt more orders and, without remembering that the buyer was a double amputee, told him that if he could sort us an order out, he would gladly take him out on expenses and get him "legless." As he uttered the sentence, Dasher realised what he had said, and whilst still maintaining the call in as brash a way as possible, he slumped forward onto his desk, a glowing bright red with embarrassment. It was the charm of the man that he could get away with such *faux pas* and be even more popular afterwards.

Another legend I worked with was Keith "Two Phone" Simpson. Keith was an expert salesman who was almost the polar opposite of Dasher in that his work rate was phenomenal. He earned his nickname by literally having two phones on his desk with a receiver at each ear. One phone was a conversation with the customer, whilst the other phone was a conversation with the Steel producer we needed to buy from; he was a human conduit. He also bore an uncanny resemblance to the famous comedy actor of the 1970s and 80s, Gene Wilder. So much so that Martyn pinned a picture of Wilder in Charlie and the Chocolate Factory to the wall behind Keith, which everyone, including Keith, thoroughly enjoyed. Keith was also terrifying to go out on the road with. I vividly recall sitting next to him as he gunned his company car at over 100 MPH on the way to visit a customer whilst he was checking stock on an early, bulky laptop computer and holding a phone to his ear, finalising a deal.

As you will have gathered, my time in the Steel trade was, for the most part, good fun, and I met some wonderful friends during that time who have remained on good terms with me ever since. It was also an industry that allowed working-class people to improve themselves and earn some money. Amongst the people I met who proved this point were Mark Bloomer, a lad from a Tipton council estate who went on to senior director-level jobs all around the world, and the aforementioned Wayne Fraser, whose remarkable sales skills and resilience led to him owning his own company, and Mark Wyatt who progressed through various sales roles to achieve a wonderful career. All great mates of mine and working-class lads who came good. I will tell you a few stories involving them as we go along.

Whilst it was still a mainly male world the steel industry did have some very formidable women involved in it. There was the extraordinary "Beer Tits", who, when I met her, was in her late 20s, had a magnificent figure suitable for a page 3 model and could drink most of the men under the table. She once famously got drunk at a Christmas party and started dancing at the tables, only to fall off and break her arm. That did not stop her from enjoying the rest of the party, though; sedated by a few more beers, she continued to dance and take part in the fun, only ending up in the hospital to have her arm cast the next day after the hangover had worn off.

On another occasion, she demonstrated her party trick of stretching a condom to go completely over her head and then inflating it by blowing it out through her nose to create a latex bubble around her head. Unfortunately, she was just reaching the highlight of this particular feat of ingenuity when a deputation from head office who had been dispatched to discuss our poor sales performance was escorted through the office to the boardroom. In fairness to her, even though the senior directors stopped and one even shook her hand in greeting, she didn't falter, and the latex dome around her head only deflated after they had gone. Doubtless, she had made a spectacular impression on the visiting dignitaries.

"Beer tits" was an example of my pretty useless approach to women as a young man, I was only in my early 20s when I met her, and of course, I fancied her, let's face it, who wouldn't? Anyway, on one occasion, we met in Wolverhampton on a boozy night out and ended up together. She invited me back to her flat, and I was extremely pleased with myself about what was about to happen. She seductively slurred to me that she was going to the bedroom to "Slip into something more comfortable." As I sat there with a can of super strength lager kindly supplied by my host, I started to get the strangest feeling. I was itching, and then my eyes began to water and eventually swell. After that, I started to struggle to catch my breath. It was only at that point that I felt something behind me; looking around, I realised that there was an extremely fluffy cat sitting contentedly on a shelf just behind the couch I was sitting on. Dear reader, there is only one thing I'm aware of being allergic to, but believe me when I say I am extremely allergic to them, and that is cats. By the time my host re-entered the room in silky underwear, leaving hardly anything to the imagination, she was rather upset to see me red-faced, gasping for breath and with tears running down my face. I had to get up and go outside, which I did at some pace, hoping to be able to breathe before I rather embarrassingly passed out on this exciting woman of the world's sofa. Sadly, she took this as a reaction to seeing her frankly extraordinarily voluptuous body, and as soon as I left the door, she slammed it behind me, telling me, amongst other things, that I was a boy, not a man. I would have liked to argue my case but by that.

point my throat had closed to such a degree it was almost impossible to talk. Suffice to say I never got another chance with the legendary "Beer Tits."

I did have more luck with women later in my time in the steel industry; indeed, by the time I had hit my mid-20s, I was flying. At one organisation, I had a huge row with a woman in our credit control department because she was unwilling to give credit to a company that the records showed as basically insolvent. Do not forget I was a salesman judged on sales, I frankly did not care if they paid that was someone else's problem. The row continued until we finished work when we stood outside in the car park. Then for some reason to this day I cannot fathom the conversation moved onto the fact that she had recently had breast implants and that they had cost two thousand pounds. Maybe she was comparing the cost to the steel I had just sold, I can't remember, but in a grumpy mood, I said words to the effect that it was a waste of money as I couldn't see any difference to which she angrily replied: "come back to my place with me now let's sort this out". When we had made the short journey to her place of residence, she marched me upstairs to her bedroom stripped off naked, literally jumped on me and pushing the cosmetically improved breasts into my face said "can you see the difference now? A couple of hours later I had to admit to her that I had a new and improved impression of her body and even more satisfyingly at work the next day she passed off my order. Now that's what I call a win, win!

On another occasion at a different company, I played in a cricket match for the works team against an opposition our MD clearly didn't like much. Do not worry this is getting round to being a sex story so cricket haters please read on a little further.

The game was played at a very high standard cricket ground with an extremely good batting wicket. As we were hiring the ground, they had placed us right on the edge of the square, meaning the boundaries on the one side were very small. To cut a long story short I scored a very quick century including technically the longest six I have ever hit, due to the ball leaving the ground and smashing through the top window of a passing bus which was on its way into central Birmingham. At the end of the game, I was thoroughly enjoying the role of being the hero of the hour and drinking heroic amounts of beer. It was clear that I could not drive home, so I was very pleased when one of the younger women from the office offered to drive me back. I was even more pleased when she took a diversion down a rather quiet lane and leaned over to kiss me. That was nice, but what followed next was a real bonus. She got up from the seat walked to the front of the car, lay on the bonnet and took her knickers off throwing them some distance into the bushes nearby. Now please keep in mind that whilst this was a quiet road and fairly secluded it was still a road with at least some chance of a passing vehicle driving by with its headlights on full beam. I deliberated over what to do next for around half a second, then leapt out of the car and engaged in some rather frantic and certainly uncomfortable carnal activity on the bonnet of a Ford Focus. I guess as it was as a result of a cricket match you could say I had bowled a maiden over even though the strict definition of a maiden is rather questionable in this case.

Just to finish the story, the next day, the MD summoned me to his office. He was not only aware of my cricketing heroics but of my exploits that followed it. I was unsure of how he was to react but was very quickly delighted by him sending out his secretary to buy us both a sausage butty to sit and discuss cricket and then at the end of the conversation his awarding me a very significant pay rise. Yes, as life goes it doesn't get much better than that really.

Mind you, it was not all fun and games in the steel industry. There was a very generous amount of insanity, stress, and violence. On one occasion, I sold a coil of steel that one of the senior sales directors had been keeping back for his best customer. As I entered his rather large glass and steel office, I was aware that the large man rather well known for his bad temper wasn't in a great mood. He started the conversation by asking me had I sold the coil to which I replied in the affirmative, he then asked me why to which I perhaps a little too aggressively replied "Because its my fucking job" This was the trigger to one of the most explosive fits of rage I've seen anywhere. He told me how much he could have sold it for, and I replied saying it was a good job Id sold it then as my price was higher. At this point he turned more purple than the ripest beetroot ran from behind his desk and through himself headfirst at his filing cabinet which he repeatedly head-butted screaming "Get out, get out" at the top of his voice. At this point, I decided that getting out was actually a really good idea.

On another occasion, I had an important order that needed to be delivered urgently. I spoke with the transport manager who had made a rare and rather risky visit to the sales office, and in a characteristically truculent manner, he told me he wasn't going to do it. Tempers flaired and we faced off with each other in the office, this culminated with me picking him up by the shoulders and lifting him off his feet to repeatedly smash him into the wall until he agreed to do it. However, the story didn't end there. In a very unsporting way, he went straight to the owner of the company and told him what had happened. This led to me being summoned over to a different but even more impressive large steel and glass office. The owner of the company was a middle-aged man who had inherited it from his father. While he had a posh accent, a nice suit, and a good education, there was certainly a little of the gangster and a lot of the psychopath about him. This was a man who had video cameras fixed on the operatives in the works and used a stopwatch to time how long they were on the toilet on one occasion, marching out to the works demanding to know whether the worker in question had bowel cancer and if not, why had he spent more than the allocated time on the toilet. This was a man who took the sales team to the Legs Eleven Lap Dancing bar to celebrate his birthday and simply told the security his name had the best table cleared, and the most beautiful dancers perform for us, but when they came too close to him had said in a disgusted, high pitch but refined voice "Don't touch me, don't ever touch me" Anyway this was the man whose office I was summoned to. He looked up from his video cameras and, in an unwavering yet strangely sinister public school-educated voice, said, "Did you attack the transport manager?" to which I replied in the affirmative. He then followed up with a strangely drawn-out "Why?" to which I replied that he was refusing to help me secure an order. He then looked me up and down briefly and said "good, shut the door on your way out."

This same somewhat peculiar Managing Director had his own ways of applying pressure. It was not unknown for him to walk in at the end of a day ask us what we had sold then make the apparently serious comment "turn the lights out I'm getting some candles I can't afford the electricity" before driving off in one of his collection of hugely expensive luxury vehicles. His tendency to demand the maximum amount of work for the minimum amount of money for his workers extended to his demand that we work extra hours as a standard. Our hours of work were officially 8.30 am until 5 pm but anyone who did not turn up at least an hour early or leave at least an hour late was severely frowned on and as for taking a lunch break, well that was considered wild extravagance to the point of rebellion. He took this very seriously and could often be seen staring out of his office window, which was on the opposite side of the street, to the sales office, checking his watch to ensure we had arrived at an appropriate time. The one person who engineered a cunning way around this was the ingenious Mark Wyatt. He had planned and rehearsed a route from the car park to the office, which cunningly kept him out of view of security cameras and the eagle-eyed stare of our lord and master. It was a routine which would not have looked out of place in a "Mission Impossible" movie ducking in and out of nooks and crannies and crouching behind parked vehicles all done at an impressive pace. He had even covered his based by leaving a suit jacket permanently draped over the back of his chair just in case anyone came into the office to check if he was there, and he could use the excuse of "Just having popped over to the works". The fellow inmates of this madhouse, otherwise known as a sales office, eventually became a little tired of this, and on one occasion, we brought in a large block of wood, drew a face on it and placed Mark's jacket around it. It was particularly effective as Mark was very keen on his weights and had exceptionally broad shoulders. It so happened that on that day, the lord of darkness himself did actually visit our office. On looking around our office he noted the wooden block on Mark's seat but did not miss a beat and simply said "Good morning, Mark you look busier than usual" and walked out.

Not everyone could cope with the extreme pressure and general lunacy of the Steel industry. Whilst the likes of me and Mark Bloomer would often battle through a day before going to the gym to blow off steam and then drinking significant amounts of wine others were not so capable. I vividly recall seeing my first nervous breakdown when a sales manager finally cracked under the pressure. The gentleman in question was a genuinely nice guy and a pretty good salesman, but a run of poor sales figures and general bad luck got the better of him. I vividly recall working at my desk going through some sales records and figures when I heard an eerie high-pitched sound starting off rather quiet, then leading up to a wild scream followed by him repeatedly smashing his head off the desk. After a couple of minutes of this he calmly stood up took his jacket and walked out of the office. Apparently, he was found some twenty four hours later walking aimlessly around Birmingham city centre. Suffice to say that was the last we saw of him.

It was all part and parcel of the game to see the occasional meltdown, to witness the occasional fight, and to endure regular, totally unnecessary bollockings. It was also standard and pretty much vital to go out drinking and partying with your fellow salesmen in order to release the stress of the day. I do remember one morning that I must have completely over done it the night before as I had got home in the early hours then seemingly just a few minutes got back up to go to work donning the same clothes. When I got to my desk, I reached into my jacket pocket and like a magician pulling rabbits from a hat pulled out a seemingly never-ending bra, it was absolutely huge and to this day I still have absolutely no recollection of how it got there but I guess it must have been fun.

I worked at a variety of steel companies with some of them being rather big international concerns whose managers prided themselves on being very professional. These were the kind of men whose hair was always perfectly combed into place; their skin had a permatan the envy of a Hollywood film star, and their suits cost more than my car. Every now and again, we would have the honour of the company of one of these demigods at a sales conference or seminar in a swanky hotel. On one such occasion I had found the jacuzzi and was thoroughly enjoying it whilst having a laugh with my immediate sales manager who wasn't a bad lad at all and had an infectious high-pitched laugh which seemed quite out of place coming out of such a big guy. We were having great fun when a gentleman with a title akin to high priest of sales for the continent of Europe or some such similarly magnificent label headed towards us, his immaculate body clad only in what are commonly known as "budgie smuggler trunks." He approached us addressing us in his transatlantic business god accent "Hi guys can I join?" Of course, we had no choice but to say yes and moved ourselves into positions where there was room for him to enter without any of that awfully embarrassing man-on-man contact a crowded Jacuzzi can regrettably initiate. As this Sales God, this ultimate executive, this commander of the European forces of a huge multinational organisation, attempted to enter the water, he somehow managed to trip and, to our shock and horror, fell head first into the jacuzzi. What was worse was that he seemed somehow stuck and was unable to move so that he was perfectly positioned head first with his rather beautiful and very manly legs posed perfectly straight upwards in the air like a synchronised swimmer. Eventually he managed to right himself and with remarkable poise straightened his still almost perfect hair, gained a seat at the edge of the water, and as if nothing had happened enquired in a very serious way "so how's business guys?" I must admit I hesitated for a moment, trying to get into character in order to reply in as professional a way as I could after having seen the most bizarre and dramatic entry to a jacuzzi it is possible to imagine. As I started to speak, I was aware of a noise at the side of me. It was only faint, but it was a sound like someone conducting a dreadful inner battle as I began to talk, trying my best to speak in the sales waffle that was the only language the great man could understand. The sound grew louder and louder until I realised that the guy I had entered the jacuzzi with was fighting and losing an overwhelming urge to burst out into hysterical laughter. I turned the bubbles up, hoping the sound would drown it out. I spoke louder and louder in a voice that could probably be heard from across the pool, but it didn't work, and it came to the point where my colleague had no choice but to run from the pool into the changing area, where he slammed the door behind him but signally failed to drown out the sound of hysterical high pitch laughter that had been battling to burst free for the preceding moments. At that point I stated with as much dignity as I could that I fancied a swim and left the jacuzzi to swim but more importantly get my head under the water to disguise the tears of laughter now running down my face.

I survived twenty years of the rough and tumble of the steel trade. Made a few quid, a lot of friends and some golden memories. Unfortunately, by the end it had been largely taken over by number crunchers who hadn't been brought up in the trade and the fun was squeezed out more effectively than the juice out of a breakfast orange. By the middle of 2009 I had lost my last job in the steel trade and as I approached forty a whole new chapter of my life was about to begin.

Womanising

I must admit that for the first twenty years or so of my adult life, I had devoted so much energy to chasing after women that if it had been employed in almost any other more productive or career-oriented activity, I would have undoubtedly become a millionaire. I felt I was failing if I did not have at least four numbers in my book with live female contacts who would be interested in going on a date or even better still staying in and engaging in some bedroom gymnastics.

During this time, I not only wasted huge amounts of energy and money but I undoubtedly messed up what could have been some very nice relationships. In fact, as soon as the prospect of a relationship with a nice kind caring woman raised its head, I instinctively made a run for it. Unfortunately, when relationships with dangerous and entirely inappropriate women beckoned, I was drawn like a moth to the Wembley floodlights. It was only when I got married and had a few years free from chasing women that I managed to focus my efforts on my career with some very satisfying results, and indeed, that career only started to go back downhill when I got divorced and started wasting my energy on chasing women again, all be it with considerable success and a huge amount of enjoyment along the way.

I had a slow start with the girls at school, and I was 17 and in the 6th form before I hit any kind of form. I'm not quite sure how it happened but it was like a button was pressed and the floodgates to the world of sexual relations with women suddenly exploded outwards and it was game on. In quick time, I was working through girls at a rate I had only previously dreamed of. I did however deeply regret that two of my early girlfriends who were from Indian families and were extremely beautiful and lovely women had to be moved away from due to some unsubtle pressure from their families who were not at all impressed with their daughters dating a white boy. They were both wonderful, and one of them is still a friend today who, during my time in politics, bravely offered to come forward to testify that I was not a racist, but I dissuaded her; she is happily married and settled down now, and I did not want to drag her into my nightmare world at the time. I remember another girl that time a 19-year-old who had only recently left the school but had come back to visit her friend, she was an absolute fantasy come true to a 17-year-old rock fan. She had an amazing figure huge blonde hair with black streaks in it and the most heavy metal eye makeup seen outside of Motley Crue. Unfortunately, she came to see me play basketball for the school team one night straight from work, she wore a lovely white top but as she approached me I could see it was smeared with blood, she was a veterinary nurse and I am sorry to say in that brief instant the spell was broken.

During my teenage years and into my twenties and thirties, I had the advantage of a mentor in the world of "pulling" Now, before we go any further, can I acknowledge that much of this is going to be very politically incorrect but not only is it a truthful documentation of how it was but I also really, really don't care! Anyway, back to my mentor, I was very lucky that my mom's brother, Bill Hickinbottom was not only my uncle and my godfather, but he was also my best friend and absolute champion pulling partner. He was a good-looking bloke in his early years looking a little like a cross between Georgie Fame and George Best (Google the names kids trust me they were cool). He used to take me into pubs when I was way too young and get me used to drinking significant amounts of beer and then a little later managed to get me into nightclubs at a similarly youthful age. He was a wonder to see, bestriding the club like he owned it, always in a suit with a crisp white shirt and seemingly always with a cigarette cooly draped out of his mouth. In the ways of pulling women, he was OBI Wan to my Luke Skywalker. It came to the point where when initially I had simply stood back and watched him wowing the ladies I eventually started joining in and such was the confidence imbued by having Uncle Bill there I very rarely failed.

After this world-class apprenticeship, I was able to do well with ladies but never quite what I wanted and never really as good as the Indian girl I had had to give up at school. I did have another girlfriend in those years, and she was lovely and kind but a little younger than me, and it fizzled out. I shan't share any stories about her because she is a kind soul who doesn't deserve to be part of this kind of book, even in a light-hearted, humorous way.

My primary activities, aside from working hard enough to be able to go out drinking in my early years and chasing women, were playing football and cricket. My chasing of the opposite sex became so obvious at the cricket club that I was given a nickname there, which has lasted to this day: "Bonking Bill." In fairness, I did work hard to earn it. The club I played at was Claverley in the Shropshire countryside. It's well away from prying eyes in the off-season and very dark. I had a favourite ploy of driving my dates out for a drink in the quaint country pubs nearby then suggesting I show them where I played cricket. By the time we had driven through the gates all the way to the boundary at the far side of the pitch under a large tree, we were really in the perfect place for carnal action to commence, and it did many times.

What could have been my greatest cricket-related romance became one of my all-time greatest romantic fails. I had been dating a lovely girl who often came with me to cricket for some time. Unfortunately, over a period, I treated her very poorly to the point that she started looking elsewhere for attention. One of the other guys at the club was a tall, posh, and handsome fellow who often turned up with his own rather beautiful girlfriend. A series of events unfolded where this guy ended up meeting my girlfriend in a club and taking her home with him. This became public knowledge, and his girlfriend left him.

A few months later, I was at a nightclub with friends when I realised I had recognised the barmaid. Tall, dark haired outrageously posh and rather attractive it was the ex-girlfriend of my former team mate he who had hastened the split up between me and my last girlfriend. I felt a splendid plan for a very pleasurable revenge forming. I spent much of the night speaking with her and by the end of the evening we exchanged numbers and agreed to go on a date. I must admit my main motivation was a very silly form of macho revenge, but I also saw the potential to have fun doing it.

The night of the date came. Unusually in my experience the lady had not only offered to drive but insisted on buying the drinks. She was charming and funny and as previously mentioned extremely posh from a very wealthy family. Not only all these things but my goodness she brushed up nicely when she was up for a night out. Remember this was the early 1990s when I describe how she looked. Already quite tall she wore thigh high black leather boots with huge heels. This was complimented by a mini dress and fishnet stockings topped off by a black basque style top. Her hair was pitch black and big, her eye makeup was dark, her skin white, and her lips very red. If anyone is of an age to remember the Goth Band, the Sisters of Mercy, she was very much the double of the female guitarist. In short, she was right up my street!

At the end of a fantastic evening, we went back to where I was living. I was still living with my parents, but I counted on the fact that it was late at night, and they would be in bed asleep. The scene was set for romance, and we started kissing. Initially I found it hard to adapt to kissing a woman who in her heels was taller than me but I was getting the hang of it. Things were starting to warm up nicely and it looked inevitable that the perfect date was going to finish in the perfect way when the mood was destroyed by the sound of my dad stamping on the floor shouting "Nock it on the head now Bill." Needless to say the mood was entirely ruined and she left shortly afterwards. I compounded the error by in what I thought was a friendly gesture giving my ex-girlfriend a lift to the cricket club where she had a great many friends the following weekend. We were seen together, and the news got back to my Goth queen. She phoned me and in a very classy but indisputably final way told me that my chance was gone and she wanted no more to do with me. I think that the only way to describe this episode is as an epic failure.

Wolverhampton was my playground for much of my twenties and thirties. I had found out that on each night of the week, a different bar would still be lively and full of women. Importantly it became evident that the women who went out midweek were the determined partiers who were out for a good night while the weekend was more likely to have "Tourists" who weren't really as wild. At one point, I had identified a different bar where there was likely to be some kind of action on each of the seven nights of the week.

On one of these infamous nights out I was drinking with my cousin who was similarly focussed on the female form. We met a trio of ladies who were attractive and good fun. I became very friendly with one of them and managed to use my most bizarre chat online ever to get things on a more intimate level. I persuaded her that I had been in an accident that had left me with a wooden leg and a real foot. To prove it, I kindly offered her the opportunity to touch my foot and to touch above my thigh to prove they were real. She never did bother to check which part was wooden as we got distracted by other and much more enjoyable activities by that point.

On another occasion, we became friends with a mother and daughter on a night out. The mother was about forty and the daughter was about twenty so as my cousin was considerably younger than me, we paired up accordingly. We all ended up on a warm summer's night over a park. I was still in my footballing days, and I could not resist when I saw the goalposts. I laid my friend down on the goal line and that evening scored more times than I had all season!

There are dozens more such events and stories, but I can't recall too many of them as to quote the Fast Show character Rowley Berkett QC "I was very, very drunk."

On one boy's weekend in Blackpool, I had a truly bizarre and, I pray, unique experience in my pursuit of women. I had got separated from my friends and found myself alone in a club, drinking huge amounts of whiskey with a local young lady. My night became something of a blur and I did not remember much until waking up in my hotel room the next day. With a pounding hangover and eyes that could scarcely focus, I looked around the room. There were definite signs of activity. There were several empty bottles of alcohol lying around the place, as well as furniture tipped over and lying on its side. At that point I decided to close my eyes a little longer to see if things were better when I opened them next, they were not. I looked to the side of me in the bed and there were several very large empty pizza boxes which appeared to be moving. I gently picked one up and put it to one side only to receive quite a shock when I saw a woman was underneath it. The woman in question looked almost as tired and hungover as me so I decided to gently shake her to wake her up. When she woke up, she looked as surprised as I was to be in the room and to see me there. Neither of us had any firm memories of what had occurred the night before. Eventually we got out of bed and agreed to meet on the evening to see if we could spend some time together and remember it this time. Fortunately, she lived quite locally, so it wasn't a difficult journey in a car. We said our goodbyes for the time being, and I met up with my friends for the day before excusing myself on the evening to meet up with my lady friend.

On arriving at her house, she summoned me in and said that she had some drinks in and was determined that I should stay there that night. This courted no objections from me. When I entered the living room, I noticed a young teenager sat on the sofa, we were introduced, and I was informed it was her brother. I was told "he doesn't talk much unless monkey does the talking" I Was a little confused by this but decided to let it ride as I had other priorities that evening. About half an hour into my visit the young man left the room and I cuddled up on the sofa with the hospitable Northern lady I was keen to get to know properly this time. Imagine my surprise when he re-entered the room with a ventriloquist dummy in the shape of a monkey, sat opposite us and started holding a quite deep and detailed conversation with us, well I say "he" it was the monkey's mouth moving but I'm assuming the voice was being generated by the human. After a while I began responding and speaking with the monkey and I must admit we got into quite an interesting conversation about Blackpool and its attractions. Eventually it was time for bed and I was led by the hand by my hostess to her room. The young man and monkey followed us until she forcibly pushed him back and locked the door. We leapt onto the bed and I assumed a night of fun was ahead. Things progressed in a very positive manner, and we were fully into the act when I started hearing a rustling sound. I paused for a moment to ask what it was. The reply was "Oh dot worry that's Polly she will settle" in a fright I looked around wondering if I was going to see another of her siblings carrying a doll observing our copulation. I was mildly relieved to see that Polly was just a parrot in a cage in the corner of the room so being ever the good sport I got back to the business of the night. However, this became rather difficult as with every thrust and movement the parrot loudly screeched and I don't know if it was my imagination but seemed to be cheering us on. Determined to achieve my goal regardless of this we finally finished the act and as I lay there quietly for a moment it occurred to me that I was quite possibly in a house full of complete lunatics. Now this is not very gentlemanly but I decided to wait for my hostess to go to sleep and then make a bolt for it. Within no time at all, she gave way to her exertions and the considerable amount of alcohol she had consumed over the last two nights and drifted off to sleep. A fact I could confirm because she was snoring extremely loudly. I saw my chance and decided to take it, slipping quietly from the bed I slowly and stealthily put my clothes on and gently oh so gently opened the door to and began to head for the front door. As I began taking the steps downstairs one of them must have creaked, within an instant I heard a voice shout "Where are you going?" I looked round and to my horror I saw Monkey emerging from the bedroom next door to where I had just been entertaining Polly the parrot closely followed by a naked young man with his hand up monkey's backside. Im not ashamed to say I sprinted down the remaining stairs briefly fumbled with the lock and ran out to my car. In my panic I just pointed the car and drove only to realise I was in a Cul De Sac. I turned the car around and gunned it towards freedom, only to see Monkey and his naked handler chasing out of the house and down the road towards my car. I swerved around them and managed to drive my car to the main road and headed at top speed back to the relative sanity of the West Midlands.

Even as I typed that last story, I found it hard to believe, but I can assure you it was absolutely true which leads me even at this point several decades later to ask myself what the hell was I doing?

During these years my woman chasing was so obsessive and extravagant it was almost a mania. It consumed all my energy and time. Looking back on it now it seems a little odd but hey a mans got to do what a mans got to do.

However, let it not be thought that I was just a boy who can't say no to misquote the song badly. On one occasion whilst in my political life I became friendly with a very beautiful, slim, blonde young lady who was in her early twenties. This was quite a surprise to me as I had never really been the kind of bloke who would attract girls of that age, even when I was that age myself. It quickly became very clear that her sexual attraction to me was all about my relative fame at the time and the potential for me to introduce her to well-known people. I did not mind that particularly and can be a pragmatist when it suits me. However, our involvement ended very suddenly when during a passionate clinch she told me that she wanted me to have rough sex with her and rip her clothes off whilst throwing her around the bed and she insisted on calling me "Daddy" Never has sexual attraction dissipated so quickly. There was not a single part of that proposition that remotely appealed to me, and the desire to call me "Daddy" made my flesh crawl. She was most surprised when I got out of there at extremely high speed and never looked back.

During my time in politics, I managed to get involved with another beautiful blonde woman who was mercifully not quite as young as the last lady but was still very much in her prime. We had some fantastic times, and she was wonderful fun. After our first sexual encounter, which had been quite a drunken marathon, she uttered the charming and romantic phrase, "What a night that was, I've got a fanny like a scrambled egg" Unfortunately, this relationship turned very sour and was an extremely emotionally damaging time for me. I made the mistake of developing feelings for her, which grew deeper when she revealed to me that she had been struggling with some serious mental health issues for most of her life. Her petite figure, blonde hair and fawnlike brown eyes brought out the hopelessly old-fashioned male desire to look after her in me.

Unfortunately, as the relationship went on, her mental health issues became more and more apparent. I actually paid for her to see a counsellor, but all to no avail. One evening she told me that she felt like she was losing herself and she needed to get to the doctors the next day. When we awoke the next day, it was almost like a very different person had woke up next to me. Her eyes were much darker, and her attitude was totally changed. From that point on, she went out of her way to cause harm to me emotionally and to my career. She even found the lowest and most snake-like person in UKIP to send messages to revealing my weaknesses and keeping him up to speed with my actions.

I remember this time with sadness and frustration. My sadness is that a woman who could at times be wonderful company is afflicted with a condition that turns her into a monster. My frustration is that I allowed the weakness of allowing myself to care to make me vulnerable on many levels. In politics and life in general, I have found it is important to keep the shields up and never show a chink of weakness. That may explain some of my behaviour and the way I am perceived but hopefully the contents of this book will allow the reader a greater understanding of why I am the person I became.

I had a brief relationship with a fantastically beautiful Tunisian woman whilst in Brussels. She had olive skin, black hair, and the most amazing dark eyes. She also had a figure which defied belief and gravity. Unfortunately, yet again I was to find that I have an unwavering ability to attract women who are mentally unstable and she was another example of this. It seemed to me that the more beautiful the woman I got with, the more certifiably insane she was

There were literally hundreds of other encounters and sexual conquests but as tempting as it maybe I don't want this whole book to be about that and about my dramatically disastrous romantic life.

I have also consciously left out large segments about women with whom I've had relationships. This is for several reasons. Firstly, they probably aren't all that entertaining to read about but far more importantly I don't have any desire to remind them of times in their lives when due to my insensitive and downright bounder like behaviour I have caused them distress. I would like it to be enough to say to any of them reading this that I apologise, and I hope that they may occasionally remember more of the good times than the bad.

Having become rather more self-aware as I've got older, I've also decided that it may not be just that I only ever felt attracted to women with slightly unstable mental health. It could be that they were the only ones who were prepared to countenance any kind of relationship with me.

Unfortunately, from time to time, feelings got involved. The bizarre thing was when a genuinely nice woman developed feelings for me, I resented it, but when a downright nasty piece of work hinted that maybe things could get serious, I used to dive in head first and repent at my leisure. As later chapters of this book will show, this was a trait which caused me huge amounts of trouble in the years to come.

Politics
Tories

In 2009 I was made unemployed and for the first time ever I could not jump straight into another job. After trying to cope with daytime TV and leading a slower life for a couple of weeks, I decided I had to do something to keep me occupied until I found work.

I volunteered for a local charity trying to pay for a historic church's renovation and upkeep and decided to contact the local Tories to see if I could help with some leafletting or general voluntary work to support them. I had always voted Conservative largely under the misapprehension that they were still the party of Thatcher that had been about Patriotism and in the case of my family at least about allowing working class people to better themselves.

My relatively brief time with the Conservatives led to some very memorable moments. The local party had a few members who were genuinely interested in serving their community but several others who had delusional notions of grandeur that were quite disturbing to witness. Their grandstanding in local council meetings attempting to put together semi Churchillian speeches about the need to increase parking charges on local council car parks or other similarly momentous issues was only rivalled by the Labour group who all seemed to fashion themselves after a cross between Michael Foot and Che Guevara.

One of my favourite moments was watching the leader of the Conservative group trying to execute a preplanned ambush on Labour in the council chamber. The idea was that when she was coming towards the end of her speech, she would gently put her hand bag down on the desk in front of her and then all of her colleagues would press their buttons to indicate they wanted to speak thus denying the Labour group speaking time. I had been in the meeting room before the event and had witnessed the whole Tory group nodding along with the plan, yet at the time the esteemed council leader gently put her bag down none of her colleagues reacted or even waivered in their glassy eyed vacant stares. She repeated the movement several times until finally slamming the bag down and in a very strong Dudley accent shouting "Oi!" at this point her startled colleagues woke up but the element of surprise was most certainly lost.

The Conservative group were very strong on law, order, and discipline within their own ranks rather than in the actual area they were supposed to be serving, of course.

I vividly remember being called up in front of a disciplinary panel made up of a man old enough to be in the Guinness Book of records, a somewhat embarrassed woman who was only there because her father was a big noise at the local party and a so-called "Whip" who was so drunk he could not form words properly or even stand up without holding onto his chair. My offence was that of delivering Tory leaflets without asking permission to do so. A rather odd offence to seek to chastise a member of the party for, after all I had driven to collect the leaflets from the local had office at my own expense and then spent my own time to go and deliver them in an area that nobody else was covering.

The meeting came to an end when the Whip became so drunk that he forgot mid-sentence what it was he was supposed to be shouting at me about and wandered off to the bar to get another beer.

This was not my last appearance in front of a so-called disciplinary hearing, but it was certainly one of the most amusing.

I was fortunate enough to be taken on as a campaign executive in the run-up to the 2010 election. This seemed mainly to involve aimlessly delivering thousands of leaflets while nocking as many doors to canvass the level of support for the party in the Dudley North area as possible. It did have its interesting moments, however. They were mainly based around campaign visits by national figures and some of the frankly bizarre moments along the way.

Michael Howard was a surprisingly good campaigner. He belied his somewhat stuffy image and the sobriquet of "having something of the night about him" by electioneering and meeting the public with great gusto and humour. He even joined and my dad on our special stand outside the butchers shop where we were handing out free pork pies obtained from the supportive butcher as long as they had a leaflet entitled "Gordon Brown's Porky Pies" with a list of PM Brown's untruths detailed on it.

Bill and a Conservative Party Leader one night

Mr Howard spent a whole day campaigning with us, confronting and good-naturedly debating all comers. The only hitch occurred when we took him to the train station to head back to London. The staff at the station simply would not believe that he was travelling standard class and repeatedly tried to escort him to business class. It was the only time that day that Mr Howard looked a little ruffled, and as the train left the station, we could still see him desperately trying to argue the fact that he did not want to travel business class.

Roger Helmer
In his own words

Back in 2005, the draft EU Constitution was put to a referendum in member states. It was a fascinating document, offering illuminating contrasts to the American Constitution, which opens with the magnificent and unforgettable words "We the People....". By contrast, the European draft Constitution started out with a list of EU heads of state in alphabetical order. The opening words were "His Majesty the King of the Belgians....".

On the 29th of May, France voted, and to the delight of Eurosceptics, the NO side won 55/45. And in the Dutch referendum on June 1st, the NO side won even more decisively, 62/38. The EU Constitution was dead in the water.

So, did the apparatchiks of Brussels do the right thing? Did they accept that the people of Europe did not want their constitution? Did they say "Well we got that one wrong. How about a Plan B?". Did they hell?

No. The question wasn't "What can we do to fulfil the wishes of the people?" Instead, it was "How can we get all the substance of the failed constitution enacted, but without giving the ignorant public the right to reject it?".

And their solution was one of great simplicity — but also of massive cynicism. "Let's just call it a Treaty, not a constitution, then we don't need referendums". And thus, the Lisbon Treaty was born. Most of the text was simply cut and pasted from the failed Constitution.

So, in 2007 this new Treaty was ratified by member state governments, and as a mere formality the European Parliament naturally had a vote on it.

Formality it may have been, but it was also an excuse for an orgy of pro-EU celebration. The Strasbourg tower block is an elliptical structure around a large elliptical open space. I called it the exercise yard. And in this central space we were to have speeches, marching bands, and general rejoicing.

We Eurosceptics were mortified. Of course, we had voted unsuccessfully against the Lisbon Treaty, but it had gone through the parliament with a massive majority. Were we to see the odious rejoicing in our place of work without at least a gesture of dissent?

Slowly, we evolved a plan to make our mark. We took a sheet of A4 white paper and printed the word "NO" about 150 times on it. We then made multiple copies of the sheet. And using a good old-fashioned guillotine, we cut up the sheets until we had maybe a couple of thousand small squares of paper, each one marked "NO".

One of our colleagues had an office on the top floor of the tower, facing inwards over the exercise yard. At the height of the celebrations, the office window was opened, and our negative confetti was thrown out.

I had positioned myself in the exercise yard, well placed to see the action. What did I expect? I hadn't really thought it through, but I suppose I expected the paper squares to flutter down quietly to the floor. But I hadn't taken account of the breeze that blew through the entrance passages and down from the sky and swirled and eddied above the exercise yard.

Do you remember those snowstorms in a bottle that entranced us as children? It was just like that but on a vaster scale. And it seemed to go on indefinitely. I wish I'd had the presence of mind to video it. A frisson of alarm seized the assembled company, MEPs, staff, various dignitaries & performers. But as the first paper fragments reached the ground, they recognised it for what it was — a protest against this blatant rejection of the voters' decision.

The next morning, the ride-on vacuum cleaners were still forlornly cross-crossing the exercise yard and picking up the detritus of the previous night's party. Politics can lead to some brutal and unpleasant rivalries and animosities, but it can also lead to some rather unusual and very precious friendships.

One such friendship that I was honoured to develop was with the long serving former Conservative but firmly UKIP by the time I arrived in Brussels MEP Roger Helmer. I had met Roger before and enjoyed his company at campaign events for the Freedom Association, which was at that time led by the admirable Simon Richards and had welcomed speakers including Phillip Davies MP (Now of GB news) and Lord Tebbit. I had always considered him knowledgeable and interesting company; however, a genuine and profound friendship grew when I went to Brussels as a rookie MEP.

Roger is a man who is unashamed to stand out from the crowd. His sartorial elegance often includes the finest of tailored suits topped off with a variety of colourful hats, cravats, and other accessories. He has often made splendid use of his now white facial hair to grow magnificent moustaches or latterly a very distinguished almost regal looking beard. His voice is as rich and powerful as the variety of fine whiskeys he made a living selling in the Far East in his younger years. In short, Roger is a formidable and impressive presence.

Highly educated and very much the archetypal raconteur and lover of life, Roger is an absolute joy to spend time with. Fortunately for me even though our lives were vastly different we forged a firm friendship which is still strong until this day and we keep in touch whenever his globe-trotting to visit opera houses, ballets, or drive route 66 in the USA with his beautiful wife Sheila allow.

As well as being allies in the political world, both being great admirers of Lady Thatcher, we also found ourselves on some splendid adventures together. Most notable of these being a trip to Jerusalem where we met likeminded souls Pastor Chris Edmonds and Congressman Scott Taylor. The trip was to speak at an international conference of Right of Centre politicians but also included a fair degree of sightseeing. Now when you sight see in Jerusalem the sights are somewhat more remarkable than the normal city breaks, I was used to in the past! Our hosts took us to see Christ's tomb, where I made a huge Faux Pas by trying to crack a joke. Looking inside, I said in a dramatic tone, "They are right. You know he's definitely not in there any more" The stern-faced religious officials around me did not raise as much as a titter, and I made a swift exit.

As part of our trip to Jerusalem, we were driven to the historical sights on a bomb-proof bus with armed escorts. I was sat next to Scott Taylor who had formerly been a Navy Seal. As we drove in, he leaned over and whispered to me that the last time he had entered this area, he had been disguised as a tribesman and was on an anti-terrorist mission. I decided he was very much the man to stay near in case of trouble!

When we arrived, we were taken into the centre via an underground tunnel. Our hosts calmly told us that this was the best way to enter the area without terrorists taking pot shots with us so I was happy to oblige. Unfortunately, it became very clear that this ancient tunnel was not built for the size and bulk of the modern-day politician. As a group of about ten we entered the tunnel in single file. As we progressed further, the tunnel walls grew narrower, and the ceiling certainly dipped. Add that to the flickering lights illuminating us, and the whole experience was getting worse by the second. To compound the issue it is fair to say I am a rather large man, around 6 foot 1" tall and weighing in over 280lbs. I am not the ideal person to be trying to traverse a tiny tunnel built for people centuries ago who would have considered someone of my size to be either a freak or a titan sent to challenge their heroes. My aim during the tunnel trip was to try to control my breathing, close my eyes, think of something less stressful and keep walking until I came out the other end. As fate would have it, though, I was trapped with 6 or 7 people behind me in almost total darkness, and in front of me was a gentleman called David Kurten. Now, for those who have not encountered David, let me tell you he is a very nice and good-hearted man who fought hard for UKIP in the London Assembly for many years. He is also the only person in UKIP at that time that I can safely say was both taller and wider than me. My heart sank at one point when the tunnel ceiling dipped considerably, the walls got narrower, and David, well, David, got stuck. If ever there was a moment to fully experience claustrophobia, that was the time. It can only have been for a minute or two but the time there was no movement forward from David and I felt people bunching up behind me whilst I was doubled over crouching because of the low ceiling felt like an absolute eternity. Fortunately, David somehow managed to wriggle his way through and eventually when we both came out of the other side of the tunnel it was very similar to corks flying out of a champagne bottle which is an analogy that Roger, who had made the journey unscathed and with his usual suave panache would certainly have enjoyed.

We certainly saw some remarkable sites in Jerusalem and the experience of walking the stations of the cross and stopping off at the points that the story tells us Jesus stopped at during his awful journey to crucifixion baring his own cross was truly moving. Having been to Jerusalem I certainly give the Bible stories far more Creedence than ever before as the places described are basically still there. It was also notable for just how geographically close the Jewish, Christian and Muslim holy sites are, they are literally as has been demonstrated many times no more than a stone's throw from each other.

Having endured a hot and arduous but fascinating day looking around, we went back to the hotel. We were all very tired but had to attend a meeting in the evening. During the meeting, I noticed that Roger wasn't looking or sounding his normal ebullient self. During the meeting, he made his excuses and left the room. We later learned he had been taken ill and was in hospital. Obviously, we were all extremely concerned and I was delighted to receive a phone call from the great man himself later that evening during which in typical fashion his main concern was that I pass on his sincere apologies to the rest of the party that he would not be able to join us for dinner. Thankfully, Roger rejoined us the next day, apparently none the worse for wear.

The trip to Jerusalem was also notable for a meeting that would lead to a wonderful lifelong friendship. Pastor Chris Edmonds attended the event largely because he was being awarded a posthumous medal of honour on behalf of his father. Chris's father was Captain Roddy Edmonds, who had served as a GI in the 2nd World War and had been unfortunately captured at the Battle of the Bulge. As the senior officer in the prisoner-of-war camp, he was the point of liaison for the Germans. After suffering unimaginable cruelty at the hands of their Nazi captors Captain Edmonds and his men could have been excused for being broken men, but nothing could have been further from the truth.

When it became clear the Germans were losing the war and having to retreat the Nazi Commandant summoned Captain Edmonds and told him they would soon be withdrawing and leaving the camp however he wanted one last role call of the men and that the Jews had to line up separately. It didn't take much imagination to understand why this might be required, and Captain Edmonds had none of it!

The next morning, all the American prisoners lined up together for the roll call as usual. When the Commandant demanded to know why the Jews were not separate captain Edmonds performed an act of almost unimaginable bravery. He told the Nazi that "Today we are all Jews". Obviously, the Commandant did not see the funny side of this and pointed his Luger in Captain Edwards face and told him that if he did not tell him he would be killed. The courageous captain responded by reminding the Nazi that he did not have enough bullets to kill every one of the prisoners, and he promised that whoever survived that day would remember him and track him down after the war. In the face of such fearless defiance, the Nazi backed off, and he left the camp, taking his men with him. Captain Edmonds's selfless courage saved hundreds of Jewish American troops.

It was to receive recognition for his father's heroics that Chris was in Jerusalem. A small man with a big personality and a warm smile, Chris was immediately a popular member of the group. Towards the start of our visit he approached me and said "You look like the bad man of the group so I think it will be more fun to hang with you if that's ok" with those words a friendship of many years which burns brightly to this day despite thousands of miles of separation began.

Chris is from Knoxville, Tennessee, a beautiful part of the USA. He epitomises what I expected a Southern gentleman to be about, but with a very liberal dose of fun and humour thrown in. In later times I visited Chris in Tennessee, and I discovered a way of life and a country I fell in love with.

Tennessee

I have been fortunate to travel around the world a great deal and I have visited many wonderful places but there is literally nowhere that can compare with Tennessee. Deep in the territory of the former Confederacy, it is not unusual to see the occasional rebel flag still flying, but contrary to what we are led to believe, that is not universally a symbol of racism or hate; in this case, it is more a symbol of a culture and way of life remembered and an enduring determination not to be changed by the fashions or demands of the modern world.

On arriving in Tennessee, we were picked up by Chris from the airport, which was a blessing as the heat was taking a little while to acclimatise to; even the locals seemed to be wilting a little. After settling down at our accommodation, my party was picked up and taken to the house of one of Chris's friends, where we were welcomed with wonderful warmth. Pecan pies and other homemade treats were served to us whilst Chris and his friends treated us to their vocal harmonies. We were definitely in the South, and it was great.

One of the highlights of our trip was to drive up the smoky mountains. The scenery was magnificent, with huge forests and steep climbs passing by deserted dwellings and following the path of streams and rivers. Whilst driving towards the top of the mountains we noticed that the traffic ahead had slowed, when we came to a halt, we realised it was because there was an absolutely huge black bear by the side of the road and people had stopped to take photos. The bear was on its hind legs and seemed at least 8 feet tall. Instinctively, I rolled up the car window and pulled my arm in, to which Chris reassured me not to worry as the bears don't go for your arm. Then, after a brief pause, he said, "No, not your arm. They will go straight for your head and rip it clean off" Of course, I felt extremely comforted by this.

Further up the mountain trail, we stopped off at a trading post-style shop to pick up some water and essentials. The man behind the counter said something along the lines of "Yall ain't from round here, are you?" to which I replied I was a visiting politician from England. His reply was wonderful as he told me, "I don't know much about your politicians, but I have heard of that guy Nigel Farage. Have you heard of him?" with a wry grin, I mentioned that I had met him once or twice, yes. Nigel's fame or infamy seemed to have spread across the globe, even to a man halfway up the smoky mountains who, I'm pretty sure, had never travelled further than to the nearest bar.

Later in the journey, we stopped off at a mountain stream where we were reliably informed Dolly Parton used to sit in a steel drum and float down from the mountains. I'm not entirely convinced, but it's a good story. The locals like a good story; I mentioned to one of them that we had seen a huge black bear, and he replied, "That's nothing. I used to see his daddy, and he was twice that big" Well, maybe he did ….

On another journey up the mountains, we travelled up the legendary Thunder Road, once famous for illegal moonshine running but now the route to a great set of bars. We went into a Moonshine bar along Thunder Road, and I found myself in a scene that could have been direct from an episode of "The Dukes Of Hazzard" Big men in overalls drinking moonshine from jars, country rock blaring from the jukebox and incredibly good looking barmaids wearing "Daisy Duke" shorts calling me "Honey" It was just joyful.

One of my favourite things to do in America, and particularly Tennessee, is to go to the gun range. Yes, guns are dangerous, and I'm sure anyone with Politically Correct inclinations will shudder at this story, but on the other hand, if you are Politically Correct, I'm not sure why you are reading a book written by me. I've shot a variety of guns, including pistols, hunting rifles, automatic rifles and shotguns with one result; I really enjoy it, and I'm really very bad at aiming. Fortunately, at a gun range, as long as you point the gun away from you, it really doesn't matter where the bullet goes. Now, the reason I mention this is that on one occasion, I was part of a party of English visitors at a range when one particular gentleman forgot this fundamental rule, which goes along the lines of always pointing it away from you or anyone else. There are occasions when guns jam, especially when the person using them doesn't have much idea of what they are doing.

American politics

On one occasion, the person next to me who had travelled as part of our group but I won't name to spare their blushes seemed to forget this straightforward rule. His gun jammed, and as I looked on in absolute horror, he turned the rifle round and looked down the barrel to see what could be blocking it. In that split second, I had about a hundred contrasting thoughts. Normally, I would, as calmly as possible, suggest that the person remove the barrel of the loaded gun from directly in front of their face, but we were wearing ear protectors, so that was out of the question. The next option was to nudge them to get their attention, but I had a vision of the nudge setting the gun off and a loud explosion followed by me being covered in someone else's brains, so I took the only option I felt I could, I walked out of the range and held my breath saying a few random prayers until I could dare to look through the window

46

and see he had put the gun down. Thankfully, after looking down the barrel and shaking the gun to see what was wrong, he eventually put it down, but that particular memory still sends a shiver down my spine.

The bars in Knoxville are great. I spent a wonderful few hours in a long bar one evening smoking cigars and drinking beer on a tab, much of it bought by locals who felt an obligation to be hospitable that I was keen to accept. As the evening went on, people started turning up with musical instruments and joined others on the stage for impromptu jam sessions, playing a mix of country and rock classics, then freewheeling off into their own versions or compositions, and the amazing thing was, they were all really good, no drunken Karaoke this! During the evening, a small fistfight broke out in the bar with a group of people going full John Wayne and trading punches. Then, as soon as it started, they were friends again and buying each other drinks. One of the locals even bought me a drink, apologising saying, "I'm sorry Yall had to witness such a weak ass fight" Yes, I must say I absolutely love Tennessee.

At the end of one of my trips to Tennessee, I was scheduled to travel on to Washington DC for meetings with political figures from the American congress with the aim of assuring them that despite the UK government consistently ignoring their efforts to arrange post-Brexit trade deals, we really were worth doing business with. Chris arranged for us to be given a send-off at his chapel. The travelling group of us attended a very joyful service with Chris on top form, and then he told me that he had mentioned his friends from England were off to DC. Several of them approached us and told us that we were in their prayers and to watch out for the Devil in Washington, DC. At first, I thought they were being metaphorical, but eventually, I realised they believed that Hilary Clinton and Barrack Obama were literally demons and who knows, maybe they were right. We were given a range of gifts, including several beautiful Pecan Pies. Then, one lovely old lady approached us with something under a blanket and asked Chris to look in the opposite direction, which he obligingly did. She then handed us the biggest jar of Moonshine I had ever seen, saying she had distilled it herself "just like Daddy used to".

The people of Tennessee may seem unusual or even strange to European eyes, but I can honestly say I've never met such warm and friendly people or anyone so determined to cling to their way of life, and frankly, I don't blame them, it really is one step from heaven.

Famous Politicians

During my time in politics, I was fortunate or maybe not so fortunate in some cases, to meet some very famous politicians and see the real person behind the public image.

In my early years, I attended events run by the Freedom Association and The Bruges group, which were both largely Conservative-based organisations designed to stand predominantly against the EU and our UK membership of it. These organisations were the catalyst for me to meet two of the most inspirational politicians of my youth, Margaret Thatcher and Norman Tebbit. I was always enthusiastically and supportively joined on these visits by my wife at the time, Star. Star had been brought up in a working-class northern town and, in a similar way to my experiences, had seen her friends and family better themselves during the 1980s, so we were both fascinated by the Thatcher era. We made unlikely Thatcherites and often stood out from the crowd due to being younger and far more working class than the rest. We were also probably the only Heavy metal fans amongst the crowd, and we were certainly the most rebellious amongst them. Star had christened us "The Sex Pistols of the Conservative party", much to the disapproval of our local Tory party chairman, but she had a point: we were different.

Meeting Mrs Thatcher was an extraordinary moment. It genuinely felt like we were taking part in a moment of history. After all, love her or hate her, Margaret Thatcher will always remain one of the most notable and remembered politicians of the 20th Century, with a worldwide fame that few politicians from the UK have since matched. It was one of the last public appearances the lady would ever make, and the air of excitement and anticipation in the room before she entered was palpable. In fact, several people were jostling and nudging each other for a position; I actually delivered quite a sharp elbow to the ribs of one grey-haired gentleman who clearly felt he should be better placed than me, only to realise shortly afterwards I had just assaulted Norman Lamont, former Chancellor of the Exchequer!

When Lady Thatcher entered the room, I was struck by how very old, tiny and frail she looked. Throughout the years of my childhood and teens, she had seemed to be something akin to a warrior queen mixing Boudicca with Queen Elizabeth the 1st, and I had been braced for an altogether more formidable presence. When she walked in accompanied by Bruges Group Chairman Barry Legg, the room went very quiet; in fact, it was so quiet I was sure I could hear the sounds of sharp intakes of breath as people realised they were in the company of a living legend. To her credit, Star was the first to break the silence. Seizing the moment, she walked forward, shook Lady Thatcher's hand and said quite a moving few words about how inspirational she had found her personally, not just as a politician but as a woman who had made it to the top from a relatively humble background. My moment came a little later as I required a couple more glasses of the excellent red wine being served before I had the courage to approach the great lady. I circled around for a while, trying to find a convenient moment to introduce myself, and after a while, I became aware she was looking at me. After this had gone on for ten or fifteen minutes, which seemed like an eternity, she beckoned me over. Amongst the noise and general excited chatter of the event, it was hard to hold a prolonged or in-depth conversation, but I shook her hand and thanked her for all she had done for the country as well as pointing out that she had made it feel possible for people of my background to achieve more and my own family had thrived during her time in office. She fixed me with the eyes that President Mitterrand of France had once compared to those of Caligula and said, "Thank you so much. That makes it feel that everything I did was worthwhile" Then, much to my surprise, she kept hold of my hand, and I became her unofficial escort around the room. I deeply regret that due to the noise, I did not pick up on much of what she said, but contrary to the abiding image and unkind media coverage, I can honestly say that in that brief encounter, I felt nothing but warmth and kindness from an old lady who knew her time was drawing near but still wanted to share what time she had left with the people who supported and respected her.

Margaret Thatcher and Bill at the Bruges Group

She wasn't quite so kind to wealthy donors to Eurosceptic causes, Stuart Wheeler, who made quite an obsequious and overly loving speech about her whilst proposing a toast. He ended his words with "If only you were twenty years younger", to which she briefly rediscovered her old booming voice and acerbic wit, replying, "If I were twenty years younger, I wouldn't be standing here next to you, I'd be far too busy."

I met Norman Tebbit at an event on a similar scale organised by the Freedom Association. Most people remember Lord Tebbit for his combative style and his famous call to the unemployed to "Get on your bike and look for work", but once again, I found the person behind the image to be far different. Indeed, after meeting him, I used to write regularly to Lord Tebbit, asking for his guidance in my political career and taking his suggestions as to who was "Sound" and worth supporting. The man himself was still remarkably sharp-witted and erudite. I told him the area I was from, and he immediately told me what the people in the Dudley area would be concerned about at election time, which was all the more impressive as I had been canvassing on hundreds of doorsteps and could confirm he was correct. Out of interest, the issues were hard-working people resenting their neighbours, who seemed to have a more comfortable existence than them even though they were unemployed and on benefits and immigration.

Bill and The Rt Hon The Lord Tebbit, CH, PC

In my conversations with Lord Tebbit, I learned that he had fallen foul of the Conservative establishment for being considered rather too common and plain speaking. Harold McMillan had certainly not been an admirer and had repeatedly made it clear he was not the right sort. This experience was one that I became only too familiar with in the following years, be it at a much lower level of politics.

Lord Tebbit was not shy of an opinion, as you can imagine. He told me that he believed the Conservative party had been hijacked by Social Democrats, whose whole aim was to stop people of principle from getting anywhere. When I asked him why he stayed as a member if he felt that way, he said there was no way he would allow anyone the satisfaction of running him out of the party. Much later in our acquaintance, when I joined UKIP, I asked his opinion. It's fair to say he was not impressed and wished that people like me had remained to fight the fight within the Tory party, and he was even less impressed with the leader of UKIP, a certain Mr Farage, who he regarded as not being at all a serious political figure.

One of the most outrageous stories I learnt from Lord Tebbit was of an encounter he had with the then-leader of the opposition, David Cameron. In the meeting in question, Tebbit had asked Cameron why he thought it was that he was not further ahead in the opinion polls against what had by then become an immensely unpopular and out-of-touch Labour government. Apparently, despite his public image of being a hoody-hugging, charming gentleman politician, Mr Cameron has a ferocious temper. Cameron's temper was well and truly lost during the meeting, and the implacable stone-faced Tebbit interrogation only served to inflame it. According to the story, Cameron was in such a rage he started throwing objects around, and security had to be called to remove the octogenarian Tebbit from the room.

Speaking of David Cameron, I was in his company several times in the run-up to the 2010 election and just afterwards. My opinion was that he was intensely unlikeable and an absolute ass of a man with a self-centred born-to-rule entitled attitude, the likes of which have inspired the French to use guillotines on the aristocracy in their fondly remembered past.

In public, Cameron gave off an attempted Cary Grant charm, which ended up being closer to Hugh Grant, but it was certainly more pleasant than the man I witnessed behind the scenes. His treatment and language towards subordinates were, in my opinion, rude, hectoring and bullying. His treatment of party volunteers was patronising and arrogant. On one occasion, he was greeted at a garden party by a husband-and-wife duo of activists who, on meeting him, mentioned the fact that they thought the husband looked quite like Mr Cameron. His response was that he was about to go on some foreign visits to places that were not particularly pleasant, and he would get his security team to send his lookalike instead, then strode off, ignoring further conversation.

Around this time, I met another future Prime Minister, the one and only Boris Johnson. Boris has made a career out of appearing to be a loveable buffoon, but I can tell you from my experience that is yet another lie that he could be labelled as perpetrating. My main experience of Boris was being part of a team of activists asked to chase around a conference, making sure he had everything he wanted. As he power walked across the room, he barked instructions at hapless staff liberally using four-letter words to add colour to his orders. Then the BBC stopped him in his tracks and asked for a word on camera. The transformation was almost instant; he shooed his lackeys away and paused just long enough to ruffle his trademark unruly blonde locks, adjust his tie to make it look less smart and change into character to become loveable, cuddly Boris. Mr Johnson is most certainly not the person he tries to make us believe he is, and I personally would not trust him even half as far as I could throw him, and as he is a big lad, that is not very far.

Nigel Farage

Nigel is undoubtedly the most influential politician of the last decade. This feat is rendered even more remarkable by the fact he has never won a domestic election despite seemingly endless efforts.

Many people are fooled into thinking they are Nigel's friend by his charm and gregarious approach. The truth is that, like any immensely successful man, he has very few actual friends and is, in fact, a very ruthless operator. Do not get me wrong; this is not a criticism, merely an observation. I was never naïve enough to think Nigel was my friend, but I do like to think that our working relationship was so close and effective for a few years that there was mutual regard and respect, at least for a while

My working relationship with Nigel was without a doubt the most effective and satisfying I have ever experienced. Between mid-2010 and 2015, we were mutually extremely useful and supportive to each other, and it will always be a time I will remember with great fondness. I've always had a problem with working under people that I do not respect or consider to know less about the job than I do. That was never the case with Nigel; it was always very apparent that he was the master politician, and I was the sidekick, learning as much as I could and being as supportive and helpful as was humanly possible, and I was fine with that.

Nigel and Bill on the Brexit campaign trail

I met Nigel briefly a couple of times, but our work together began in earnest mid-2010 after I had left the Tories and delivered a reasonably well-received speech at the UKIP party conference berating Political Correctness. I had rather persistently badgered Nigel to come to Dudley to make a public appearance, believing not only that he would be well received but that it would do me a power of good to be seen next to the emerging figurehead of the Eurosceptic movement. In typical Nigel fashion, he eventually accepted my invitation but with a rather demanding challenge attached. He would come and speak in Dudley as long as I could get a crowd of over one hundred and fifty in attendance and cover the costs for the whole event by charging people to attend a dinner with him directly after the public speech. I accepted the challenge with trepidation but felt this was the ultimate Carpe Diem moment; it was a chance to fly high and make a name for myself or to completely

52

wreck my political career within UKIP before it had properly started. How could I resist?

As it turned out, we managed to get over two hundred and fifty people crammed into the Dormston school theatre in Sedgley, Dudley and then sell more than enough tickets to attend a dinner with Nigel at a rather nice Italian restaurant a few minutes down the road. At the time, it was the largest public meeting Nigel had ever addressed, and the reception was nothing short of ecstatic. I think we both realised we were onto something by the end of that night.

In the years to come, I was Nigel's go-to man in the West Midlands, being tasked with a range of challenges from helping to organise more public meetings to quelling dissent in renegade UKIP branches, which for some reason still harboured loyalty to renegade and frankly absurd serving UKIP MEP Mike Nattrass. During my time with the Tory party, the Labour party in Dudley had labelled me "Bill the Tory Hatchet Man" While I had enjoyed the title, I never really lived up to it until I started travelling UKIP branches in the West Midlands, bringing them to heel. Of course, many of the branches were more than supportive before my intervention, but the ones that weren't very soon realised that no dissent was to be tolerated anymore, and it was a case of following the party line or being in for an extremely unpleasant visit from yours truly.

I was also tasked with visiting potential donors in the area and having the initial meeting before deciding whether they were serious enough to broker a meeting with "The boss" As well as potential donors, I went out to persuade former members that Nigel believed were worth bringing back in that it was worth coming back. Most notable of these people was Jill Seymour, who later became an MEP in 2014.

Nigel persuaded me to stand in as many elections as possible, rightly saying that even if we didn't win, we would still be spreading our message across the West Midlands. This was the reason why I ended up standing for the role of West Midlands Police and Crime Commissioner in the first such election. This long and protracted campaign showed me, not for the last time, that you can win as many hustings as you like, but it has very little impact on how people eventually decide to vote, but more on that later.

Whenever there was a by-election anywhere in the country, I was sure to receive the call from Nigel normally along the lines of "I'm in (fill the space as appropriate) get yourself here straight away Etheridge we need you nocking doors" I really didn't mind in fact I thoroughly enjoyed the experiences as in those years Nigel still lived by the motto "If its not fun its not worth doing" and by God we had fun. Yes, we campaigned long and hard, but every day was concluded with world-class drinking, eating and party sessions that tried the stamina of everyone except the apparently invincible Nigel. I will make the boast that I never went to bed before he had finished the session and went drink for drink with him, but whilst I was a complete mess the next morning, he seemed as fresh as a daisy, leading to ask him on one occasion whether he had cloned himself and had separate bodies to do the drinking and the campaigning. On one occasion, I awoke in a hotel aching, hung over and barely able to compute where I was; realising I had slept a little late, and it was about 8 am, I quickly started getting dressed and turned on Breakfast TV only to see a grinning, fresh as a daisy and sharp as a tack Nigel sat on the sofa looking nothing like a man who had drunk at least twelve pints of Guinness the night before!

After one campaign session, we all retired to a hotel bar for a night of drinking. Noticing that the TV news appeared to be on a loop on several screens, we challenged Nigel to down a pint and balance the empty glass on top of his head every time he was mentioned. He was delighted to accept. None of us had realised just how often he would be on and how much coverage he had secured, but nonetheless, at least ten pints later, the empty glass was still being balanced atop the Farage ahead with great poise and a cheerful laugh.

Unfortunately, as time progresses, people move apart, especially when one of those people achieves a form of global superstardom. Nigel and I spent much less time together after the 2015 General Election, an election at which for most of the way until a catastrophic fall off late in the day due to a Tory scare story about a Labour/SNP pact I had looked like winning in Dudley North.

After that election, Nigel became more distant not only from me but from the group of hard-core supporters who had considered ourselves his Pretorian guard. This included the hard-drinking, straight-talking, working-class duo of Paul Nuttall and Ray Finch. We were extremely loyal and would have done anything, probably up to and including taking a bullet for the Boss, but gradually, our services were less appreciated and required.

I was fortunate enough to be there during one of the most famous Farage moments. I was in the bar at the Strasbourg parliament having a drink before we had to enter the parliamentarian for yet another savage and ultimately pointless exchange of views when Nigel walked in with a huge grin on his face. He summoned me over and, in a stage whisper, told me that he had decided to really wind them all up this time. This was the first major Euro Parliament session after we had won the independence referendum and was bound to be a packed house. Nigel informed me that his speech was going to be a lot of fun. He had turned up with the intention of making a conciliatory and statesmanlike speech, but the comments and behaviour of the other MEPs had prompted him to a late re-write. Basically, he had decided there were going to be fireworks, and he was not disappointed. His speech included the classic line. "Isn't it funny...when I came here seventeen years ago and said I wanted to lead a campaign to get Britain to leave the European Union, you all laughed at me... Well, you're not laughing now !"

The whole place erupted with UKIP MEPs and our fellow Eurosceptic MEPs from other countries cheering wildly but being drowned out by a chorus of booing, abuse and general rage from the rest of the parliament. While people watching on TV or video probably could not pick up the full extent of the noise due to the parliament microphone and noise filtering system, let me tell you, it was like being an away fan at Millwall. It's fair to say the establishment lost its heads and threw its toys out of the pram in grand fashion. It was an absolute pleasure to be there.

Another notable occasion when I was chatting with Nigel in the bar was after one of his visits to see President Trump. The whole building was awash with panicked discussion about the fact that Trump had Tweeted words to the effect that he was considering hiring Nigel for an Ambassadorial role to deal with the EU on his behalf. Chuckling Devilishly into his wine glass, Nigel told me how the whole thing was simply a wind-up, and after the tweet, he and Trump had thoroughly enjoyed seeing the horrified reaction almost worldwide. In fairness to some of the very few members of the Euro parliament, quite a few of them did address Nigel as "Your Excellency" for a while with their tongues firmly in their cheeks, and Nigel laughed along, thoroughly enjoying the humour of it all.

Over time, Nigel started to promote people above me, whom he obviously considered to be more appropriate for a serious political figure. Unfortunately, they were almost all either personally disloyal to him or diametrically opposed to the political principles we were supposed to be campaigning for. Nigel is a great speaker and an inspirational leader but a disastrously awful judge of character. His ability to choose people to be close to him who would, without hesitation, stab him in the front, back, and any angle possible was uncanny and only matched by his ability to treat those who were immensely loyal like dirt.

For all his brilliant communication skills and ability to put the thoughts of everyday people into words, Nigel is prone to being a snob. He does not mean to be a snob, and he really tries to make everyone feel comfortable and part of his team, but maybe because of his public school education and wealthy upbringing, he simply cannot help himself. On one occasion, when telling me he could not support me for a leadership bid after he had quit the role, he said words to the effect that while I was the most politically engaged and attuned of the candidates, I simply was not the right sort.

This may have impacted his decision-making in later years when he spent huge amounts of time with millionaires like Aaron Banks and world leaders, notably Donald Trump, but basically ignored those of us who did the day-to-day work to keep the whole machine of UKIP running. I genuinely do not think this was done with malicious intent. Its simply he was inevitably attracted to the company of those of his own type and probably didn't even realise he was shitting all over the team that had helped to make it all possible.

When Nigel left UKIP and went on to the Brexit party, I was keen to continue supporting his efforts. Despite my reduced standing in his eyes, I felt that I could still be useful in achieving the goals we had both worked so hard to achieve, particularly seeing Brexit through to its conclusion. I had a conversation with him where he advised me to abandon some of my more controversial plans for foreign visits as it would be beneficial to go forward with the new party with as little aggro around me as possible. I agreed and put my name forward to stand as a Brexit party MEP at the upcoming Euro Elections. When the list of Brexit party candidates was announced, I was completely excluded. Even then I did not throw my toys out of the pram. Rather, I prepared a full team to fight the Dudley North seat again at the not-too-distant UK general election. I had a telephone conversation lasting some half an hour with Nigel, during which I managed to leave the garden centre I was in, deposit the rather spicy curry I had eaten the night before in the public toilets and walk back out into the public car park so seamlessly he was unaware of my challenges. I asked him on at least five occasions in five different ways if he was sure he wanted me involved. The answer was an unambiguous yes.

Having received this assurance, I phoned the Brexit party Headquarters to secure my candidacy for Dudley North, a seat in which I had achieved some of the highest scores UKIP had received anywhere in the country in previous elections. I was put through to an obnoxious, deeply conceited clown going by the name of Toby who informed me that was nothing certain, and they were being very careful to make sure they didn't get "Too many UKIP nutters" Apparently, they had a stellar list of candidates including TV personalities, doctors and airline pilots who were cut from the right kind of cloth. I was informed I had to attend an interview in London at their Headquarters to apply for the seat. Being a good sport and wanting to be cooperative, I agreed. My interview was conducted by a deeply unpleasant character going by the name of Ajay, who spoke to me in the most rude and hostile way imaginable. In fact, I was convinced it must be a role-play exercise to see if I still had the balls for the rough and tumble of the election campaign. At least ten minutes of this interview was taken up by him accusing Nigel Farage of being a racist and me rather forcefully refuting this nonsense. Needless to say, I was not selected to stand for the seat but was asked to do the campaigning for a rich, privately educated farmer from down south by the name of Rupert...yes, a candidate in Dudley called Rupert. It beggars belief.

When I told Nigel, he said it was not in his control, and it was all down to Richard Tice. Richard Tice is the ultimate example of Nigel's poor judgement in who to trust and work with. He is broadly detested in the pro-Brexit movement by most people who have met him. Many of us share the opinion that he is an egomaniac who is solely motivated by massaging his own ego and posturing on TV rather than achieving meaningful change. Having said that, it is nice to see someone who is part of the deepest and most loving relationship I have ever witnessed; Tice and his mirror are so deeply and passionately in love that it really is quite moving.

Nigel Farage has achieved great things for this country, and I have had some wonderful times with him. However, I cannot help but believe that he is an unfulfilled potential. Without the almost suicidally poor decisions surrounding himself with people who are either solely in it for their own gratification or who genuinely despise him, he could have achieved so much more. As I write this, Nigel is excelling at eating grubs and camping in the Australian Jungle on the ITV celebrity torture show that appears so popular with its diminutive hosts Ant and Dec. Despite his rather shoddy treatment of me personally, I truly hope that this is not the end of politics for Nigel, he has so much more to give, and I believe that in these times of quite terrifying state overreach into all of our lives we need someone with his libertarian instincts and powers of persuasion more than ever. My journey in politics would certainly have been less successful and much less fun without Nigel Farage, and for that, I will always be glad that I have known him.

UKIP 2010 to 2014: "It's not worth doing if it's not fun."

The early years of my involvement with UKIP really were great fun as well as very productive in terms of the work we were doing growing the party and its appeal.

Around 2010 and 2011, a few very significant new faces joined UKIP. They helped to reshape and organise the party. Yes, it had been in existence for some time beforehand with fantastically dedicated volunteers and activists, but the arrival of these bright young things made a huge impact.

When I first joined UKIP, it was a far cry from the formidable campaigning organisation it would become. It was mainly made up of older people sitting in side rooms of pubs, agreeing with each other that the country had gone to the dogs. The belief was that because the UKIP message was right, there was no real need to persuade people; simply to be seen with the banners and leaflets should be enough. There was a need for modernisation and up-to-date techniques.

Now, I refer to the group of newcomers as "Bright young things" They weren't all necessarily young, but bright they certainly were. Many of them had been driven from the Conservative party by the dreadful betrayal of its values encapsulated by David Cameron's coalition with the Lib Dems. Others had come from senior roles within the media or think tanks and felt that the time was right to stand up and be counted on the electoral battlefield.

National stage

Amongst the newcomers were Jamice Atkinson, a former "A list" Tory candidate who defected post the coalition. A strong and formidable woman, Janice would later become an MEP.

Another was Tim Aker. Formerly known for his work in Right of Centre think tanks, Tim certainly perfected and fitted the description of a bright young thing in every way. A clever and determined young man whom I formed a firm friendship with, he also later became an MEP.

Lucy Bostick joined us from the Tories. Incredibly intelligent, principled and spirited, Lucy was, in my mind, symbolic of the change in UKIP. Young, vibrant, educated and very attractive, she was a fantastic addition to the party. She ascended as high as the NEC before eventually leaving the party disillusioned with the latter in fighting. Lucy's role in the change the party went through in those days must not be underestimated.

Around this time, a gentleman who would hit many headlines in the years that followed joined us. A suave, well-dressed, charismatic and devilishly good-looking lawyer by the name of Stephen Woolfe. He later became an MEP, but more on him later in the story.

The group of new, experienced political campaigners merged very quickly and effectively with most of the old guard and were welcomed with typical warmth by Nigel.

The energy we generated was tremendous. Whenever a by-election was called, we would descend on the area with our teams of volunteers from all over the country and campaign with passion, humour and determination. The days would last very long hours, and we would cover so many miles. Blisters and worn-out shoes were the norm, but we still managed to finish each day with some serious drinking and partying. Nigel was at the front of everything; he was out there campaigning with us with the occasional break for media, and he was always at the forefront of the partying.

I remember one occasion when a group of us were racing across London on Rickshaws with our cycling drivers being paid handsomely for it with the promise of a bonus for winning the race. Unsurprisingly, my guy came in last as he had something of a weight handicap carting me, but I still gave him the extra money and had a laugh and a joke with him while he caught his breath, and I made sure he wasn't going to have a heart attack. The endpoint of the Rickshaw race was a very posh jazz club where we consumed huge amounts of alcohol, and I tasted the most expensive hamburger of my life.

We also turned party conferences into celebratory positive events, the likes of which I had never attended before and very much doubt I shall attend again. Hard-hitting but humorous speeches, lunches with activists or potential donors, then evenings in bars and clubs. I shall never forget one occasion when we were all tiring a little; we decided to hit the rather small and dated dance floor in the hotel we were staying at. Almost like Wonder Woman changing in a phone box, Lucy changed her business-like shoes into some killer high heels and led us all onto the floor, dancing for the next few hours. She looked classy and stylish; I suggest those of us following her onto the floor looked a little more like the Happy Mondays at the end of a long tour, but we gave it our best. It was fun.

"You Just Got Lucky"

The number of times I've heard people say with a faux air of wisdom and a sardonic smile that I "Just got lucky" to be elected and had not done anything to deserve it probably needs to be addressed briefly at this point.

Yes, we had fun building UKIP to the point where it could be challenging to win elections. Yes, I've always been inclined to being something of a hedonist and tried to gain the most pleasure from everything I've done, but lucky? Read on and decide for yourself.

The primary factor that everything depended on was Nigel, so in the respect that I was involved with him at the peak of his campaigning powers, he decided I was worth being part of the team. I guess you can say that's luck. The rest of it was all about extraordinary hard work, and I'm put in mind the famous quote, "The harder I train, the luckier I get", attributed to many, but I believe it may have first been said by South African Golfer Gary Player.

When I first joined UKIP, the branch in Dudley was, in my opinion, one of the better ones, and I was glad to be with them. Being one of the better ones meant that there were more than two or three of them, and they were aware of the requirement to go out and campaign at elections. That was not the case with many of the other branches.

Dudley UKIP had grown to be a significant force in the local area largely on the back of a former Councillor called Malcolm Davis. He has galvanised public opinion against the proposition to develop a huge "Mega Mosque" on a hill which would have overshadowed the whole town, including Dudley Castle. I had my differences with Malcom. In fact, in my opinion, he was a grotesque neo-Nazi embodying most of the bile and prejudice that people tried to label UKIP as a whole with, but credit to him, he was an effective campaigner and managed to help UKIP come close at council elections. Interestingly enough, Malcolm had been a Lib Dem prior to joining UKIP, and when he left because he was sick of me "Strutting around like a Peacock", he joined the Conservatives.

I was far more impressed by the branch chairman Phil Wimlett who worked long hard hours for the cause and was the glue that held everything together. There were other members of that branch who were worthy of praise and support, and I do not wish to offend anyone by going through a list and running the risk of missing any of them. Suffice it to say they were passionate patriots who tried very hard but were not only in need of but broadly embraced a modernisation of their process and message. I was happy to work with them, and we adopted many of the more modern approaches to campaigning I had learnt from the Tories, along with the focus on very local issues I had observed working well for the Lib Dems.

For much of the first two years, I covered a large part of Dudley on my own. The rest of the activists were fully occupied in other areas, so I volunteered and took on the part that was closer to Wolverhampton and, coincidentally, more conservative-minded and totally uncoincidentally where I lived. I went out canvassing doorsteps and delivering thousands of leaflets with only my dog, Bruce, for company. Bruce was an odd-looking Terrier of mysterious breeding and a very independent character. We became well-known across the area, and I often thought that if I put Bruce on the ballot paper, he would certainly gain more votes than me.

Bill and Bruce

After a while, I developed a team of helpers. My dad decided that it was time to get stuck in and spent many hours delivering leaflets and canvassing; although I do suspect that he derived a strange pleasure from trying to canvass people who would never vote for us, he could have a good old row with. I approached other people to join us, and the team began to grow.

I made use of my Uncle Bill for canvassing on doorsteps. As a veteran and legendary salesman who had sold everything from double glazing to nuclear fallout shelters, he was superb at selling the message that it may be worth voting for us even though he really didn't have much idea of what our specific policies were other than leaving the EU. He did it for me; he did so much for me in his life, and this was just one more thing he was happy to do for "Our Bill."

I recruited Dean Perks to the cause. This is the same Dean Perks who, some years later, would absolutely beat me senseless whilst sparring in the boxing ring. He was a fantastic addition to the team. A big man with a big personality whose family was hugely respected in the local area, Dean was brilliant and showed himself to be a very smart political operator as he later became a regional organiser for first UKIP and then the Brexit party.

Other key members of the team were Alex, my cousin, who had enough of Uncle Bill's ability to chat with and persuade people to make him a very valuable asset, as well as being the first to keep our spirits up at the end of long days by guiding us into the pub and entertaining us with his rather eccentric take on life and funny stories.

They were joined by the twins. The twins were Zoe and Natalie. Very small and extremely pretty, they were well-known characters in the local area. The kind of people that everyone knows and everyone has time for a chat with. They were also capable of walking and leafletting like nobody else. They seemed to have their own internal nuclear fusion energy that kept them going when the rest of us were dropping like flies. On one occasion, we leafletted through a thunderstorm after an eight-hour session, walking up and down a very hilly part of the area. We retreated to the pub, and Natalie very nearly collapsed from exhaustion. This was symptomatic of the amount of effort and energy that went into our work. The twins were the engine of our local campaign machine and later would be requested to join them by branches all over the country when it was campaign time as the Dudley UKIP team became the ultimate campaigning force.

There are other people who helped, and I only leave their names out to preserve their anonymity as they are now settled back into civilian life and may not wish to have people reminded of their association with me.

I recruited, organised, coached and led a growing team of activists. I designed and paid for tens of thousands of leaflets, and I engaged with hostile or indifferent local media as much as I could to get us noticed.

I stood for election for Dudley Borough Council three times before finally being elected, and I stood for West Midlands Police and Crime Commissioner as a dry run before running to be West Midlands MEP.

On European election night in 2014, I was the last person in the whole of the country to have their election confirmed. I had been put onto the UKIP list at number three, behind Jill Seymour, who I had actually brought back into the party and Jim Carver, who had as much to do with the West Midlands as Del Boy Trotter from Only Fools and Horses. I have nothing against Jill or Jim, even though I certainly don't agree with much of what I at least understand to be their politics, but when people say to me they think the UKIP candidate selections were somehow crooked or corrupt, I merely smile and say "You may say that, but I couldn't possibly comment."

So when people say I just landed in Brussels as an MEP and that it was all pure luck, I do feel just a brief moment where there is a desire to express myself in what is referred to as "Industrial Language."

The Temple of Vanity
Life at the European Parliament from 2014 to 2019

My time as an MEP was largely spent at the European Parliament in Brussels, with a monthly visit to the European Parliament in Strasbourg. As far as I can see, the trip to Strasbourg had nothing to do with the practical running of a parliament and everything to do with keeping the French happy, which, as we all know, is a constant and largely thankless endeavour.

The parliament in Brussels is a magnificent structure, a masterpiece of Steel, glass and concrete. It sits at the head of a parliament square full of bars and restaurants and is often used for craft and food fayres alternating with all manner of protests and marches.

The inside of the building is truly huge; it has to hold the thousands of staff, politicians, and visitors who are there for three weeks every month. Bridges through ornate glass tunnels link various parts of the building, which exists on several floors. These floors incorporate parliamentary offices, meeting rooms, a rarely used parliamentarium, a hugely expensive state-of-the-art TV studio, at least four canteens and restaurants, a shopping centre, a gym, a travel agent, several different bars, a number of glass smoking booths and a downstairs car park housing dozens of parliamentary cars and their chauffeurs. I've probably missed a few parts out, but I think it's enough to get the drift, it's huge. Over the road from it is a similarly huge building which the secretariat occupies, thousands of them.

My office was conveniently placed near the bridge that linked the offices to the main concourse. It meant I could see everything that was going on and also meant that anyone could look in and see what was happening. I decided that using this vantage point, I would make sure my office was distinctively marked. I hung the Black Country flag outside my window. This flag meant nothing to most of the people there but its distinctive red and black colours with a centre piece of a cone for glass making and chains to represent the local chain makers attracted plenty of attention. I also made sure that I had prominent pictures of Margaret Thatcher and Winston Churchill in sight. If people wanted to look over, I wanted to make sure they got a clear message of whose office they were looking at. It did have its occasional humorous moments; on one occasion I received a call from Paul Nutttall on my mobile phone. I was working late and hunched over my computer, I picked up the phone to hear a boisterous scouse voice say "Im standing on the bridge and I can see the back of your head. Its just like a monkey's arse. Now pack up work, and let's go to the pub."

I placed the Gadsden flag outside my office with its "Don't Tread on me" quote as a symbol of my libertarian anti-big-state ideals. After a period of time, I noticed that it was continually being ripped down, so I continually put it back up. The vandals then moved on to scrawling "Racist" and other similar abuse on the flag, so I simply bought a stock of them and kept putting them back up. It took a while to realise who was doing it until one evening whilst working late, I heard a group of distinctly middle class voices chatting and giggling outside my door. I waited a moment, then opened the door to see a couple of rather young women dressed in the kind of clothes that you would expect to see at Glastonbury and with faces full of so many piercings I could not quite understand how they had managed to get past the metal detectors. I followed them stealthily and surprise surprise they ended up going into the offices of those kind and gentle Earth saviours the Green party. These Eco-warriors had been daily going out of their way to attack our property, a pattern of behaviour they seem to have adopted on a much larger scale in London over more recent years.

This went on for some time until we finally caught them in the act. Interestingly their heroics soon dissipated when confronted by a large growling and in their eyes particularly evil MEP. It was very pathetic but symptomatic of the kind of gesture politics the whole building was dedicated to.

Whilst the European Parliament is a hugely expensive building with ambitions that are beyond grandiose it does have frequent issues in as much as it doesn't always work. On one occasion, our office was infested with a grotesque smell. Martin Day, one of my Brussels-based staff, tells the story here in his own words.

"If ever there was an anecdote that summed up the two years I spent in Brussels working for Bill, it would be this;

With long days and late finishes, it was not unreasonable that there was a shower room off each MEPs office. Unless Bill was having meetings, he was kind enough to allow the two of us Aides to use it, too.

What many people don't know is that the main rectangular Parliamentary building was not one building at all; it was four, with a roof and linking walls bringing them all together.

This development had led to a number of changes in routes for the plumbing and there were places where pipes just led to a dead end. In addition, some facilities were a long way from a boiler, and water did not always stay at the desired temperature to stave off germs.

In time, an almost predictable missive came to the office instructing everyone not to use the hot water as Legionella pneumophila bacteria was rife in the system.

In short, the people who purported to run a continent couldn't even manage to run a warm shower!"

On another occasion, the gym, which I had taken to using and was extremely expensively equipped, was closed down on inquiring as to why I found out that it was due to Legionnaires disease. It never did reopen.

The TV studios were absolutely state of the art and cost many hundreds of thousands of Euros. Unfortunately, they were regularly out of action and lay in darkness.

Brussels: The Ultimate Playground

I am aware that I have covered a few serious issues and that many people who are reading this book aren't reading it for that reason. I understand that the intrigues of politics and the excesses of the European Parliament aren't all that exciting for most people. If you are reading for sensational content, then now is the time to shake off the onset of boredom because the nightlife in Brussels really is sensational.

Before any sour faced puritans try to use this section to moan about the fact that I was out there having fun rather than representing my voters let me just remind you that a typical working day for me and my team was 9.30 am until about 8 pm with no lunch. I'm in agreement with Gordon Gecco when he said, "Lunch is for wimps."

When we left the parliament building, both my team and I were normally far too wired from a long day of doing everything we could to put as many spanners in the works of the EU as we could to simply go home and go to sleep. Instead, we found a wide array of places to go and unwind.

It's important to note that while I was very keen on my team enjoying a beer, we never engaged in the hard drugs that are so prevalent around the EU parliament. It seemed that the place was entirely fuelled by Cocaine most of the time. Whilst I'm no Puritan, I saw the result of people working and playing fuelled on this drug and the inevitable crash down afterwards, and neither I nor my team went near it.

Nor did we engage in the regular visits to the red-light area that many of the other staff and parliamentarians enjoyed. Some of them were there so regularly they struck up friendships with the sex workers and even got to know their families. I have a rule that I have applied all my life: I love women, and I love sex, but to pay for it is a humiliation which takes away all of the pleasure. I much prefer to persuade a woman to sleep with me than pay for it. Having said that, I'm not against Prostitution or the people who use their services. It's just not for me.

Now, let's get around to what we did. We found some amazing bars, the likes of which are unrivalled on my travels. The hardest core drinking could be done in a place appropriately called Delirium Alley. This alley is home to the famous delirium bar with its famous Pink Elephant symbol. Delirium boasts more varieties of beer than anywhere else in the world, so if your taste extends to drinking coconut beer, wheat beer or a variety of splendidly fruity beers, that is the place to be.

Just over the road from Delirium is the Absinthe bar. Splendidly opulent in its faded grandeur with art deco designs and paintings still adorning the wall, this is the ultimate place for Absinthe. This is the real stuff, by the way, not the weakened versions available in the UK. We are talking about 70% alcohol-by-volume shots of the kind that can bring on hallucinations and allegedly led to Van Gough parting company with his ear.

I discovered these places on my first night in Brussels. A group of us decided to hit the town. I shall not mention names, but if you are reading this, guys, you know who you are. We started with a very nice meal washed down by far too much wine. Brussels is a wonderful place for seafood, and we shared a mountain of seafood between us at a very nice restaurant with several bottles of wine to wash it down. Then, the decision was made to find Delirium Alley.

On entering Delirium Alley, we politely declined the drug dealers offering us their wares; this was the last sensible decision of the evening. We entered Club Delirium on a mission. We were determined to try as many different beers as possible, and after around seven or eight drinks each, we felt we had done the place justice. As we left the bar, we saw the Absinthe bar and decided we should try a few chasers; this was a mistake. We started steadily enough with a couple of shots, each observing the traditional way of drinking it. This entailed dowsing a sugar cube in the drink then bringing it out and placing it on a perforated metal implement atop the glass and setting fire to it. Once the sugar has caramelised from the burning, you stir it into the drink, then swig it back in one. The trick is not to breathe straight away directly afterwards; if you do, it feels like your throat and lungs are on fire and are immensely uncomfortable. We had mastered this by the second drink.

Seeing that we were game for a bit of fun, the bar challenged us to use a glass funnel for a drinking game. The idea was that the Absinthe was put into the far side of the funnel and then set alight. This led to a jet propulsion effect, with the shot being fired down the tune at high speed into your throat. My first colleague did it, and whilst he tried to maintain some dignity, you could see it had hit him hard, and his drinking was done for the night. Then I did it; I can honestly say it felt like being physically thrown backwards. I slumped against the wall and focussed very hard on getting my eyes to work. Then, the final member of our group did it, and something went wrong. At some point, he lost control and spat the absinthe out in a very wide spraying motion. The flame was not out, so the flying absinthe caught fire, and briefly, the whole antique bar appeared to be alight, but this was not the worst of it. When I looked at my colleague it was clear that he must have sprayed some of the potent liquor into the air and it had landed on his head and caught light. For a brief but eternally memorable moment the whole top of his head appeared engulfed in flame then went out. It is an image that will always stay with me, doubtless enhanced by the hallucinogenic qualities of the Absinthe. Just for a short period of time he had looked like a Marvel Super hero or a human Olympic Torch.

My recollections of the rest of the night are approximately zero. In fact, the next thing I remember is being in my office at the Parliament, being violently sick. I have no recollection of what happened between the Absinthe bar and then. That day was perhaps the most exceptionally violent hangover of my life, but being a trooper by about 8 pm, I was recovered enough for another night of much more subdued drinking.

On another occasion, several team members based in the UK came out to Brussels to join us for an experience of the parliament and, of course, just as, if not more importantly, an experience of the nightlife. We started the evening drinking in an unusual Cocktail bar called the Pharmacy. The pharmacy was furnished and decorated in a style more suited to the nineteenth rather than the twenty-first century. Comfortable armchairs and drinks waiters dressed in uniforms suitable to another era. It also had a fascinating display of books lining the walls interspersed with what appeared to be scientific specimens in jars ranging from snakes to items of the anatomy of various creatures. A stag's head was the main decoration, and the whole effect was to give the impression we had entered a gothic horror story, some kind of hybrid between Frankenstein's laboratory and Sherlock Holmes's drawing room at 221B Baker Street. The drinks served were unique. Stange concoctions that often emanated steam or had parts of plants or trees appearing to be growing out of them. After setting the tone there with a few drinks, we moved on.

We then savoured the delights of Delerium Alley. Needless to say, the alcohol was kicking in hard by then, but still, we ploughed on. We managed to drink unusual beer and then try a couple of shots of alcohol without anyone's head being set alight on this occasion.

After that, we moved on to my favourite bar in all of Brussels, "The Coffin Bar". You enter the bar through a small doorway and walk up the darkened staircase until you see the dim red glow of the main bar. As you approach the bar, the booming sounds of Heavy Metal greet you with German Rockers Rammstein, a particular favourite. The walls are decorated with images of skeletons and demons painted onto a red background. The finishing touch is that each table you sit at is glass-topped and coffin-shaped. Peering through the glass, you see that each coffin table has a skeleton inside it. I assume the skeletons are stage props, but who knows? This is Brussels, and anything goes. When we had all seated ourselves, rather the worse for wear, we began ordering drinks. The house special was the appropriately named "Death Cocktail", a creamy drink with several different spirits in it and laced with Absinthe! After we had been there a little while and the drinks had continued to flow, it was clear that one of the members of our group was about done with the drinking. Gazing blankly into space, she continually started saying in a very matter-of-fact voice, "I'm going to be sick, I'm going to be sick" I tried to avert disaster by looking her straight in the face and suggesting she make her way to the toilet to which she replied quietly but in a very matter of fact way "Why can't you understand, my eyes aren't working, and I am going to be sick" Looking at her I believed her. Her usually piercing blue eyes appeared to have turned into Kaleidoscopes. On reflection, maybe that was the Absinthe affecting me, but that is what I saw. Eventually, one of the members of our group tried to help her to the toilet, but it was all too late. For a rather petite lady, she managed to vomit out an almost impossible amount of fluid. She left her trail all the way from the bar to the corridor leading to the toilets and then completely covered the toilets in her vomit. The angles of the spray-covering walls and even the ceiling were seemingly impossible. I was left with a very strong impression that it was a scene that would have fitted nicely into the movie "The Exorcist". Amazingly, the barman was really cool about the whole situation and was actually delighted when one of the members of our group asked for a mop and sponge to make some headway in clearing the mess up. We may have been drunken louts, but we were considerate drunken louts.

UKIP Civil Wars Part 1:
MEP meetings the seeds of destruction

UKIP really was different to the other parties in Brussels. In many ways, we were outliers for a more democratic approach. While other parties had their decisions on how to vote decreed from high, we had regular MEP meetings to discuss the issues.

The Whips team led by the inimitable Stuart Agnew MEP would recommend to us how they thought we should vote, and we could then discuss the issues after a brief explanation of the details from the relevant staff member for that particular issue. The staff members were all exceptional people, highly educated and prepared to work long hours to break down what the hundreds of pieces of legislation we were expected to vote on actually meant. Much of the legislation had cunningly hidden measures hidden away within hundreds of paragraphs of seemingly harmless waffles, and it took a careful eye to spot it and advise us as to how to vote. It was the equivalent of a five-hundred-page document which started by saying we all love our mothers and ended by saying we all love apple pie, but somewhere in the middle had a clause that was effectively a contract to sell your soul to the Devil.

Stuart Agnew, or "Aggers" as he was universally known, was a classic ex-military man. He was prepared to tolerate debate within set parameters, but he insisted that whatever we did, we all voted as "One Squad" He was excellent for the role of Chief Whip. Honourable to a fault, he never let his own views or agenda get in the way of his position and responsibilities.

"Aggers" was a farmer, and it's fair to say that he was not a fan of modern trends for organic or free-range farming. The other MEPs often privately joked about him and his methods, stealing lines from the famous Alan Partridge episode about farmers and suggesting he had huge genetically modified chickens locked away in darkened buildings or that they had an extra leg and ran so fast he could not catch them. On one occasion, we managed to make Tim Aker the butt of the Aggers jokes. We were aware that journalists had been investigating the Agger's farming operation in an attempt to cause more trouble for UKIP. In a typically formal fashion, Aggers informed us that he was going to make a formal statement about the investigation to us at the next MEP meeting. In the gap between him announcing this and the statement being made to use, we had somehow persuaded Tim that Aggers had been caught having sex with a giant genetically modified chicken. When the actual statement was made, revealing that nothing serious had been found, Tim erupted into relieved laughter, roundly calling out most of his fellow MEPs for winding him up. Aggers took the interruption in his stride and, in his formal military fashion, called for order to be restored, and we continued with the business of the day.

I grew to have a huge degree of respect for Aggers. Yes, he was very formal and rather stiff, but he was truly honourable and a straight speaker. As the saying goes, he is the kind of man you would want next to you in the trenches, and I have a sneaking suspicion he probably fought in the trenches at some point. An example of his decency and fairness came when I was standing for election as party leader. He attended every husting to ensure that fair play was being done. At the end of observing a seemingly endless stream of hustings, he declared publicly that he would support me to be a leader. Apparently, at the beginning of the process, I was about the last person he would have backed, but he cast a fair eye on how everyone performed at the hustings and declared I was the one who had won that series of battles. Honest, fair, principled, and honourable, they don't make them like Aggers anymore, and I was very proud to have been part of his squad.

Initially, although we all had our say at MEP meetings, the argument would be settled by Nigel expressing his opinion and everyone falling into line. This was a metaphor for the party as a whole; UKIP was never a group of people with one settled set of opinions but rather a loose amalgamation of disparate views united in their desire to leave the EU and their support for Nigel as a leader. In years to come, it became apparent that literally, nobody other than Nigel could hold this alliance together, which is both a tribute to his abilities and a condemnation of those of us who tried to fill his shoes or even keep his seat warm for him.

As time went by and Nigel became more popular and in media demand, he attended MEP meetings less and less often so that by the later part of our term in Brussels, he wasn't there at all. This allowed the huge differences and alternative camps within the party to be seen in a microcosm, with the most prominent figures from each faction clashing at MEP meetings.

The MEP grouping between 2014 and 2019 was split in so many different directions that it was almost impossible to imagine we were in the same party. Indeed, I think our fatal flaw was that some of these people were actually at the party. There were a significant group of MEPs who had absolutely no idea about political principles and were solely in UKIP because they were inspired by Nigel. These people became the floating voters in our internal battles, as without Nigel being there, they simply had no idea of what they were supposed to think or do.

Then there were a group of MEPs who were akin to Left Wing Nationalists and would probably have been more comfortable in Madame Le Pen's Front Nationale. The most prominent and effective of these people was Patrick O'Flynne. Patrick is a guy who, outside of politics, I have a lot of time for and can be great company. I also have huge respect for him as a communicator in the written word and his debating ability in a meeting. My issue with Patrick was that his opinions, with the exception of his desire to leave the EU, had absolutely nothing to do with the principles and constitution of the party I had joined. Over a period of years, he worked with his acolytes, most notable of whom were Lisa Duffy and Suzanne Evans, who would later be joined by London Assembly member Peter Whittle as a formidable force for change, pushing party policies towards Authoritarianism and more state power while all the time very skilfully portraying themselves as moderates and "the adults in the room."

The other segment of opinion was largely led by me. I considered myself to be standing up for the Libertarian principles of the party I had joined and had been grown by Godfrey Bloom and Nigel Farage. Classically liberal economic policies and an emphasis on the individual having more power restored to him from the state whilst maintaining a patriotic love of country was what I believed we stood for and should continue to stand for. I stood my ground in many a heated debate, prompting Ray Finch MEP to call me "The conscience of the party" due to my insistence that we stand by the principles laid out in our constitution.

The other segment of party opinion represented was in the brooding figure of Gerard Batten. Economically to the left and a ferocious Nationalist, he had much in common with the views espoused by Patrick; however, his loathing of Islam was so fanatical, and his dislike of homosexuality was so extreme that, in my opinion, he was the person with the most over the top, and hard-line views I have ever met. Picture Alf Garnett with an elected position, and you would not be far from the man. Fortunately, for much of the first part of our term, Gerard kept himself very much to himself, only ever involving himself in discussions to do with the EU and how to get out of it. I wish he had maintained that position indefinitely.

After Nigel had started absenting himself from the MEP meetings, the tide changed dramatically towards the Oflynn camp. Try as I may, I simply wasn't up to stopping them. Even when I was winning a debate, he would use the killer line "In light of the coming referendum" and then shut down any policy idea or approach that was in any way radical or different to the mainstream parties. Even when we were asked as a group whether to back Aaron Banks's bid to run the leave campaign or to support the Tory-dominated "Vote Leave", and Nigel won the day for Aaron by throwing his weight behind him, Patrick and his devotees supported Vote Leave. Let us not forget that Vote Leave was, in some people's opinion, predominantly a vehicle for getting Boris Johnson into office and that its mad genius in chief, Dominic Cummings, was unequivocal in his plan to sideline UKIP and Nigel. This should have been an obvious sign that some of our colleagues were not interested in the success of our party, yet they were not only allowed to continue in place but also gained more power.

In one of the many examples of Nigel being a disastrous judge of character, he allowed Oflynn's acolyte, Suzanne Evans, to take control of policy before the 2015 General Election. She proceeded to produce the most bland and unimaginative document possible, with the headline policy being to throw more money at the NHS. This is the one topic that every party engages in a bidding war on, so by joining in with the money-burning madness, we simply indicated we were the same as all the rest and lost any possible competitive edge. Almost all the libertarian-themed policies that Godfrey Bloom and Nigel had championed for years were removed. The 2015 manifesto was the biggest missed opportunity in modern political history. By making us seem like the other parties, it made the voter's decision even more than usual about which personalities you trust to govern, and as almost every one of our senior figures had been under constant character assassination from the media for years, it wasn't our strongest card.

The First Post Nigel Leadership Campaign

After the Leave vote won the Referendum, a campaign covered in much more detail later in this book, Nigel stood down from party leadership with the famous line, "I want my life back". I sat next to Paul Nuttall, who was deputy leader at the time and said to him, "This is it then this is your time, mate" I worked with Paul and other MEPs to muster large portions of the membership behind him, and it appeared that the overwhelming backing from the party as a whole gathered behind the cheerful Scouser would ensure a coronation with no serious opposition. Then, out of the blue, without warning, any of us Paul took to the stage at a party conference in the North of England and stated that he would not be leader with, the reason being it wouldn't be fair on his family to bring so much pressure and attention onto them. At that moment the cells to the lunatic asylum all opened simultaneously and every faction, every simmering resentment and every weakness in our party structure was revealed.

Stephen Woolfe was an early favourite for the leadership but he somehow managed to fail to get his papers in on time. There has been much speculation and theorising about this and while its true a number of senior figures in the party organisation had no time for Stephen the fact, he left it to the very last minute to get his entry to the race formalised was a huge mistake on his part.

A wide range of candidates declared for the leadership race, including me. My aim was initially to argue the case for the libertarian approach to politics and hopefully secure enough votes to have a position of influence going forward, but as the race went on, I actually began to believe that I just may be the best person for the job.

The Oflynn puppet candidate for the role was Lisa Duffy. Patrick was always too smart to stand for leadership himself. He much preferred to be a backseat driver. Lisa and her team ran a very unpleasant campaign with mud and smears flying everywhere, all appearing to come from people near to her.

Liz Jones, the queen of London UKIP, put her name forward. Liz is a unique individual. Her views are rather on the libertarian side of the party, and her approach is eccentric. She managed to combine ferocious debating skills with humour and charm and was always the candidate with the most swagger and style. I thoroughly enjoyed the hustings where she was involved and found myself wishing she was on my side.

The latecomer to the race and instant favourite was Diane James MEP. It was clear that several senior party backers were not at all keen on seeing me in the running for leader and wanted to put in someone far more respectable. I was furious about this as I had spoken with Diane some months earlier suggesting she should stand for leader and she had effectively said she didn't have the belly for it. To be clear I liked and respected Diane she was on the surface at least everything that should have worked as a top politician. Attractive, smart, well educated, intelligent, experienced and a good speaker she was almost perfect. The only problem was I knew she didn't really want it, and she wasn't great with confrontation. Indeed, there had been an occasion in one heated inter party committee meeting where she had been confronted aggressively by rival MEPs and I had intervened to stand up for her. The last words I heard from Diane before her declaration on the subject of leadership were that she wouldn't do it without me by her side. Her team offered me a mid-ranking position in her administration if I backed down and supported her, but it was too late by then.

I would have backed another MEP, Jonathon Arnott rather than going the full course myself but his campaign lacked traction and just wasn't working. I liked Jonathon. He is a great guy, a really genuine soul and technically has the IQ of a genius which he shows in his high mastery of chess. He is also rather sound politically and more my wing of the party, so I would have been very happy with him as leader, but it wasn't going to happen, so I continued the fight.

The campaign itself was a long, drawn-out affair with hustings arranged all over the UK. I attended every event and gave a different speech each time. Most impartial opinion had me winning the majority of the hustings but the trouble was Diane James did not attend any of them. I personally think a candidate for leadership should be forced to attend at least some of the hustings to show respect to the membership, but Diane's handlers felt that exposing her to debate with the other candidates was a no-win situation for them. They were right. Diane had a huge lead in terms of recognition amongst the membership particularly as the party officials had done everything, they tried to starve me of airtime outside of the West Midlands ever since Id joined the party. Allowing her into the same room as opponents could only be a negative for her but all the same it really should have happened as it may have saved us all some of the embarrassment that followed her election.

The period of this internal election campaign was one of the worst of my life. While being almost constantly on the road and travelling from Brussels or Strasbourg to virtually every corner of the United Kingdom and surviving solely on various stimulants and no sleep, I was being constantly bombarded with very hurtful attacks. It was an immensely difficult time which had an impact on my mental and emotional health I still feel the repercussions from to this day.

The worst part of it was the smear, which was picked up on and spread far and wide by the Lisa Duffy team involving Viagra. My girlfriend of the time was extremely erratic and prone to fits of almost psychotic rage; I really know how to pick them. She was constantly convinced that I was cheating on her, even though it was one of the few periods in my life when I wasn't chasing other women. Nothing would change her mind. Going through my car looking for evidence of infidelity, she found a pack of Viagra with two tablets missing and assumed that as I hadn't been with her for the previous week, this was evidence of me being with other women. What it actually was evidence of was the fact I had been to a Rock festival with a friend of mine without telling her, and my friend had convinced me that taking Viagra was not just good for helping to maintain an erection, but it heightened the experience of being at a rock gig making the senses more alert, he was wrong. I couldn't explain this to my girlfriend as I had gone to the festival without telling her as I had wanted a break from her constant paranoia. She posted the part-empty packet on Twitter with a caption accusing me of being a no-good womaniser or words to that effect.

This was bad enough, but the post was picked up by Lisa Duffy's supporters and spread around with the very clear implication that the MEP for the West Midlands and torch bearer of the libertarian right could not get Led in his pencil. They also ensured that the story reached the national media and of course they revelled in it. I was nationally and internationally labelled as being sexually impotent and generally ridiculed.

I have two very serious issues with the way this was handled. The first and by far the most important is that there is a major concern over suicide in the male population of the UK, and one of the biggest causes of this is issues to do with potency and manhood. Why did nobody consider the fact that there are some men who on reading every newspaper in the country declare them as impotent may well have already been in a depressed state and this could have led to yet another tragic suicide. Fortunately, I was in a better place mentally than that, but it certainly was not pleasant to read. The only thing that made it somewhat better was that my hero Ian "Beefy" Botham wrote a piece in the national press stating how appalling their coverage of this issue had been and reminding them of their responsibilities. This was not the way I had dreamed of coming to the great man's attention I confess but it still cheered me up.

The other and far less serious reason that I was unhappy with the coverage was that it all assumed I took Viagra because I was incapable of an erection. That could not be further from the truth. I took Viagra because the young lady I was with at the time felt that she had not been properly made love to until you had worked through at least half of the pages of the Karma Sutra and been at it for at least two hours. Now I was a pretty fit and healthy bloke for my age but I couldn't keep that work rate in bed up without a little extra help. So, there you go, that's the true Viagra story.

An unintended but very welcome effect of the Viagra story was that wherever I went in the country, there appeared to be a generous number of women who were keen to see whether or not I was capable of performing to standard in the bedroom. The few months following the story where particularly productive in terms of new female friends so for that at least I am most grateful.

The Duffy camp continued with their dirty tricks with them, spreading the rumour that I was going to quit the race as I could not stand the stress. A rumour they repeated at a meeting of regional organisers, at which Dean Perks was in attendance. Straight talking and Black Country through and through Dean jumped to my defence saying "That's a load of bollocks. You've got more chance of seeing Nessie swimming down the Thames than that stubborn bastard quitting" He was right!

On another occasion we were in the heat of a hustings and Duffy was pursuing her favourite past time of demonising Muslims. She asked what I would do if terrorist suspects fled into a Mosque. My answer was "Id go right into the Mosque after them" Duffy's crony tweeted that I had said I would "write into the Mosque". These pathetic and petty dirty tricks were constant and demoralising, but I kept going. I have a great many weaknesses as this book undoubtedly highlights but I'm no quitter!

One great advantage that I had been gifted during the campaign was the support of Mike Hookem. The tough ex-forces MEP for Yorkshire had joined my campaign when it was clear that Jonathon Arnott was not going to be the man to win the battle. He allowed me the use of his staff, and one person in particular from his team helped to step my campaign up to a whole new level. Annabelle Fuller also known as Trixie Saunderson was something of a UKIP legend. Her media work had been vital in the early years helping Nigel to get the airtime and coverage he made such excellent use of. She has spectacularly fallen from grace when an alleged affair between her and Nigel had been spoken about and fed to the media by rebellious former MEPs, but make no mistake, she was still a formidable personality and huge talent.

Thanks to Annabelle, I managed to get TV airtime despite the efforts of UKIP head office to stop us. At one point I had a series of interviews arranged around London and we were always just a few minutes ahead of the head office media guy who was desperately trying to head us off. She also arranged my favourite ever interview which strangely enough was with the Guardian newspaper. She had used every ounce of influence and persuasive power to get the interview which ended up being one of the very few to ever actually portray my political views and didn't label me some kind of insane NAZI.

Annabelle also travelled around the hustings with us and was a brilliant aide. It was during my time working with her that I genuinely felt I was at the very top of my game. On one occasion at a hustings, I fed her a question to ask, which I knew would trap the other candidates. The UK had recently purchased the steel for new tanks from Sweden. This had caused an uproar amongst some of the more blindly nationalist UKIP members with them screaming from the roof tops that British tanks should be made from British Steel. However, my knowledge of the Steel industry led me to understand that the very best quality of steel for armour plating is manufactured in Sweden. Annabelle persuaded one of the crowd members to raise the issue, and I sat quietly and patiently as each of the other candidates launched into patriotic speeches about how we should have used our own Steel before it came to my turn when I calmly and with great delight lectured the other candidates on the fact I would rather our servicemen have the best protection possible, and that meant buying the Swedish Steel in this case. As I was revelling in my moment, I saw Annabelle laughing hysterically then proceed to lie on the floor kicking her legs in the air. All I could see at the back of the room was her incredibly long legs and trademark "Killer Heels" kicking up in the air. It was a good moment.

Annabelle had also distinguished herself when Suzanne Evans was laughing and showing people the Viagra Twitter post at one of the hustings events. As I looked out over the rather large crowd, I saw the tall, extremely stylishly clad UKIP legend descend on the seated Ms Evans and exchange heated words. It was spectacular to see.

As well as all this, Annabelle brokered a meeting between me and Godfrey Bloom, which resulted in the great Libertarian himself giving me his personal backing.

This was a huge honour for me, and regardless of the end result, it is something that is very meaningful and a great source of pride to me personally.

At this point, I want to dispel yet another of the rumours swirling around at that time. I can guess where it came from, and it was yet another attempt at a destructive smear from within our own party. Let me state categorically that my relationship with Annabelle was strictly professional. While we developed a good level of friendship during the campaign, we were never involved in a romantic relationship. After the number of nasty smears and rumours that lady has had to deal with, I feel honour bound to clear that one up once and for all.

The results of the leadership election were announced at the party's national conference. As I entered the main auditorium, I had a little trepidation about how the crowd would receive me after such a damaging campaign. I was very pleasantly surprised by the warmth of the membership and particularly the number of ladies coming over to give me a hug and whisper in my ear that they didn't believe a word of it. All contenders were ushered into a back room to be privately told the results; well, all contenders except Diane were kept separate from us even then. This genuinely hurt me as I had genuinely thought that Diane and I had a pretty good relationship as colleagues, and I had even thought we were friends at one point. Anyway, the results were read out and as expected Diane came in a resounding first with Duffy second and me third. Liz Jones came in fourth with enough votes to save her deposit and uttered the wonderful words "Fantastic. Ive had all of the partying with none of the hangover" classic Liz and part of why she is so popular. On later analysis, it would appear that I was most people's second choice and would have had an outstanding chance of victory if Diane had not stood. Phillip Broughton, a relatively unknown young man from Hartlepool, had come in fifth with a very creditworthy share of the vote, also keeping his deposit.

When the results were read out Diane's handlers allowed her to briefly enter the room to accept our congratulations then she was ushered away to prepare for her Coronation. It was at that point that the most extraordinary thing of all happened. After Diane left the room, the door was locked, and we weren't allowed out until after she had been anointed. I had prepared a generous concession speech pledging my support, but I couldn't deliver it. Yet another insult from the party I had dedicated so much time and effort to.

We were finally allowed out of the back room after Diane had delivered her first speech as leader. We made our way to the side of the stage, at least hoping to smile and wish her well as she walked off. As we were jostled by the crowd, Liz lost her footing and literally fell into my arms. Some TV coverage made it appear that we were locked in a passionate embrace, so I would like to take this opportunity to set the record straight and spare Liz any more embarrassment. It was nothing of the sort.

Diane's leadership of the party lasted eighteen days. During that time, she was constantly shielded from her colleagues or, if you look at it another way, held hostage by a small group of backers who didn't want her mixing with us. Rumours abound as to why she quit so early, including one particular one about her receiving a death threat on the London tube, which I have no idea whether it is true or not but is rather frightening.

During her brief time as leader, Nigel approached me and asked me to try to calm her down and show that I wasn't going to undermine her. I was somewhat surprised by this because, as far as I was aware, I had never done anything to undermine her. The closest I had got to distressing her was challenging her via social media to a head-to-head debate, which she ignored. At this point I still believed that I was there to support Nigel and his vision for the party and country so of course I agreed. I could not get a meeting with her but I was informed by one of her handlers that the best thing I could do was start a petition stating that in our opinion Diane James was the leader of UKIP. I was flabbergasted by this. We had just had a long and hugely expensive election, which Diane had won by a considerable margin; what possible good could be served by this petition? I reported back to Nigel, telling him that, in my opinion, it was a mistake to organise such a petition as it may look sarcastic, to which he agreed.

After this, Nigel papproached Diane, and after much obfuscation on her part, they went for a meal and a meeting. Shortly after that Nigel said that she would have to go and go she went.

UKIP Civil Wars Part 2:
The descent into madness

After Diane had left the scene, there was a brief pause before it became apparent Stephen Woolfe was to be the chosen successor.

I asked Nigel why he preferred to back Stephen over me, and he said words to the effect that whilst I was very politically aware and strong on the issues, Stephen looked and came across better. I was actually quite relaxed about that. Stephen is a good-looking guy, and he does come across extremely well on TV.

I like Stephen. He is a nice bloke, and politically, we were quite similar. My only misgivings were that similar to Diane, I wasn't sure how he would cope with the immense pressure of the top job at the party. I knew I could handle immense pressure as I had been subjected to a huge trial by the media for the preceding few years and was still standing, but nobody else amongst the serious contenders had been battle-hardened that way. Still, under the circumstances, I was happy to go ahead and back Stephen to lead in order to restore some kind of order.

I vividly remember the day In Strasbourg when we had all had the chat with Nigel and knew that we needed to back Stephen. He went around, discussing what position we should have in his leadership team. I settled for Trade and Industry but later heard that he was supposed to offer me, Deputy Leader.

It was the end of a long day, and Stephen let out the fact that he had been in discussions with the Tories about joining them but had now changed his mind as he saw the leadership was his for the taking. This was overheard by some of the other MEPs, who were furious. Tim Aker called for a special meeting the next morning to discuss the situation, and one was urgently convened.

We all attended this extraordinary meeting, and I'm sure most of us were there to hear Stephen out and have the matter put to rest. The meeting began, and Tim laid out his concerns. Stephen responded but was clearly nervous and not his usual erudite self. At this point, the ever gruff and direct Mike Hookem intervened and asked in very direct terms if it was true that Stephen had been on the verge of joining the Tories. I think Stephen must have misinterpreted Mike's tone because he took off his jacket, put it on the back of his chair, and said words to the effect that if Mike was going to be like that, they should go outside and "Settle it like men."

"Settle it like men" is a phrase that has been hotly contested as to what was meant ever since. Stephen maintains he did not mean violently but rather directly and face to face. However, the gesture of taking his jacket off before leaving the room was not a good signal to give out.

Mike was sitting next to me at the time, and after a moment's hesitation and a slight smile, he said, "All right then," and walked out of the meeting room. There was a brief pause of perhaps no more than a minute. I sat very near to the door and didn't hear any words being said, but I did hear the sound of furniture being moved, and I assumed it must mean that things had progressed to being heated. I turned and dashed out of the door and was the first on the scene. I saw Stephen just finishing a fall towards the door he had exited the meeting room from and a slightly bemused-looking Mike standing above him. I don't believe anyone was closer or had a better view than me, and I cannot say what happened to this day. I have always got on well with both men in question, so it is not my intention to point the finger of blame at either of them; I am merely recounting what happened.

Stephen left the meeting straight after the incident, and the room soon emptied with totally confused MEPs heading off to the bar or to their offices to think about what had happened. One thing was certain: the consensus for backing Stephen had evaporated, and we never did get an answer about the link with the Tories.

Several hours later, we had a typically long Strasbourg voting session. Towards the end of it, I saw Stephen running up the stairs to leave the parliamentarian. This was a typically Stephen energetic and dynamic move and I assumed he was rushing to catch his train or aircraft back home at the end of a busy week. I left the auditorium about five minutes later, having seen it through to the end of yet another interminably long and pointless voting session, but I figured that was the job, and we should see it through to the end of the week. As I left, I saw a group of people gathered around a prone figure on the footbridge leading from the parliamentary area to the exits. I wasn't aware of who it was or what had happened until a little later. Apparently, Stephen had collapsed, and the photos of the event became quite iconic. He was soon taken to hospital, where he remained for several days.

The rumour mill started in full crazy swing after that. The story was that Mike Hookem was on the run from the police and was trying to leave France by car. Images of the former squaddie having to abandon his car, don full camouflage, and yomp across Europe to avoid capture were discussed. Of course, nothing of the sort was true, and Mike had travelled back in his normal fashion, but it was an interesting rumour for a while.

The chaos surrounding the Stephen Woolfe incident was the icing on the cake for the members, who had already begun to be disillusioned with their MEPs due to the very visible fighting, and hostility towards us from the members became much more widespread. This was added to by party officials who were always hungry for a slice of the MEP's pay packet circulating attacks on MEPs who they didn't think were coughing up enough cash.

Initially, I didn't mind this as it was funding the party, but after a while, rumours of hugely excessive lunches, opulent offices and high wages, meaning that very little of the money we donated went to the party, began to frustrate many of us. I continued to pay towards the main party as well as donating to the youth wing and funding election campaigns in my own part of the West Midlands, as well as paying for the transport and accommodation of teams of activists from my area to by-elections all around the country but it left a sour taste in the mouth particularly as unlike most of the other MEPs I was not an independently wealthy man.

We had one last chance to get it right. I was all geared up to stand for leader and had garnered significant support across the country to the point where I was rightly considered one of the strongest candidates. Then, my plans were scuppered again by a candidate being persuaded to come forward who was considered more sensible than me. Paul Nuttall had decided that this time, he was going to stand. Of course, there was no question I would stand against Paul, who I considered a good friend and pretty much politically sound. I also believed he had the kind of charming personality that would bring the party together and appeal to the general public.

Sadly, the Red UKIP acolytes of Patrick O'flynn didn't see it that way, and they unveiled their big hitter. Suzanne Evans. Ms Evans was an accomplished media performer and very good at appearing moderate. She worked hand-in-glove with Patrick and Lisa Duffy and was a significant opponent. On her declaration to stand, Patrick put out a press release with the chilling words, "The Adults have entered the room."

Despite another tough campaign, Paul Nuttall ran out the winner by a significant distance. His campaign was backed by a wide range of people from across the party, but his most vocal supporters were from the Libertarian Right. We went into bat for Paul in a massive way as we believed he was not only the right man for the job but also the man capable of finally crushing the threat of an O'flynn puppet taking over the party. I remember celebrating long and hard when the victory was won.

And then a strange thing happened. After having roundly trounced the other wings of the party, Paul reached out to them and brought them back into the fold. He managed to snatch defeat from the jaws of victory. He gave Suzanne Evans control over policy, and Peter Whittle was brought in in a senior role. Peter Whittle's views are hugely authoritarian, and he lives to fight culture wars. Patrick O'flynn was given a senior role as a key advisor.

While all of this was happening, my importance to Paul's team plummeted. I went from a point where I had been promised Deputy Chairman with responsibility for policy and whatever spokesman role we could agree to, being told Suzanne Evans had got the policy role and that I could not be a spokesman with anything to do with Economics as "Paddy won't stand for it" I ended up with a promotion to being Defence spokesman, but it was a role that kept me out of the inner circle.

It was a demoralising feeling. It felt like we had defeated our enemy conclusively in battle, only to invite them into our castle and give them all the keys.

Relations between Paul and me declined a little after this. With great credit to him, he realised this and invited me to join him for a day of drinking in his local area. We had a fantastic day, just a couple of friends ironing out their issues over multiple pints and a curry. I felt like we had our friendship back on track.

The next day, I saw a report on social media that the PM was going to make an announcement. I immediately texted Paul, saying let's get ready to saddle up, and the election is coming. He responded by saying he had asked Patrick, and I was completely wrong. There was no chance of an election. A few hours later, the Prime Minister called an election. I immediately texted Paul and asked if he wanted me to drive over to help with preparations and battle plans. He texted back, saying not to bother as Patrick was already on his way. I can honestly admit I felt crestfallen and deeply disappointed, but I was still willing to throw all I had at the coming campaign.

We were caught on the hop by the early election. No policies were ready, and we needed them fast. I was informed that every department had to prepare detailed policies that would stand up to scrutiny within three days and then send them to Suzanne Evans to collate.

My team did a magnificent job of pulling together a brilliant defence policy. I say very deliberately it was my team. I gave them direction as to what I was looking for, but it was the team that pulled the whole thing together, pulling all-night shifts to get it done and reaching out to significantly experienced military figures to confirm our details. Our immensely detailed policy demanded an increase in defence spending to the levels of GDP last seen in the mid-1980s. Special provision for improved barracks and mess facilities to help retain recruits is a well-researched and important piece of work. The building of a hospital ship by British shipbuilders provided tens of thousands of jobs and gave the navy a multipurpose vessel similar to those in the fleets of the Chinese and Americans, which could also double up as an emergency ready-made hospital for the NHS in case of a crisis or as an effective part of a practical foreign aid policy in case of natural disasters. We spelt out a policy of improved provision for veterans and a determination to stop the prosecution of soldiers for issues that had taken place in past conflict zones, including Northern Ireland. Perhaps most pertinently of all, considering the current controversy about small boats bringing illegal immigrants to the UK, we put forward a policy to build a small fleet of patrol boats in the UK to patrol our post-Brexit waters. All of the policies were costed, and all of them had multiple positive benefits to the UK, including a much-needed boost to the shipbuilding industry.

After all of the hard work, we were very excited for our policy document to be submitted to the NEC for approval. Suzanne told me she had submitted it and informed me that the NEC had enthusiastically supported it. Imagine my delight when I actually saw our defence policy printed in our manifesto for the first time at the official election launch. I opened the page for the defence section and saw one paragraph stating that we would look to take better care of our veterans. That was it, nothing else. She had completely ignored our work and submitted her own one-paragraph policy. Fuming with rage, I went to Paul to complain but could not get an audience as he was surrounded by O'flynn, Evans, and Whittle at all times. It was like he had been kidnapped by a cult. By the time I managed to speak to him, it really was too late. I decided that rather than damage the party's election efforts, I would stay in place until after the election and then quietly resign and see out my term as an MEP focussing on representing the interests of the West Midlands.

This plan for a quiet departure was totally derailed by what happened next. Margot Parker is an admirable lady for whom I have huge respect. She wasn't really part of any faction but was of a strand of old-fashioned conservative thinking I could relate to. Poor Margot was dropped into the mire of a massive controversy by the cabal of Oflynn acolytes now so clearly running the show. She was given a policy to announce in front of the media, which she hadn't been given advanced notice of the content of. When she was given the policy with the media waiting for her at a pre-arranged press conference, she had little choice but to read it out. The policy was a ridiculously clumsy effort to focus attention on Female Genital Mutilation. Obviously, FGM is a very important issue and a dreadful crime; however, the policy was nothing more than a thinly veiled attack on the British Muslim community. The gist of it was that Muslim girls would be subject to regular inspection of their genitals without the consent of their parents. Imagine the response of any segment of the community at being told the state was taking free licenses to look up their daughters' skirts; the response of the Muslim community really did not bear thinking about it.

I was amongst a majority of MEPs utterly horrified by the policy and the way it had been sprung on us, and I vocally expressed my opinion. Even if the policy was not as hard-line as it had come across, it was guaranteed to be portrayed in a dreadful light by the media, which were always keen to label UKIP as hostile to minorities. This was a massive own goal, and it was obvious for anyone to see this.

Totally unprompted, MEPs started pouring into my office to express their horror at the policy. I was not so naïve as to not understand what was happening; they wanted me to be the one who put his head above the parapet and most likely get it shot off. The meeting in my cramped office became heated, and passions rose; I was actually arguing that we should avoid public dissent and seek to speak to Paul about it. I spent quite a lot of time trying to persuade Jim Carver not to resign as a spokesman, but in a typical fashion for Jim, he either ignored or didn't understand my argument and resigned. While I was in the middle of fighting to keep what Aggers had always referred to as "The Squad," Ray Finch entered my office and completely misinterpreted what I was doing. I love Ray. He is a great guy, but he is also an aggressive Scouse Rottweiler when he gets going. He started shouting, accusing all of us of betraying Paul, and it took me some time to explain that the idea of our conversation was to keep things under control until we had had time to speak to Paul. Unfortunately for all of us, unbeknown to all of us, a reporter from the Daily Mail was lurking outside my office and had recorded much of the argument. I was only to find this out a little later.

It was agreed that a special meeting would be called to discuss the issue. This meeting was to become one of the most extraordinary I have ever been involved with. On one side of the large meeting table sat Patrick and Peter Whittle, and sat slightly back from the table was Paul looking ashen and very concerned. Nigel was also in the room on Paul's side of the table but slightly to one side. On the other side of the table sat the majority of the MEPs, and surprise, surprise, they had nominated me to be the spokesman against the policy. Aggers was the chairman of the meeting.

I began the meeting by making what I considered to be a very calm and measured argument against the policy and a complaint against how it had been foisted on us with no consultation. I was halfway through my comments when a furious Patrick Oflynn shouted, interrupting me, saying words to the effect that my libertarian ideas had been rejected by the party membership and I should stop going on about personal freedom and liberty. This was the one and only time I have seen Patrick genuinely angry. I responded calmly by saying that it was me personally that had been rejected by the party members, not my ideas.

After that, the meeting broke down into a huge row. Peter Whittle accused

Jim Carver of being a traitor, which sent Jim into an absurd rage and led to him appearing to be on the verge of becoming violent. Whittle also engaged the Scottish MEP David Coburn in a similar fashion, and I have a vague recollection of Coburn suggesting he was prepared to throw Whittle out of the window, but I may be wrong; I doubt it, but I may be.

In the midst of the Bedlam, Gerard Batten stood up and walked out, declaring it was all a waste of time and suggesting that although he supported the policy, it would never be applied, and he would rather talk about Brexit. When Gerard Batten thinks a policy is too strong to ever be applied, it's a fair hint that you are past the point of madness.

The meeting wound to a close with Nigel diffusing the situation by basically saying it would all be okay and letting's just move on. It was entirely unsatisfactory, but it brought the chaos to an end.

When I left the meeting, I was phoned by the reporter from the Daily Mail. They informed me that if I could not give them a statement, they would go to print detailing a meeting they had heard with a scouse accent that they had heard screaming and shouting at fellow MEPs and ascribe the angry Liverpudlian to being an out-of-control Paul Nuttall. I was in a no-win situation. I could tell the truth and throw Ray under the bus; I could say nothing and allow a false but damaging headline about Paul to be printed, or I could make a statement and take the heat myself. I took what I thought was the honourable thing and made a statement, determined to take the heat for the statement myself.

The next day, when Nigel read the story in the newspaper, he exploded with rage. He called Paul Nuttall into a meeting where he expressed his preference that I be metaphorically hung, drawn, and quartered. Well, I hope it was metaphorical, but when Nigel loses his temper, you can never be sure. He settled on sending one of his assistants to deliver a brief note to me expressing his disappointment, which finished with the sentiment that he had contacted me in this way so that it was impossible for me to leak what he had said to the press. I was furious and deeply offended. This was a man who I had run through brick walls for years and who had used my parent's home to take a break and sleep during his tours of the West Midlands. I angrily texted him, saying I would say no more on the subject but that his anger might be better directed at the people imposing utterly disgusting policies on our party. It was a turning point in our relationship, and it was never quite the same again.

This newspaper article also prompted the wildest argument I ever had with Paul Nuttall. He phoned me about it late in the evening after having seen another UKIP member questioning his leadership on TV. He vented all his frustration on me. I was sitting in my favourite Sheesha bar in Brussels at the time, smoking a Turkish blend and downing unidentifiable cocktails to wind down after an awful day with a couple of members of the staff. Our tempers both flared out of control. We screamed abuse at each other, and I've no doubt had we been face to face, there would have been some serious violence. At the conclusion of the call, I punched a hole in the temporary partition around my cubicle at the bar and ended up paying my Turkish hosts quite a few Euros to accommodate its repair.

The next day, Paul phoned me, and I pre-empted the conversation by apologising, saying, quite rightly, that I had no business speaking to him the way I had. I apologised unreservedly and offered my immediate resignation. To Paul's great credit, he would have none of it. We talked for some time and ended the conversation with a semblance of respect and friendship restored. Paul Nuttall is a good man, and at the end of the day, that is what really matters to me. Political differences are one thing, but respect for another good-hearted human being is another, and we never exchanged harsh words again.

UKIP Civil Wars Part 3:
The end of the party

After the disastrous 2017 General election that saw Theresa May's Conservatives massively reduce our vote share with the ridiculously meaningless slogan "Brexit Means Brexit", Paul Nuttall resigned as leader, and once again, we were plunged into chaos.

This time, the field of candidates was absolutely huge. It seemed that literally, everyone who had been a member of the party for five minutes thought they should be a leader. The big danger was that one candidate had been working very hard touring branches and persuading people that her own brand of extremely poisonous politics was what we needed, and he had gathered significant support. Anne Marie Waters was the candidate with momentum. She was extremely hard-working and dedicated to her cause. Her presentations were passionate and obviously persuasive. She was, however, the ultimate single-issue politician, and that politician was Islam. She was so focused on that single issue that when, at a point, she was asked a question about the economy, she complained that it wasn't fair to ask her about this as it wasn't her best subject. I found this odd from a person who wanted to lead a political party that had been the third most popular in the country for the previous five or six years.

It's important that readers aren't under the impression that I am soft on Terrorism or, as some of our more insane members suggested, a secret Muslim. I believe in the death penalty for terrorists and those convicted of treason. I believe in a shoot-to-kill policy when dealing with potential terrorist threats. What I don't believe in is demonising millions of people based on their religion. Religious freedom is a vital part of a free society. I have strong memories of the powerful role Pope John Paul the Second played in the downfall of the Soviet Union with his insistence on religious freedom, which was the opposite of what the totalitarian Communist state believed in. So, for the avoidance of doubt, I am neither a closet Muslim, Catholic, Sikh, Hindu, Buddhist, or Satanist. I'm of no particular religion, although I must admit that my friend Chris Edmonds has impressed me so much that I am rather fond of Southern Baptists and their style of worship.

I believed that it was important Anne Marie Waters did not take control of UKIP. I believed it would electorally destroy the party and allow national prominence to someone I considered dangerously obsessed and full of hate. With that in mind, the other candidates had to be looked at.

I looked at the other candidates and considered none of them credible. The well-known ones were authoritarian Nationalists, and the libertarians were completely split, thus meaning no single one of them had a chance of victory, particularly as they simply weren't well-known enough within the party. Once again, I felt I had no choice but to put my name forward.

My belief was that the less well-known libertarian candidates would see the sense of dropping out and supporting me as someone who was at least experienced and well-known. Early in the race, one bookie put out odds, showing me as the clear favourite to win the race. I felt that this could well be my moment. Then it turned out that there was a rumour that Nigel was supporting someone called Henry Bolton, although I never heard him say it. The rumour was enough to get Bolton into the race. Now, I can honestly say in around ten years of party membership, I had literally never heard of Henry Bolton, and I didn't take him seriously. More on him later

I approached the other libertarian candidates in order to try to forge a unified team. I guess it may be symptomatic of libertarians that they do not play well with others, but I found them all locked in a particularly spiteful feud and in no mood to unite behind me. I found John Rhys Evans to be a pleasant and talented individual and was disappointed that he would not see the sense of joining me. Ben Walker and David Coburn were, in my opinion, simply delusional, power-mad or both.

I decided to start the campaign but was not as enthusiastic as in the past. I must admit I was battle-scarred from the previous gruelling and unpleasant contests. To add to this, I was yet again in a relationship with an amazingly unsuitable woman. Blonde, slim and beautiful with a great sense of humour and a belief in UKIP, she was unfortunately also genuinely mentally unstable. Without going into the gory and deeply unpleasant details, she decided that it would be fun to betray me to my opponents, feeding them information and details of what I was doing whilst doing everything she could to destabilise me emotionally. She even sent a voice clip of me rather aggressively criticising one of my opponents to the gentleman I was talking about. He used it to try and blackmail me into supporting him, but fortunately, he was idiotic enough to put his threat into a text, which I then shared with senior party officials, ensuring that he encountered some very significant difficulties with them. I may have been gradually driven insane, but I was still far better at fighting, dirty or otherwise than some of the political pygmies trying to get the better of me.

Eventually, I reached breaking point. I simply could not go on with the leadership election. The combined effect of the years of fighting, the new bout of particularly vicious internal sniping, a relationship with a deeply emotionally disturbed woman who was trying to ruin me, combined with the day-to-day duties of being an MEP and a Councillor, were just too much. I decided to throw my support behind John Rhys Evans. If nothing else, he was an honourable and decent guy, and believe me, those were commodities in short supply at the time.

At this point I want to sincerely apologise for the people who were backing me to run for leader. It was only later that I realised how many there were and how passionately they were backing me. My apologies extend to everyone but particularly the branches in the North of England who were extremely disappointed and felt that I had let them down. I guess I did let them down, but at that particular point, I just could not carry on. I was burnt out and, frankly, very close to a breakdown.

To cut a long story short, the election was eventually won by Henry Bolton, narrowly defeating Anne Marie Waters. At the time, I still had absolutely no idea who he was other than he claimed some kind of military background; maybe he has. I have to admit, to this day, I still have no idea where this guy popped up from. I was so delighted that Waters had been defeated that I really didn't care who Henry Bolton was; I figured he couldn't possibly be any worse than her.

My first serious meeting with Henry Bolton was when he came out to meet with the MEPs. We sat in a meeting room for around four hours, listening to him drone on about his ideas for restructuring the party organisation. I must concede to being so bored I was genuinely struggling to keep my eyes open. Eventually, there was a pause in the seemingly eternal droning, and I took my opportunity to ask a question that I thought was rather important. I asked him who his political hero was and what his philosophical influences in politics were. His answer absolutely amazed me. He said words to the effect that he had never really thought about that kind of question, but if he had to pick a politician he really admired, it would be Paddy Ashdown! For those with short memories, Paddy Ashdown had been a fiercely pro-EU leader of the Lib Dems who had ultimately fallen from grace due to his dalliances with the opposite sex. It was not the kind of answer I had ever heard anyone in UKIP ever give, but the part about how the man who became known as Paddy Pants Down fell from grace was eventually proved to be rather pertinent.

Bolton soon set to work organising his team of spokesmen. I had picked up on the grapevine that I was going to be moved from Defence, and I was fine with that. I know this theme keeps repeating itself, but all I really wanted to do at this point was quietly see out my term and support the party in a much quieter way than previously. When I received the call from Bolton, I was a little surprised at his offhand tone. He told me that I was being moved from defence, and I had a choice between two roles. One had to do with culture, and one had to do with sport. When I asked him what the culture brief was, he was specific that it did not include the BBC or anything that was actually important, but as he put it, it was more about "Castles and stuff". I decided not to rock the boat and said I'd take sport. After all, I've always been a massive sports fan, so at least it gave me an excuse to indulge my hobbies.

Now, I know I'm not a paragon of virtue, and politics does allow lots of opportunities to meet women, but this guy wasted no time. He was like a kid with the keys to the sweet shop he dived straight into. Within a very brief period of time, he was involved in a very public relationship with a very attractive UKIP member who was less than half his age. He very publicly split with his wife, and a new power couple was formed. Many of us knew Jo Marney, and she was indeed a good, fun person to know and spend time with, but she was also very forthright in her views to the point of being extreme. When some of the texts she had sent with some very outrageous comments on them were released to the media, a perfect storm ensued.

As I say, I'm not a hypocrite, and I know I've done more than my share of reckless womanising both before and during my time in politics, but the key was to admit it and tell the truth to the media and more importantly, to the party membership. Maybe it was Bolton's lack of experience in politics, or maybe it was because he was lovestruck. Still, he managed to release a series of questionable statements to the media and directly to the membership about his relationship with Jo and her views. They even exposed poor Jo to a live appearance on a prime-time TV appearance, seeking to justify herself. It was an absolute shambles, and he had to go.

A dramatic Extraordinary General Meeting of the party was held in

Birmingham, and Bolton was voted out as leader after another embarrassingly short term in office. He appeared to have spent his entire time in the office chasing after a pretty girl and then justifying himself whilst abandoning his family. What an appalling waste of an opportunity that this man from nowhere should have seized with both hands and made the best of.

This led to the final death of the party as an effective political force. Gerard Batten persuaded the NEC to place him as interim leader. I can understand the temptation. Gerard is not the kind of person who will be caught up in any dramatic personal issues and has successfully served as an MEP for a very long time without being in any serious trouble. He epitomised the concept of a safe pair of hands. If only the NEC and the broader party knew Gerard the way his fellow MEPs across the parliament knew him, where he was generally written off as a slightly sinister madman.

After a brief period as Interim leader, it was time for another leadership election as demanded by the constitution. There was no great appetite for another damaging and costly internal battle, but there was a significant amount of concern amongst the MEPs about what a Batten-led party would look like. I was approached by a group of MEPs who offered to bankroll me in a campaign to take Gerard on in yet another election campaign. Still, I was under little illusion that there was much chance of me beating him, and I knew the best I could do would be to expose him as a Fascist lunatic during our debates. I wasn't convinced that was the best result for the party, so I decided to speak to Gerard to seek assurances about his conduct as leader. He made categorical promises to me and other MEPs that he would limit himself to pushing for a true Brexit. With that in mind and still feeling like I couldn't take on another battle, I ruled myself out of the race.

Straight after his election, Gerard went back on his promises and spent most of his TV interviews quoting from the Quran and discussing the perceived dangers of Islam and Muslims. This was not to be the last time I found his conduct to be dishonest and deplorable.

As with most of the other UKIP MEPs, I found Gerard's leadership deplorable. He made a point of telling me I wouldn't be one of his spokesmen as he disagreed with literally everything he had ever heard me say, which I found very pleasing. The idea of being on the same page politically as a man that appeared to be motivated by hate and simmering anger is not something of which I would be very proud.

Once again, I decided to quietly see my term out and remain in the background as much as possible. I spoke to Gerard, asking him to come to the Dudley borough during the forthcoming council election as we were defending seven seats, but he responded that he was basically too busy. I was intrigued as to what could be more important than helping to defend a significant UKIP presence on a major Borough council. After all, we weren't discussing parish elections with a few dozen voters. These were council wards where there were regularly around five thousand plus votes cast, and I would have imagined they were quite independent to a party with so few domestically elected representatives. Gerard thought otherwise; perhaps he was too busy memorising the Quran to venture north of Watford Gap.

A short while prior to these elections, I had been on a visit to a huge economic and trade conference in Crimea in my capacity as an MEP. This enraged Gerrard, and we had an enormous row during which he effectively implied I was a traitor to my country and a Russian operative. My response was along the lines that he was insane and not fit for public office. On reflection, it may seem to some people that Gerard was far too close to his long-time aide and was being influenced by the attractive Ukrainian lady, but of course, I have no evidence for that, so I would not dream of making such an accusation.

At the end of this exchange, I was under the impression that we had agreed that we needed to have it out in a very big way with a confrontation that would quite probably get very nasty but in the interests of the UKIP councillors seeking to retain their seats in the Dudley Borough we would put this off a few weeks until after the local elections.

Just an hour after we had agreed this, I was told that local newspaper "The Dudley News" had got hold of the story and was going to print with the UKIP press office having no choice but to make a statement. Whilst "The Dudley News" was very effective and credible as free newspapers limited to a very small geographical area, I found it unbelievably impressive that they had reporters in Brussels overhearing arguments being held in Belgium. Of course, if that wasn't the case, then Gerard must have leaked the story almost immediately after we had made our agreement, which would make him a liar, a scoundrel and a man devoid of any honour. I shall leave the reader to decide which of these options it could possibly have been.

The story blew up across the local press in the West Midlands with front page headlines showing my face with a rather war-like expression on it and the headlines reading "Bill Tells UKIP leader to go to hell!" which I must say was very accurate reporting of what I said.

Unfortunately, when you combine an existing decline in UKIP support with a lack of campaigning support from the party and headlines with the party leader effectively suggesting the region's best-known UKIP man was effectively a Russian stooge, it doesn't bode well for local election results. Our councillors were wiped out, with six seats reverting to the Tories and one returning to Labour. One of the Labour councillors on the night made the very telling observation, "Thank god for that we can go back to business as normal now."

I was defeated in my own council seat, with my vote collapsing down to about a third of what it had been when I won it back in 2014 and almost exactly what it had been when I had first stood for UKIP in that ward back in 2012. Standing in front of a crowd of wildly celebrating young Tories poking fun at me as I made my concession speech was not an enjoyable moment. Still, I prided myself on the fact that I retained a semblance of dignity rather than leaping into the crowd, wiping the smug grins off their silly, childish faces. It was an almost overpowering urge, and it took every ounce of self-restraint and willpower in my possession to resist. Probably a good job I did, or I may well have been writing this book from jail, and autobiographical books about their struggles written by politicians in jail don't have a great reputation.

Eventually, I had no choice but to leave UKIP. Other MEPs had been haemorrhaging ever since Gerrard took over, and the point of no return came when I was very close to being caught in the middle of a battle between Nigel and Gerard. These two had been fighting each other seemingly forever, and the idea of me being caught in the middle of another such clash was just too much to take. I had this image in my head of Godzilla and King Kong coming to blows with me stuck in the middle. I left with a stinking resignation letter addressed to Gerard, which, in typical fashion, he replied to with complete contempt. By this point, I was done with UKIP.

I briefly joined the Libertarian party and hold the distinction of being the only member of a Libertarian party to be in a significant position in Europe ever, I think. It also assured that some sources very briefly listed me as the UK's number one libertarian figure, which was quite a nice accolade. Unfortunately, it soon became apparent that the Libertarian party was effectively owned and run by one man whose enormous ego was only matched by his lack of political experience. I just had not got the energy to fight yet another clown for the honour of being the biggest fish in a diminishingly tiny puddle of a party, so I left.

I briefly lent my support to the Brexit party in order to back Nigel but I have discussed elsewhere in this book that did not go well. I was done with party politics after a decade which had included some phenomenal highs and some desperate lows. Burnt out and exhausted, it was time to move on.

UKIP still exists in a much-diminished form, and I am glad that the party still has some flickering embers of life. Credit for this must largely go to the remarkable Neil Hamilton and his truly formidable wife, Christine. They are extraordinary people who have absolutely no quit in them.

The fact remains that despite attempts by many to rewrite the history books, there would never have been an EU referendum without the rise of UKIP. Our ability to get significant vote shares across the country frightened the Tories into offering a referendum in order to "Shoot the UKIP Fox" I also believe that the result may not have gone the way that it did without the extraordinary determination and commitment of the UKIP activists.

I shall always be thankful for the many hours of unpaid work the members of UKIP put into the battle to leave the EU. Yes, MEPs like me and leadership figures like Nigel and Boris got the limelight. Still, our efforts would have been pointless without the amazing support from people who, in many cases, took time off work or unpaid leave to commit their time and energy to the cause. The people who went out onto the streets and sometimes encountered real hostility and abuse from Remainers were the real heroes of the cause, and I will never forget them or the feeling of pride I got from standing side by side with them, campaigning for the freedom of our country and its people.

Dudley Council, Otherwise Known as the Clown House

I achieved election to Dudley council at the same time that I had been elected as an MEP.

It was clear that I would not be able to work full time on the role as I had to spend so much time in Brussels, but I was determined to make a difference if possible.

Unfortunately, it soon became very apparent that achieving change through election to Dudley council was considerably more complex than achieving it through being elected as an MEP. It was also notable, but perhaps in hindsight, it is unsurprising that the general hostility towards me at Dudley Council was far more visceral than at the European Parliament.

Each month, the Councillors for the whole of Dudley Borough gather for "Full Council" at the Dudley Council building. A building more different to the one I attended at the European Parliament is hard to imagine. The Council house is a dour, barely functional old building with absolutely no frills. On one occasion, the whole electricity and microphone system was shorted by one of the councillors, spilling some water on their desk.

The Tories line up on one side of the chamber, and Labour sits facing them. The "others" are seated across the middle area. The whole set-up is designed to be confrontational in a similar way to the Westminster Parliament, but as I found out, the real confrontation was between the established parties and councillors with anyone who dared to challenge the status quo.

Each month the minority UKIP group would put forward suggestions of new policy ideas for debate and each month the Tories and Labour Councillors united to vote it down. I became convinced that if we had attended a meeting with a cure for cancer combined with a policy for eternal world peace, they would have still voted it down.

The real motivation of many of these Councillors was to take pot shots at UKIP and more specifically me. I had to sit through hours of tedious amateurish speeches with the only moment jolting me back out of my descent into sleep being the inevitable shot at me. On one occasion the leader of the Labour group referred to me and a challenge I had put out to other local politicians to take me on in public debate. He skewed his speech so that he could refer to me as "The master debater" and accompanied it with hand movement and laughter. The whole council chamber cheered and the mayor who was supposed to be impartially chairing the meeting joined in by saying "and so say all of us" I actually found this fairly amusing but it was an example of just how petty they were. I was regularly referred to as "the Councillor for Brussels" and the UKIP benches as "Etheridge Enterprises."

The atmosphere was absolutely poisonous. I handled it and simply waited out the time until the meetings ended but it was certainly an unusual and unhappy experience for some of my newly elected colleagues. Of course, it wasn't all one way and I occasionally made the effort to get up and make a speech dripping with as much contempt and venom as I could but towards the end of my term I simply couldn't be bothered. The one positive thing was it increased the interest in local politics in the area a little and even got the meetings some media coverage, as an angry playground-style atmosphere always makes for a good headline or video clip.

Of course, not all the Councillors were mindless, petty idiots. There were a few on both sides of the political divide or who were genuinely there to serve their communities. Unfortunately, a greater proportion of them were either frustrated politicians using their two minutes of fame to grandstand and massage their engorged egos or ancient, almost fossilised relics who were simply Councillors because they enjoyed having the title.

The general gist of every meeting was that we would put an idea forward, which would then be rubbished by Councillors from the Tory and Labour sides who would queue up to tell us that all this had been tried at some point in the last hundred years and hadn't worked. It was a wholly negative atmosphere. The general approach seemed to be that they would do whatever the council officers recommended. To me, this was the wrong way around, and the elected representatives should lead the agenda, but that idea was so radical to my fellow councillors as to almost blow their minds.

The greatest achievement of our time as UKIP councillors was to head off a Labour motion aimed at banning the purchase of any item with parts manufactured in Israel. Of course, this was more about gesture politics than anything else, but it is surprising how many components in IT systems have parts manufactured in Israel in them.

The Labour group in Dudley, as in many other areas of the West Midlands, heavily relied on support from the local Muslim community. They had failed to deliver planning permission for a new "Mega Mosque" in the area, so the next best thing was to symbolically have a go at Israel. We sent the word out to the Jewish communities in the area and nearby and managed to get a significant number of supporters along for the debate. I even managed to get a friend of mine from UKIP in the North West to come along, and as an Orthodox Jew who always dressed in the undisguisable garb of black clothes, wide-brimmed hat etc. certainly made a big visual impact. We managed to force the Labour group to back down and won the day.

We also won a battle to keep a local pub open despite an application from a large Supermarket chain to demolish it and build on the land. We organised a series of protests and public meetings, even getting Nigel involved at one point. We eventually won the day despite the local Tory Councillors who had pretended to be on the side of the pub campaigners changing their vote on the night of the planning application to support the Supermarket. The reason they switched their vote? Was it because they thought the application was for the good of the community? Of course not! They changed it because the Save the Pub campaign had become associated with me—petty, vindictive and pathetic behaviour.

Incidences of childish behaviour from Councillors in Dudley were too many to be able to write down without the whole book being about them, and let's face it, that's a book I wouldn't want to read, let alone right.

I will give you a good one that more or less sums up how petty their behaviour could be, though. A perfect example of childish squabbling and protecting what they thought was their turf rather than being bothered about the people.

After being elected as a Councillor and an MEP on the same day, I realised it was impossible to be in Dudley as much as I had hoped I could be, but I still wanted to make a difference where I could.

The Sedgley ward that I had been elected to represent, as do many others, always has a display of Christmas lights, decorations and a tree. Interestingly, the tree is planted in what is known as the Bull Ring, which in centuries gone by was the place the gallows would be for a public execution, or at least that's how the story goes. After dealing with the other local Councillors, it was a tradition I was sorely tempted to consider bringing back.

Each borough ward had three councillors with a four-year electoral cycle and one fallow year. My other two Sedgley Councillors were Tories. Indeed, I had campaigned with them a few years earlier at the 2010 General Election. To say they were both veterans would be an understatement. They were over Seventy years old, and one of them had actually been first elected the year I was born. There is no problem with older people being politicians. In fact, one of my heroes, Ronald Reagan, was no spring chicken when he led the free world and brought the Soviet Union to its knees. Unfortunately, these gentlemen were about as far from Ronald Reagan as it is possible to get. Dour, grey-suited old men whose only aims were to keep everything as it was and to enjoy the kudos of being Councillors.

The ancient Sedgley Tories were intensely critical of everyone and everything, with the only activities they considered worthwhile being the ones they had initiated themselves. Sadly, it appeared that they had stopped thinking any new thoughts at least a decade earlier. It would have been an easy comparison to suggest they were local politics answer to Stadler and Waldorf, the old men characters who used to hurl insults from the balcony during the muppet show. Truly the Muppet Show analogy is a tempting one as the whole council did seem to resemble a particularly surreal version of Frank Oz's creation. However, it would not be fair to the Muppet show to compare the Tory Councillors in Sedgley to such amiable characters. No, they were far more like Dracula and his servant Renfield. One of them was clearly the leader and his presence emanated gloom and malevolence whilst his sidekick was a snivelling, wretched little man who would follow his master's bidding with a permanent and totally insincere smile glued to his thin lips.

Many years earlier, they had been instrumental in organising and getting funding for the lights in our ward. Of course, this is a very good thing and something I applaud them for. Sadly, the funding did not stretch to cover the whole shopping area, and one street was left in gloom. It also happened that this street was near an infant school. It occurred to me that it would be a nice gesture to use some of my MEP salary to help with the lights and boost the area covered. After much shopping around, I found some appropriate, rather large and colourful Christmas lights that could be added to the display and spent just over £2k of my salary on purchasing them.

In order to get the lights put up on display, a simple request has to be made to the council officers and given approval by the majority of the ward councillors. Now you may think that my fellow councillors would be delighted at the addition of more lights and particularly it would give the area outside the school an extra bit of festive cheer. So, you may be as amazed as me that when we had to gather for a ward meeting to discuss this and other issues, the Tories voted against the lights being added to the display, with Renfield smugly commenting, "We provide the lights in Sedgley" and after snivellingly turning round to his master following up with "They are our responsibility, not yours."

A petty story about petty people. The conclusion was that I eventually donated the lights to a charitable organisation operating from within the ward, and they have made use of them ever since. Ironically, The institution is the local Blind Institute!

Dudley Council and my Impression of Guy Fawkes

It was the general air of obstructionist negativity during council meetings that led to me being reported as a possible terrorist threat. As I read it back, that sentence seems quite unbelievable, but it's true.

The main issue that the people in my area faced was overgrowing trees. Hard to imagine that in the Black Country, but it made up at least ninety per cent of the correspondence I received. In some areas, the trees had overgrown so badly that whole streets were plunged into semi-darkness during the day, and at night, they were frighteningly dark.

As well as the issues with light, the trees also presented issues for car owners, with sap dripping onto their car bonnets and causing corrosion. The leaves and twigs from the trees were blocking gutters. On one particularly worrying occasion, a heavy branch fell onto a woman's car, causing significant damage, and she only narrowly avoided serious injury.

I tried to get the issue discussed at full council as I could not get the council officers to cut the trees back. Instead of discussing this issue properly, the council wasted over an hour discussing a motion to send a letter to the Prime Minister demanding more women in positions of authority. Not only was this a useless piece of posturing, but it was laughable as the Prime minister at the time was a lady called Theresa May.

I left the meeting and did a Facebook live video venting my frustration and anger. I suggested the best thing for the people of Dudley would be for the council chamber to be knocked down and all of its functions shut down. At least, that would provide a significant tax cut. This video became the subject of howls of outrage, particularly by the Labour members, some of whom claimed they feared for their lives, implying I was going to become some kind of modern-day Guy Fawkes and blow the building up with them in it. One of them provided a perfect piece of drama demonstrating the term "Snowflake" by tearfully asking to be moved further away from me as she feared for her life.

The council spent a couple of thousand pounds hiring an investigator to look into what I said. This seemed quite futile as it was all on video. When he asked me about what I had said, I simply sent him a copy of the video and told him I stood by every word.

The council very seriously referred me to "The Standards Committee", which judged I should be banned from sitting on committees. This was fine by me as not only did I have no interest in committees, but I had already stated that I didn't have time to sit on them.

After I had effectively laughed in the faces of the moaning councillors, they decided to call in the big guns. They reported me to the local Bishop! Apparently, due to some bizarre and ludicrously old-fashioned decision, the Bishop had some right to be involved in disciplinary matters. He made an appointment to see me at my office, and I was delighted to receive him there. He began the meeting pontificating to me about standards in public life and other similar subjects in a tone so obnoxiously self-important that it really drove me to anger. My response was very direct and my tone extremely hostile. I asked him who had elected him and told him I don't take lectures from the establishment church in the UK. I suggested he would be better off worrying about getting congregation attendance increased than lecturing me on how I should behave. He attended the meeting no doubt thinking I was a bad guy and I'm pretty sure he left it thinking I was positively demonic. That suited me just fine; I was not in politics to toe the line; I was there to rock the boat, and I was determined to do everything I could to make an impact.

The European Parliament. The Joy of Committees

The EU parliament loves a great many things. It delights in proclaiming its own importance and what better way to do that by express its enduring love.

Possibly the greatest love of the European Parliament is committees. There are committees to cover virtually every subject of governance. Of course, all of these committees are treated with reverent respect and seriousness, no matter how obscure or pointless the topic they are designed to cover may be.

Part of the process of the parliament is that committees will create reports taking many months to put together then discuss them internally before voting on them. Once they are approved the report is then presented at a parliamentary session and subject to several hours of discussion followed by a vote the next day. Most of the reports pass the vote as the content has already been discussed and agreed upon by the larger political groups. The truth is that you could have a parliamentary speech the equivalent of Churchill in his prime and it would make absolutely no difference to the final result of the vote as the MEPs are whipped to vote a certain way by their groups well in advance.

At the end of this long, drawn-out process, the result is that absolutely nothing happens. This is because the elected members of the European Parliament cannot propose legislation or laws. The passed committee reports simply end up at the In tray of the European Commission, where the real power lies. The unelected members of the commission are the people who can propose new legislation and it is possible that they may base that on the reports passed to them from the Committees but a little unlikely.

The truth is that for all of the grandeur and cost of the European Parliament its only power is to either rubber stamp legislation originating from the commission or in vary rare cases it can vote against it to send it back for them to have a look at making a few changes. It is actually almost a mirror image of the British system where the elected representatives can propose legislation, and the unelected House of Lords scrutinises and rubber stamps it. The UK House of Lords has far more strength and ability to hinder legislation than the EU parliament, but there is a similarity.

My role in this system was to be sent as the representative of the group UKIP was part of to sit on the Regional Development Committee. The aims of this committee appeared to be all about how they could take money from the contributions of richer member states and redistribute them across the whole European Union.

I made my mark at the first meeting of the committee and probably didn't make any friends but I wasn't there to cooperate in the squandering of UK taxpayers' money I was there to be a spanner in the works. The main political groups had already sat down behind closed doors and done some horsetrading about who was to hold the senior positions on the committee. One of the first items on the agenda was for the members of the committee to nod through the appointments. I seized my opportunity to object and raised a point of order demanding that each position be the subject of a discussion and vote. There was some confusion in the checking of notes by the secretariat before they were forced to yield to my point of order and put each position forward for discussion and voting.

The whole process took hours. I made a point of putting myself forward for every position and demanding a vote on each one. I knew that I had absolutely no chance of winning or even gaining any votes, but I wanted to make a point, and I was feeling in a particularly devilish mood. There were long delays when it came to voting as they had never had to vote on these issues before, and the committee wasn't sure how the votes should be conducted.

At the end of several hours, I had lost every vote but my share of the vote had risen from zero to three or four of the thirty plus delegates gathered in the committee room. During one pause, a very tall and absurdly handsome Dutch MEP called Olaf Stuger approached me. He was laughing uproariously and told me that he and his colleagues were enjoying the show so much they had started voting for me and even lobbying others to do so just to keep the fun and games going.

By the end of a long day each of the originally nominated appointees had been voted in to place but it had been done in a way that was at least a little more democratic. I rounded off the day by thanking the committee for its time and informing them that this was just the first of a series of lessons about democracy I intended to teach them.

Yes, I was being an arse but that's what I was there for and frankly it was fun watching these pompous, entitled Eurocrats scrambling around trying to figure out the rules when a challenge arose that they weren't used to.

Amongst the momentous issues that we discussed at the committee was the provision of Broadband in Transylvania and a dog training and health centre in Hungary. The volume of bizarre and peculiar projects to spend money on was almost impossible to keep up with. The general tone of each debate was that most of the other committee members would be in favour of throwing money around like lottery winner after ten pints and I would be a lone voice saying that this money was in large part extracted from British taxpayers and it was outrageous that they were making so free with it. As you can imagine I lost every vote but I kept hammering away at them.

One of the more intriguing debates was based around the fact that the committee had promised far more money to projects around the EU than it actually had in its budget. This led to companies who had undertaken work on the projects not being paid on time, causing them serious cashflow issues. I made the proposal that if they must spend so much money, surely they should tailor the amount spent to fit the amount in the budget. This seems a reasonably sensible point to me and I made it in a very calm and measured manner which made the response I received even more surprising. Speaker after speaker got to their feet to condemn and attack me, claiming I was a heartless extremist. It was actually quite entertaining.

The end result of this discussion was that an irate motion was passed to be sent to the European Commission demanding yet more money to waste and what is worse it was actually favourably received and more funds were released. The overwhelming desire of the committee and the EU as a whole is to involve itself in every aspect of life across the European Union and demand that their adventures be subsidised by the handful of member states who were actually giving more money to the pot than they were taking out.

I hope that next time you feel unhappy at a lack of hospital beds in the NHS or disconcerted by the amount of tax taken from your pay packet, you can console yourself with the knowledge that the Broadband scheme on Transylvania is probably well underway now, and Dracula can spend his time watching Netflix rather than the activities we traditionally associate him with.

Occasionally, an association with a committee can allow you to get access to information that can be actually useful. Quite early in my term, I was invited to an event where EU commissioners were discussing a project called City Regions. I was intrigued to see the leader of Birmingham council as well as some other West Midlands elected officials there with their entourages.

The City Regions project is a simple one. Each area across the EU has a large city surrounded by smaller cities and towns. The map had been partitioned into regions that would be classed as attached to a nearby major city. In the eyes of the instigators of the project, the scheme was highly beneficial as it facilitated easier flow and administration of EU funds and regulations. For this very same reason, I found it an extremely disturbing prospect.

It was clear from the meeting that one of the main areas who would benefit from membership of this scheme was Birmingham and its surrounding areas which were classed as Greater Birmingham for the purposes of the demonstration. I was horrified. Not only by the prospect of greater EU intrusion into my area but the thought of my home region of the Black Country being consumed into a catch-all term of Greater Birmingham was extremely unwelcome.

I gathered as much information as I could and instructed my staff to turn it into a report that I could pass on to the local authorities and media in the West Midlands. I really felt that I was on to something that would at least warrant serious discussion back in the UK, and my information would be useful to inform any such debate.

This was an issue that would directly impact on the lives of everyone. Amongst the terms and condition of being a city region were various politically motivated changes involving diversity quotas and a whole raft of green issues that would impact on waste collection and lead to the introduction of more congestion charging to reduce the volume of traffic.

I contacted the BBC on the issue and was involved in a heated debate on BBC Radio West Midlands with a Labour councillor from Sandwell who basically wrote off everything I said as "Typical UKIP scaremongering" That was about the extent of the coverage we managed to get in advance of these huge changes.

Unperturbed, I printed out copies of the report and distributed them at the next Dudley Council meeting. I was informed by the mayor at the meeting that I would not be allowed to raise the issue and when I left the chamber I was appalled to see that a very large proportion of the members had either left the report behind or ripped it into pieces without even looking at it. This kind of ignorance was symptomatic of the place, if it had my name on it they simply did not want to know.

Of course, in the years that have followed, we have seen the creation of the West Midlands combined authority. Guess what? It has introduced a whole raft of Green policies, including changes to waste collection and the introduction of congestion charging. They also distribute funds in line with diversity targets. We may not be a member of the EU officially any longer, but we are still following their edicts.

I don't tell this story to say "I told you so" I tell it to point out that we are still EU rule followers and none of our elected representatives from the establishment parties have challenged it. Actually, I found it very difficult to explain the importance of what was happening to many of my UKIP colleagues as well. I guess if you make something complicated enough and involve a lot of reading in it people just cant be bothered to understand it and oppose it. Oh and by the way particularly in connection to congestion charging in Birmingham I am going to say it, "I told you so!"

Immigrant Camps in Calais

The topic of the illegal immigration into the UK is an ongoing and highly controversial issue. The opposing sides in the argument broadly breakdown into those that feel we should offer safe refuge to those fleeing persecution and those who feel that illegal entry to the UK is dangerous criminality.

As you may imagine, my initial instinct was to be with the side that believes illegal immigration should not be tolerated. However, I felt it was such an important issue that I needed more facts in order to get a better understanding of what was going on.

At this time, I was working quite closely with Mike Hookem and his team. We decided to go on a joint expedition to Calais to actually visit the immigrant camps and if possible, talk to the people there.

The mission was arranged and Mike was joined by his team members including Annabelle and a cameraman to record our findings.

When we arrived at a large migrant camp in the Calais region, I was struck by just how close it was situated to the channel tunnel and the coast. It really was a perfect point to plan to enter the UK from. I was also taken aback by the fact that the French police would not enter the camp and we were basically told once we entered the grounds we were on our own.

I must admit to being concerned that we were entering a place where no law and order was present. Mike is a pretty tough guy and I can handle myself but neither of us were under any illusions that we were safe.

As we walked through the camp, it was immediately noticeable that our presence had not gone unnoticed. We were walking along paths deeper into the camp as dozens of young men were following and keeping an eye on us from the ground above us on either side. They appeared to be communicating with other gang members and keeping them informed of our movements.

The camp itself was as unpleasant as has been reported by the journalists who occasionally ventured in. We walked through much and passed a hundreds of small tents that appeared to be sinking into the mud in some areas. The smell was grotesque and the people were clearly not enjoying anything like civilised living conditions.

I was intrigued at one point, which I believe was somewhere near the centre of the camp when we found the equivalent of a shopping centre. Food was being cooked on open fires and items of clothing we being bartered for. It reminded me of the camping grounds for a rock festival by about the third or fourth day. Muddy and unsanitary, the whole place was very unpleasant.

We decided to try to speak with some of the people inhabiting this site. The estimate was that there were up to ten thousand people at this camp, so we reasoned that maybe one or two may wish to speak with us. I was a little concerned when ever enthusiastic and determined Annabelle ventured ahead of us trying to find people to speak to, the looks she was getting from some of the mainly male population suggested we really needed to keep her in sight.

We did manage to speak to a few of the would-be immigrants to our country. With each one of them I started off by asking them why they wanted to leave France and whether the French were in anyway treating them badly. All of them recognised that the French were not hostile to them and in fact gave them a surprising amount of freedom.

My follow-up questions to the camp dwellers were even more revealing. I asked them why they needed to come to the UK if the French were treating them so well. Every one of them came up with a similar answer which was long the lines of the famous cliché about the streets of London being paved with Gold. They told me that in the UK they would get better housing, healthcare and education as well as stating as a fact that it was a far better place to earn money and do business. I decided it was probably best not to enquire as to what kind of business they had in mind.

Some of them kept in touch via Mobile Phone with friends and family who had already made it across to the UK. The reports back were that it had been worth the effort to sneak into the back of a lorry or brave the small boat crossing as once they were in the UK, life was fantastic.

In one way I was very pleased that people believe the UK is the best country to come and live. I tend to agree with them, although the changes in our country over recent years have led me to question that conviction.

It was also interesting to me that these people wanted to risk life and limb to escape the EU mainland and come to the UK. People are still doing that to this day. It is interesting to see the reality of where people actually think is the best place to live rather than listen to the nonsense that is constantly spouted about how wonderful the EU is and how the UK is missing out by not being part of an "Ever closer union."

The key point in my mind was that none of these people were actually seeking to come to the UK to flee persecution. They were looking to enter our country to get a better life. That means that they should be classed as economic migrants, not Asylum seekers. What is more concerning is that none of them had tried to immigrate to our country through official routes, and very few of them had any identification or papers.

The key point of this story to my mind is that these people are determined to get to our country because they believe it will be a better place to live and raise a family. They believe that the housing, education, health and welfare prospects are better. They are convinced there are business opportunities for them to exploit and make money. None of them want to come to the UK for safety; they are already safe in France.

In the full knowledge that what they are doing is illegal, the inhabitants of the camps were determined to force entry to a nation that had not invited them in.

Undoubtedly, some of the people seeking to come to the UK have been fed a whole banquet of lies about how great the living conditions are here by people traffickers. The gangs organising the traffickers are vile criminals preying on people's dreams of a better life, but those paying the traffickers to get them to the UK are also engaging in criminality.

If a person's first act on entering your country is to be part of an illegal enterprise and break the law, it doesn't bode well for how they will behave when they are here. The striking fact that so many of these people have no documentation should also be a source for concern. I have no doubt that the handful of people I spoke to in this huge camp were fundamentally decent human being just trying whatever they could to get to a better life but there were approximately ten thousand people in that camp and who knows what all of their motives were.

As a point of clarification before Im accused of being a racist, for about the millionth time. Let me point out that I would be concerned about any large group of people of any nationality, ethnicity or face seeking to illegally enter a country with no paperwork. This is obviously a concern shared by governments and people all over the world otherwise why do we bother with passports or border checks?

I approached politics with the belief that if I was honest and straight-talking, not only would I stand out from the crowd, but people would understand what I was all about, and even if they didn't agree with me, they might respect me. Let me tell you in no uncertain terms that approach simply does not work, and whilst I don't condone it, I can now understand why politicians stick to set lines and very rarely give honest and direct answers.

My experience in politics is proof positive that virtually anything you say can be manipulated or taken out of context to make you look like the Devil incarnate.

As much as it grinds on me to have to rehash some of these stories and my defence for them, I really couldn't write this book without mentioning them, so here we go.

Golliwogs

Me and Star joined the Campaign Against Political Correctness early in our political journeys. The campaign was run by members of the Conservative Party, and its most prominent member was Phillip Davies, MP. We organised meetings for the campaign in the Dudley area.

One of the Campaign Against Political Correctness's main talking points was how words and ideology had changed the significance and meaning of things in our society, creating division where there should be none. One of the best examples of this was the Golliwog doll. It had been the subject of great debate some years earlier, so we felt on safe ground revisiting it. We had our photos taken holding a Golliwog doll and contributed them to a mural of people from many different ethnicities doing the same thing.

The point was that whatever the present feeling and controversy about these dolls when we were kids, we had thought of them as totally harmless and, in many of our cases, literally had no conception that there was a link between these loveable toys and the oppression of black people. In fact, I vividly recall Dean Perks saying that if he had thought these dolls were representative of a human his childhood would have been haunted by nightmares as they were nothing like any black person he had ever met and he had no idea they were meant to be human.

I posed for the photo with absolutely no trepidation. I had led a life so full of relationships, friendships and dealings with people of a wide variety of ethnicities it never even crossed my mind that anyone would consider me racist. In hindsight, this was very naïve.

The photograph was seized on by members of the Dudley Conservative party who reported us to the party head office basically accusing us of overt racism. It would appear that the energy and enthusiasm my wife and I had thrown into the Tory cause had unsettled some of their semi fossilised senior local figures and we needed to be nocked down a peg or two. Little did they realise that in the words of Obi-Wan Kenobi to Darth Vader on Death Star, "If you strike me down, I shall become more powerful than you could possibly imagine."

We received letters from Tory head office suspending us pending investigation. Our response was to resign sending stinging letters saying that we thought we had joined the party of Thatcher and Tebbit but ended up in the party of Blair with a blue rossette.

The incident led to my first major encounters with the media. It actually made the news worldwide which even now seems a massive overreaction. It did however give me the chance to meet controversial journalist Rod Liddle for the first time. I travelled to Westminster, and he interviewed me in a pub over several glasses of wine and many a chuckle. Rod is a brilliantly flamboyant character who was one of the very few who reported the incident fairly. I would come across him several more times in my political career and always found him to be one of the very best in the business and a genuinely nice bloke.

Adolf Hitler

My link to Hitler is almost immediately apparent if you google search me. I must say it isn't the most helpful connection in this modern age when everyone appears to be judged on their internet history. To this day I am still baffled as to how I managed to be associate with the evilest tyrant in history by media outlets worldwide over a few words in one supposedly presentation to UKIP members. Unfortunately, our good friends in the media had sneaked someone in the presentation and they managed to put their own legendary and unique spin on what had been said.

I was asked by the party to give a seminar-style talk to its younger members about public speaking shortly after my election as an MEP. At that time, I was considered to be quite a good public speaker and was still allowed to actually speak at Party conferences before I was blacklisted and ignored for several years by the chairman and his officials.

I was demonstrating the various styles and approaches to public speaking. I was working my way through well-known figures and their speaking styles; I even spoke a little about Tony Blair. Then came the part of the talk which caused all of the trouble.

In preparation for the talk, I had cast back to public speaking lessons and seminars I had attended when still in the world of business and sales. They had almost all focussed on one particularly important area: the start. They mentioned how it was a long-standing technique for teachers to stand silently in front of a class before beginning a lesson. The idea is if you stand silently looking at people for long enough, they will eventually settle down out of curiosity as to what it is that this silent figure standing in front of them wants to say. If you think about it, I'm sure you can come up with a huge number of examples of speakers who have done this.

I decided to go with the most famous of the adepts of this school of opening a speech and the person that professional coaches had almost all used in their presentations. Yes, I did it; I committed the crime of mentioning the name of Hitler. What is worse is that I compounded it by assuming that my audience would probably appreciate the fact that by remarking on his skills as an orator, it would not mean that I was actually secretly tattooed in Swastikas, was wearing Jack Boots or that I had designs on invading Poland. It never crossed my mind that anyone might think I returned home each night to a home decorated with NAZI war memorabilia and statues and painting of The Fuhrer. I stupidly thought that a remark about his oratory may be taken entirely in context.

As I type out this section of the book, I'm aware that simply by speaking about history in the context of discussing Hitler, I run the risk of my door being smashed down by police, my books being piled up and burnt, and yet another public inquisition and torture by the Politically Correct media but the story is out there so I may as well tell the real version of it.

In my presentation, I spoke about the historical fact that Hitler was a very effective and powerful speaker. His presentational methods were not only ahead of their time, but his technique and style of delivery had been practised meticulously. His rallies were attended by tens of thousands of people, and he persuaded vast numbers of people to back him. With this in mind I focussed during my presentation on the very deliberate way that he would pause at the start of a speech staring passionately out at his audience, He would not speak until there was silence. Now, here's the rub. What I neglected to say because I assumed it was stating the bloody obvious was that the message he was seeking to get across was evil, demented and totally insane. I was under the impression that the fact Hitler was a "baddie" was pretty much a given.

In fact, my audience at the presentation included a wide variety of people, including a Jewish family. Not one of them blinked an eye at what I was saying they were all perfectly well aware that I was not saying Hitler was a role model they totally understood that what I was saying was his speech making technique was an interesting one to look at. I blame myself for one sentence where I said, "He achieved a great many things" At the time, I stopped myself from saying that those things were, broadly speaking, the evilest crimes that had ever been committed on humanity. I actually thought that by saying that, I would have been insulting their intelligence.

I was warned that the story was breaking the next day, and I immediately phoned the UKIP top man in the media and press, the splendidly named Gawain Towler. After ringing several times, I finally received an answer from Gawain, who, over the sounds of clinking glasses and an obviously very lively party in the background, informed me that it was nothing to worry about and was a non-story. This was advice that I reflected on at length over the next few weeks as the story spread worldwide with headlines such as "UKIP urges its young members to copy Hitler" and other such edifying titles.

The BBC contacted me and asked for an interview on the subject. I was delighted and thought this would be my chance to fight back. They attended my office and took a pretty strong two-minute statement from me saying how appalled I was. Unfortunately, when the piece aired, it was inter-spliced with clips of Hitler in full flow, making a particularly intense and wide-eyed speech.

This particular story, out of all of the hit pieces that were done on me, was the one that hurt me the most. When I first saw the headlines being discussed on TV news, I had the most singular feeling as if I had been punched very hard in the stomach; it was a distress that was not only emotional but physical. Remember, my much-loved Grandad had spent years fighting Hitler's NAZI hoards, and I believe myself to be the very opposite of a NAZI. I was very deeply hurt and distressed.

I knuckled down and tried to continue with the job. Two amusing incidents stand out that helped me weather the storm. One was a phone call from Paul Nuttall, who was Deputy Leader at the time. He began by asking, "Hello, am I through to evil Nazi headquarters" and then continued with him telling me to keep my chin up. The other happened at Wolverhampton Train station as I waited for a train to London. It was apparent that a gentleman on the platform recognised me; he approached me then walked past, whistling the theme from Dad Army, bringing that familiar refrain "Who do you think you are kidding, Mr Hitler?" to mind, then turned around, winked, and burst out laughing. Both instances certainly lightened my mood.

The story was effectively rebutted when I was invited to be interviewed by British TV's most feared and well-prepared interviewer, Andrew Neil. I had a long wait in the green room and noticed that the guests due to go on before me, who were far more experienced and from established political parties, were literally trembling with fear. One of them actually had to leave the room to be sick. As you can imagine, this didn't fill me with confidence. When my time came to enter the arena, I was somewhat relieved to see that the "Talking head" who was a guest on the show to deliver his verdict on the political performers was none other than Rod Liddle. As I took my seat, Rod gave me a slight smile and a wink, which really helped settle my nerves. Just imagine if I had walked into a lion's den with both Andrew Neil and Rod Liddle intent on going after me; the thought of it makes me shudder as I type it. Fortunately, Andrew confronted me with the story, took my explanation and settled the matter by saying that it might be an idea to say that I "Misspoke" and move on from there, which we did.

Enoch Powell

The MP for the area of Wolverhampton near where I grew up in the 1970s was the now-infamous Enoch Powell. I had spent much of my early years being aware of how controversial a figure he was.

In adulthood, I looked into him in more detail, including having prolonged conversations about him with Christopher Gill and Neil Hamilton, who had both known him quite well.

My opinion of the man is that he was an interesting figure in modern political history. He was right about the problems that joining the Common Market would lead to. He was dramatically wrong in his belief that the UK should unilaterally disarm its nuclear weapons. His views on immigration had some truth to them, but his language and the images he created were deliberately repugnant in order to create publicity for his stance.

Now, to be clear, when I say his views on immigration had some truth to them, I mean in the context of his predictions that certain parts of the country would change in ways that nobody had ever voted or asked for if immigrant populations were too focussed into their areas rather than being evenly disturbed. His words about race and some of his overly dramatic language talking about "Rivers of Blood", etc, are not anything that I would ever want to be associated with, and I certainly don't agree with them.

Keeping this in mind, I can now tell you the truth behind the story covered in many newspapers that I had said the infamous catchphrase "Enoch was right."

In the early stages of the Brexit campaign, attendance at public meetings and press coverage for the leave campaign was sluggish. I had been speaking at a series of public events across the West Midlands with fellow speakers Jill Seymour MEP, Jim Carver MEP, former MP Christopher Gill and chairman of The Freedom Association. While the speeches were good, we weren't getting enough coverage, so I decided to take one for the team to stir up some attention.

Unfortunately, just like what had happened with Powell's comments, the media attention soon became negative, and I had to spend most of my time explaining myself rather than arguing for EU withdrawal.

I had issued a carefully worded statement to the press saying that Enoch had been right about the danger that immigration would run out of control and the potential loss of sovereignty and freedom incurred by joining the Common Market. Of course, that wasn't how the headline writers had it, and soon enough, I was the twenty-first-century Enoch Powell being roundly criticised by all sides, including my own party. To put it plainly, the ruse was a mistake that backfired. I guess you live and learn.

The most bizarre part of the whole incident was when I was invited to a debate hosted by a large regional Newspaper, the Express & Star, some years after my statement to discuss whether there should be a blue plaque in Wolverhampton marking the fact Powell had been our MP. My argument was that he had been that as an important historical figure, it should be marked, and perhaps there should be a yearly conference or debate held in Wolverhampton to discuss where he had gone wrong or whether any of his predictions were coming true. The debate was hosted at the Wolverhampton Polytechnic, where I was a student. I was advised to park a distance away and walk in in case of any possible attacks on my car. In reality, I was held up on the way in by a crowd of people wishing me well and supporting my opinions. On entering the room later than invited but still before the scheduled start time, I was astonished to be told I had to sit in the crowd rather than at the table on the stage that had my name written on it. I was effectively "empty-chaired" at an event where my comments had sparked the debate and one where I was actually in attendance. This petty behaviour, which I learned was instigated by the editor of the paper, is the kind of nonsense you have to grin and put up with in politics. It was particularly ironic that although they only gave me two minutes to speak from the crowd during the hour-and-a-half discussion, it was still my picture and comments that carried the headlines the next day.

Women

As mentioned in other parts of this book, I've had more than my share of dramatic relationship issues. That's perhaps not surprising and certainly not unique, but the amount of media coverage it attracted was quite a shock. As with some of the other issues the media picked up on, I had honestly thought that headlines about politicians and their marriage breakups and various girlfriends were very old-fashioned and out of date. I'm still pretty convinced that the reading public, in general, wasn't remotely interested, but the newspapers absolutely loved it.

I had one girlfriend who actually got the full Paparazzi treatment with photographers camped outside of her house. They were even going through the bins for some bizarre reason. They did manage to capture a very unflattering photograph of her early one morning, presumably going out to get the milk in; she wasn't impressed. The neighbours on her council estate were fascinated, though; they had never seen the like of it.

It seemed every time there was some kind of sex scandal anything to do with UKIP; I had the media phoning me to check if I was somehow a part of it. I did remark to one reporter that it was all immensely flattering, but I could only wish I was as successful with the ladies as they seemed to think I was

The only really lasting effect of this coverage was that it seemed to permanently put off quite a few nice and respectable ladies from being seen with me and encouraged quite a few of the other kinds of ladies that I was a good bet to further their ambition for media coverage.

Jimmy Saville

When the media first broke the story about what a monster Jimmy Saville had been, shortly after he had died, there was even an attempt to smear me with some connection to the disgraced TV star.

A friend of mine had posted on his Facebook account, "Jimmy Saville burn in hell". I noticed it, and as the stories were only just coming out about what a beast Saville had been, I commented under the post, "Now then, now then". I learned from this that Jimmy Saville's impressions were no longer acceptable and that they did not work when typed anyway. The local press picked up on it and attempted to stir up a big outrage about it, but it was such a weak reason to try to publicly humiliate me that on this occasion, the horror at what an awful person I was didn't last very long.

Peter Lundgren and the Spice Girls

Peter Lundgren is a man with a big physique and an even bigger personality. A former Lorry driver, he had been elected as an MEP to represent the Sweden Democrats party.

Well above six feet tall and weighing in at a rough estimate at somewhere above Three hundred pounds, Peter is an imposing presence. For all his rugged looks and appearance, Peter is a warm and friendly man with a great sense of humour. He was a great friend to me during my time in Brussels, and we have kept in contact ever since.

We would make a point of going on what became known as "Duck hunts" at least once a month, which were basically a mission to find the Chinese restaurant serving the best crispy aromatic duck. These meals would be entertaining and convivial nights that we invited our staff along to, and we had great nights. At one point, when I was seriously dieting and exercising in preparation for my boxing debut, Peter sent a message saying he needed to see me urgently that evening. Wondering what the issue could be, I cleared the diary for that evening and met with him. He informed me very seriously that he was concerned about my weight loss and feared that I was wasting away. I told him that as I still weighed somewhere near two hundred and seventy pounds, I was hardly in danger of malnutrition, but he would have none of it. With a serious expression on his face and a strong voice heavily laced with his Swedish accent, he told me, "You need meat, my friend. Tonight, I am buying us much meat" True to his word, he took me for an enormous meal with so many different types and cuts of meat that I probably had enough protein that night to last me a year, but it was a sign of what a kind friend this big man was

Do not be misled, though; Peter was no softie. When it was time to speak in parliament or meeting rooms to represent his constituents, he was a truly formidable advocate with an imposing presence and a booming voice. On one occasion, he was having a heated conversation with his staff, who had not delivered the performance he was expecting on a particular issue. I sat at the same table but kept my head down until the discussion was over. It ended very abruptly when the big man pounded his fist into the table, making the whole room appear to shake, and loudly declared, "I don't give a shit" However, in his accent, it sounded like "I don't give a sheet" either way the message had come across loud and clear. Incidentally, the one thing that all of the nationalities at the European Parliament seemed to agree on was that English is the best language to swear in, so at least they admire us for something, I suppose.

Having mentioned Peter's assistants and staff, I feel they deserve a mention. They were an absolutely excellent team who were more than happy to help other MEPs other than just their boss. Highly educated and intelligent, they were genuine stars of the parliament, and I'm pleased to say they became friends of mine.

Christopher was one of the Sweden Democrats staff. Highly intelligent and thoughtful, he would often stay at the same hotel as me on our monthly stays in Strasbourg, and we enjoyed many a pleasant meal and bottle or two of wine together. From my conversation with him, I learned about Swedish cooking and the tendency to focus on meat that they would grill on the barbeque, regardless of the time of year and weather. He also spoke of hunting his own food and enjoying the wonderful Swedish countryside, leaving me with the impression that Sweden must be a hell of a place to live.

Then we come to Peter's Spice Girls. Peter had two main parliamentary assistants, Natalie and Laura. These ladies were recognised by virtually everyone in Brussels. They were both tall and slim with remarkable figures. Natalia had a rare kind of exotic beauty, and the fact that she was often seen walking the corridors with Laura, who was a remarkably good-looking blonde-haired, blue-eyed beauty, made them hard to miss. Peter gave them the name the Spice Girls, which they were more than happy to adopt. It may be easy to think that these ladies got their jobs based on their looks, as was the case with many other very attractive parliamentary assistants, but nothing could be further from the truth. They were excellent at their jobs, and both were highly intelligent and well-educated people who helped many of us navigate the issues facing us in the often incomprehensible bureaucracy of the European Union.

Such was the loyal friendship that I struck up with Peter and his team that they even came over to the UK to help us with our campaigns. Peter had played quite a significant role in the Brexit campaign and was very proud of his efforts in helping us campaign for independence, and in return, we were proud to have his support. He also brought a team over to help me with my 2015 General Election campaign to win the seat of Dudley North.

Much of the campaign saw a neck-and-neck battle between UKIP and Labour in Dudley, with a poll just three weeks before the election showing us just one percentage point behind the incumbent Labour MP, Ian Austin. Unfortunately, a combination of a national scare campaign by the Tories suggesting a vote for anyone except them would allow a Labour/ SNP coalition into government, ferocious and quite brilliant local campaigning from Ian Austin and the local Tories who knew they couldn't win deciding to target UKIP votes to gain second place led to ultimate failure. My vote in Dudley North topped eleven thousand people, but we slumped into third place, and Labour retained the seat. The celebrations of the Tory activists when seeing that they had stopped us from winning and dumped me into third place tells you all you need to know about modern politics. They would rather have a Labour MP in place than a UKIP one.

Peter, Laura and Natalie spent a few days on the campaign trail with us, including a public meeting at which Peter spoke. The meeting was at a social club, and Peter very much enjoyed the atmosphere. One of the locals asked him if he wanted a pint. Unsure of what English beer to go for, he decided to copy the order of the person in front of him. That order had been for a pint of Shandy, but unfortunately, our Swedish guest had misheard and, much to the mirth of the assembled crowd, asked for a pint of "Shaggy" I took great pleasure in explaining to him later what the word "Shag" meant in English slang and to his credit Peter exploded in fits of laughter.

A visit to my home area wouldn't be complete without a big night out in Wolverhampton. Peter and his team joined me and other members in the centre of town. Large amounts of alcohol were consumed, and a brilliant night out was had. It was notable for Laura and Natalie taking to the dance floor and absolutely stealing the limelight from the somewhat unimpressed local ladies. They dragged me onto the dancefloor, and for a short period of time, I felt like Eighties Pop star Robert Palmer in his iconic music video for "Addicted to Love", self-consciously swaying whilst surrounded by very cool beauties.

We finished the night in proper fashion with a drunken curry. Peter stepped up the drinking, moving onto the spirits, and at least one of my team members collapsed, unable to match the pace.

Considering both the Sweden Democrats and UKIP were labelled as far Right xenophobes by the press, it was a wonderful friendship between a group of people that the establishment would have the public think should hate each other.

Beatrix von Storch

Beatrix is a formidable lady. A German MEP, she was a member of the AFD party. Another of those political parties, the Tories, would label far-right extremists until they got the chance to work with them and they happily joined a group with them.

Beer, Beatrix, Bill, and Brussels

Not tall or big in stature, the lady packs a political punch. I first noticed her when she repeatedly stood up to make defiant speeches against Politically Correct measures, such as measures aimed at positive discrimination to promote more women. She was also one of the few people who suffered and argued against a whole afternoon debate in Strasbourg where the EU parliament was arguing for a European directive dictating how much housework a man should do and equating a lazy husband with domestic abuse. Yes. We spent a whole afternoon on this madness.

I had complimented her a few times on her speeches with a very stoic, typically German nod until things changed one afternoon after I had made a speech. As I left the parliamentarium, she leaped out from behind me and gave me a hefty smack on the backside and, with a big grin, said, "Great speech" From that moment on, we became great friends and allies. Despite her rather stern initial appearance, Beatrix is great fun and a loyal friend. She came to the UK on one occasion to make a speech in favour of one of my runs for Westminster Parliament. We started the evening with several pints of very strong beer in the Beacon Hotel in Sedgley. Its real ale is famous across the country for its distinctive taste and high alcohol volume. She entertained the locals with her sense of humour and fun attitude before crossing over to the working men's club where the public meeting was to be held. She delivered a speech in English that lasted around forty-five minutes and was greeted with a standing ovation.

A great friend and ally as well as an outstanding politician, Beatrix showed that belief in freedom and independence was not simply confined to the "Cranks" of UKIP but was a Europe-wide movement.

Marine Le Pen

Madame Le Pen was never a personal friend of mine, and I differed in my politics from her Front National in many ways. Our only similarities came from a shared desire for national independence and a loathing of the EU.

She was notorious for standing up in the parliament and making magnificently grand speeches oozing defiance. In fact, she was very typically French. Indeed, on one occasion amidst a chorus of boos and abuse for her latest speech, she simply stood up tall and declared, "I am France", with a look of stunning defiance.

Regardless of whether we agreed with her speeches, we all used to make sure we were in place to hear them. It really felt like you were in the presence of an important figure in political history; I guess time will tell on that.

She oozed magnetism and charisma, prompting Nigel to remark on one occasion that she was "Really rather sexy" In order to understand this, you must be in her presence. She isn't the most physically attractive woman, but there really is something intoxicating about people who emanate power, and it's rather refreshing to talk about a woman rather than a man in this context.

On one occasion, I had made a barnstorming anti-EU speech and had retaken my seat. I received a tap on the shoulder, half expecting to be in some kind of trouble, only to see that it was a member of the Front National with the whispered words, "Madame Le Pen wishes you to know she approved of your speech" I looked around to where the magnificent lady was sat and received the smallest of regal nods and a slight movement of the mouth which I interpreted as a smile. It was a nice compliment from an important person, but it also felt just a little intimidating.

That Christmas, I received a Christmas card from the lady herself. I've kept this in safekeeping just in case she ever beats the electoral system and wins the French presidency. After all, she may be looking for an Ambassador to the UK!

Possibly the most moving moment to do with Le Pen and the Front National was the first parliament session after Brexit. They and other members of the anti-EU parties gave us a standing ovation, and one of her deputies came over to me and said, "Vive Britannia Vive Libertie" In response, I said, for certainly the only time in my life ", Vive La France" The desire to leave the EU has never been about hating other countries it is about wanting each of our friends and neighbours to live by their own democracy and rules.

Guy Verhofstadt

The guy is the MEP most anti-EU politicians and activists love to hate, but I must break that pattern and say I rather liked him.

A passionate and senior Belgian Liberal, Guy makes no secret of his desire for the United States of Europe. His speeches are always dramatic, with his mop of hair flying around accompanied by expansive hand gestures that could easily black the eyes of colleagues sitting too close to him if they don't duck. In short, his beliefs and mine are polar opposites.

Keeping an eye on Guy Verhofstadt

So why do I like him? Well, maybe like is too strong a word, but I certainly respect him. The reason is simple. He is honest. He doesn't hide his aspirations for a Federal Europe or seek to disguise what the project is all about. Instead of hiding his dreams, he shouts them from the rooftops. In every debate, he argues for more Europe and more centralisation, and he does it with fire in his belly.

He is also unique amongst senior Euro politician frontbenchers in that he will take questions and debate points. In order to engage in a question or raise a point at the parliamentary session, you have to raise a blue card, which is then noted by the chairman, who will ask the speaker if they are prepared to take the question once they have finished. A question is allowed to be asked for thirty seconds and the answer one minute; that is the extent of the debate allowed. The guy always accepted the question and always turned round to face me directly when answering; that takes some guts, and I've always admired him for that.

On one occasion, Guy had been ranting about the need for combined EU foreign policy to much applause. I asked the question as to whether that would require an EU army, knowing that the next person scheduled to speak was Nigel. Guy responded very positively that he was all in favour of combined EU armed forces. This was the perfect set-up for Nigel, who then piled in, savaging the idea and supporting the continuation of NATO. At the end of the session, Nigel walked past me and, with a wicked grin, said, "Well, that worked out rather nicely, didn't it?"

I can respect people that I disagree with. Especially people who are prepared to look me in the eyes and argue their opinion forcibly. Guy Verhofstadt is a very rare example of a politician who says exactly what he thinks, and I very much respect him for that.

President Juncker

Jean-Claude Juncker was a remarkable man to witness in action. As President of the European Commission from 2014 to 2019, he was a regular speaker at Parliamentary sessions and a hugely important figure in the EU.

He was also capable of speaking multiple languages fluently. He regularly displayed this ability by swapping between languages mid-speech.

His behaviour was rather odd, which is the only way to describe it. He would often pause mid-speech to respond to heckles in whatever language they were made in, and on many occasions, he seemed a little unsteady on his feet. Another of his habits was to give big hugs to the senior politicians sitting on the front benches, whether they wanted him to or not. Nigel was occasionally the recipient of a big hug and kiss from the esteemed president, and I'm pretty certain it wasn't among his happiest moments as an MEP.

There were rumours that President Juncker enjoyed a drink, regardless of the time of day. His behaviour occasionally appeared very similar to that of a man who had a couple of Shandies too many. This was particularly unusual as most of his speeches and appearances took place quite early in the morning. Of course, these are just rumours, and I would never accuse such an esteemed figure in European politics of being a drunk myself.

I was quite flattered that, on one occasion, he responded to a heckle from me. I was a little late for the session, and as I walked down the steps to my seat, I heard him say in perfect English that the British Conservative party had been taken over by UKIP. Laughing loudly at this preposterous idea, I said, "I bloody wish it had been" He stopped mid-speech and replied, "Yes, I'm sure you do, Mr Etheridge, but to the rest of us, the idea is horrific" He then reverted back to his prepared notes.

Whether he was drunk much of the time, in fact even more if he was drunk, Jean Claude Juncker was incredibly well educated and quick-witted. He is another man on the opposite side of the argument that I can at least have some respect for if not by any means be bosom buddies.

Godfrey Bloom

Godders is one of the most extraordinary people I have ever had the pleasure of meeting. Highly articulate and exceptionally well educated, he is a joy to spend time with.

A man whose educational attainments can stand comparison with anyone, he also had a distinguished military career before using his exceptional understanding of the economy to make a considerable fortune in business. He was one of the most impressive and devastating speakers in the European Parliament during his political career.

The speeches made by Godders were a mixture of a detailed understanding of the subject matter combined with dripping contempt for the European establishment. They are still available on YouTube, and I recommend you have a look at them; they are exceptionally entertaining.

My rise through the ranks of UKIP sadly coincided with Godfrey's dramatic fall from grace. I had a bird's eye view of some of the incidents that led to his demise within the party. It was a spectacular fall if you keep in mind that this man was a huge favourite with the membership, with only Nigel more popular and not by much. Indeed, he and Nigel had shared living quarters in Brussels for many years.

The first incident I witnessed with Godders getting into huge amounts of trouble was the infamous "Bongo Bongo Land" speech. The speech was actually made at a UKIP meeting that I had organised in the Dudley borough, and I feel a little guilty about the repercussions suffered by the great man. It was one of my innovations to video record speeches at our events and shared them on social media. I was one of the first in the party to appreciate the reach of social media outlets like Twitter and Facebook. I can actually remember one conversation with Nigel when he told me it was a waste of time, which is rather ironic considering the amount of support and money he has gained through social media in recent years.

The speech itself was rapturously received by a crowd of around a hundred people. The value of these public meetings can be shown by the fact that only about half of the people in the crowd were current members of the party. There were a significant number of people there hearing the UKIP message in person for the first time. I felt sure the video of the speech would make a huge impact when shared on social media. Unfortunately, it wasn't the entirely positive impact I had hoped for.

Godfrey has a particularly old-fashioned vocabulary and turn of phrase. You could put that down to his age, but I prefer to think it has more to do with his life experience and the circles he has moved in. He is about as far removed from modern-day pop culture as is humanly possible, and changes in the meaning of certain words and phrases most likely passed him by. Having said that, I very much doubt that he would choose his words differently, even if he was more up-to-date with times.

During the speech Godfrey was making a point about how wrong it was for us to be sending a significant amount of our national treasure out to other countries in the form of indiscriminate foreign aid. It was at this point he referred to "Bongo Bongo land". Now, anyone who has ever spoken with anyone before around 1980 would realise that this term is a catch-all describing distant lands with often dictatorial and inefficient governments. There were people of different ethnicities there who took no offence whatsoever at the term, including one rather elderly black lady who applauded the sentiment vociferously.

Sadly, the video clip was captured and sent to the mainstream media, who used it to fit their narrative that UKIP was a racist party. Much to the annoyance of the UKIP head office and media managers, he insisted on engaging with the media and arguing his case rather than following their one consistent policy, which can be loosely paraphrased as "Let's ignore it and hope it goes away."

At the height of the controversy, I was sitting in a pub grabbing a quick pint or two of real ale when I overheard a group of men discussing the issue. At this point, I could sit in a pub relatively anonymously, so it was easy to listen in to what was being said. It was clear that the comments were very popular, and the efforts to smear the party had actually backfired. Of course, this conversation was being held between a group of middle-aged working class males who were having a pint straight after leaving a factory, so there are opinions that were immediately deemed to be worthless by the media and establishment elite.

The next time I saw Godfrey, I was in the reception area of the building hosting the UKIP conference, and he burst through the door with Annabelle Fuller desperately trying to find a ravening press pack off him. It was an unbelievable scene, and it was only later that I realised this was the follow-up to Godfrey having clipped Channel 4 journalist and former Labour activist Michael Crick round the ear with a rolled-up copy of the conference programme.

Later that day, we learned that Godfrey had used the word "Slut" at a fringe event when describing women who did not clean behind the fridge. It was blindingly obvious that it was a remark made as an attempt at humour. It also needs to be noted that the modern meaning of the word is not the one he was using. He was using "Slut" with its original meaning of being untidy.

At the end of that eventful day, party chairman Steve Crowther took to the stage and announced the party had suspended Godfrey. His announcement was met with a huge chorus of boos and shouts of derision from the membership. His bacon was saved by Nigel taking to the stage and calming the crowd, but emotions were running very high.

If we then fast forward a few years to my leadership bid, Godfrey became my highest-profile supporter, referring to me as the only genuine libertarian in the race. I was extremely honoured by this and thankful to Annabelle for brokering the meeting that led to this endorsement. If I had won the election, it was my intention to bring Godfrey back into the party and into a senior role within the leadership team, but sadly, it was not to be, and besides that, I do not know whether he would have accepted the offer. He had made a promise to Mrs Bloom that he would not go back, and he is a gentleman of his word, but I would have given it my very best shot. Politics needs brains and experience like Godfrey can offer.

I often thought during the ideological battles that took up much of my time as I tried and failed to stop the efforts of Patrick Oflynn and Suzanne Evans to drive the party into a middle ground inhabited by bigger and more established parties that Godders would have been the perfect ally and maybe the result might have been different. The intellectual vigour and oratorical skills of Godfrey Bloom on your side of an argument are the equivalent of being able to deploy tactical nuclear missiles in a battle.

One more thing about Godfrey. He is the only person who has ever referred to me as "Dear boy" and certainly the only person I would ever allow to call me that without a slap. Coming from Godders, it felt like a badge of honour, and I am proud that I was in some small way associated with this exceptional man.

Lobbying at the EU

Apparently, there are more lobbyists and lobbying organisations working in or around the EU than there are in Washington, DC. There was certainly a huge amount of very obvious lobbying going on. If you were of a mind to, you could spend the whole week being wined and dined by various groups in return for listening to a brief presentation on the subject that they wanted to sway your opinion on.

As a general rule, I gave the lobbyist events a swerve. Yes, it was cost-effective never to have to buy your own drinks or food, but on the other hand, it did entail having to spend time listening to political pitches and even more tediously spending time with other MEPs, which, with a few exceptions got very "old" for me very quickly.

I did tend to have an open door to listen to lobbyists during my work time, though. I felt that it was probably my responsibility to listen to what they had to say, even if I thought it was garbage.

The one lobbyist event that I did attend fairly regularly was the tobacco industry one. It had a lot going in its favour, including free handouts of tobacco products, a decent buffet and plenty of free booze. This was not unique, but what I particularly enjoyed about it was the absolute absence of them actually trying to persuade us of anything. On one occasion, I saw a British MEP turn up with the most insanely huge pipe I have ever seen and proceed to stuff it with as much free tobacco as he could lay his hands on. He also stuffed his pockets with freebies, and when he left, he seemed almost weighed down to the point that he couldn't move,

Amidst all the greed and generally repulsive behaviour of the tobacco event, I actually learned something that was really fascinating and showed that things are never what they seem through the EU-looking glass.

I struck up a conversation with a representative of a small German firm that had been making cigarettes for a century. I expected him to be very much in favour of the tobacco lobbyists, but actually, he was there to tell anyone who would listen that these people were actually quite the opposite of what we thought they were.

The organisation had been lobbying for a standardisation of the health warnings printed across cigarette packets rather than the different standards we currently see in different states. The argument was that they were being responsible for public health but helping the tobacco industry with exports because they only had to print one label. This proposition seems quite reasonable at first; however, the reality of the situation was that the standard of labelling being lobbied for only made sense to large multinational corporations who, due to the size and scale of their operations, could absorb the cost quite easily. Unfortunately, the costs incurred by smaller firms who did not have the benefits of economies of scale were so significant that they feared they may be driven out of business.

The lobbying organisation was not lobbying for the tobacco industry as a whole. It was lobbying for measures to be imposed by the EU that would drive its smaller competitors out of business.

Who Could it Have Been?

Shortly before I pulled out of the fateful leadership race that elected Henry Bolton as leader, a very strange thing happened. As I recount the story here, I wonder what conclusions you may reach as to who may have been responsible and why.

At this time, I was mainly based in my parents' home whilst in the UK. There really didn't seem much point in buying a property when I spent my whole week in Brussels or Strasbourg, and when I returned to the West Midlands, I would either be staying with a girlfriend or out at the pub catching up with mates.

Distressingly, during this time, my parents' home was broken into. It was a very unusual form of break-in.

There was no obvious sign of how the trespassers had gained ingress. Even more strangely, nothing had been taken.

The plot thickens. The only way that we knew there had been a break-in was because the draws on a filing cabinet had been opened and paperwork moved and leafed through. This was odd as there was money left out quite openly, a fair amount of rather expensive home entertainment equipment, including laptops and TV, left untouched, and the keys for two relatively expensive cars were left out on the sideboard with the cars very obviously parked on the drive.

Even more intriguingly, it was clear that the doors to each room had been opened and the alarm disabled. Perhaps the most peculiar thing was that my very alert and rather aggressive Terrier Bruce was staying at the house, but he never heard anything. We know he couldn't have heard anything; otherwise, he would have charged whoever was in the house and given them an extremely uncomfortable time.

The police were called. They inspected the house and found that the intruders had accessed the building through the garage. There were minute signs of where doors had been forced. There were no fingerprints, though, anywhere. When we asked them if they would investigate the matter, they smiled knowingly and said they don't investigate things like this.

At the time this happened, the bookies had me as their favourite to be the next UKIP leader, and I was publicly stating that I was going to run for the position.

So I'll leave you to ask yourselves the question. Who would break into a property so silently and expertly? Who would ignore easy opportunities to make money, valuables and cars? Who would only be interested in accessing computers and a filing cabinet?

I guess we will never know, but we can have a bloody good guess, I think.

Adventures on the UKIP Brexit Bus

As soon as people hear the words Brexit and Bus, they immediately start thinking about the seemingly endless fuss created by Boris Johnson standing in front of a bus suggesting we could add another £350m per week to NHS spending if we left the EU. Don't worry. This story is far more interesting than that.

Before I start on the fun stuff, let me say for about the millionth time Boris Johnson, his bus, and his promises had nothing to do with me. Not only was I not a Tory, but I was not cooperating with the official Vote Leave campaign. I personally think the promise was a ridiculous waste of money, which has been rendered worse, in my opinion, by the fact that the post-Brexit increase in NHS spending has actually turned out to be closer to £500m per week.

Magic bus

No, the Brexit bus I'm going to tell you about was the UKIP Brexit bus. This was an altogether different enterprise and, in my opinion, much more worthwhile and certainly more fun.

A supporter had very generously offered us the use of his tour bus, which had previously been used as a tour bus for Motorhead. A covering was designed and fitted around the bus, showing the faces of the MEPs backing it and a large UKIP logo. As it turned out, although several MEPs were backing the bus endeavour, only one of us completed the whole tour on it; yes, you guessed it, I was the one.

The bus tour was carefully planned to cover towns and cities from the West Midlands to the Northwest over a two-week period. The adventure started in Dudley, where we loaded up with essential provisions and a group of volunteers, all male.

Essential provisions, in this case, consisted of several bottles of whiskey and a great many cans of beer. After all, it had been a Motorheads tour bus, so we had a certain standard to maintain.

On the night before we set off on our adventure, we occupied the bus, chose our beds on the upstairs deck and decided to have a quiet drink and some food before we set out. Several hours and a significant amount of alcohol supply later, we had finished off the takeaway pizzas and collapsed into our beds.

The next morning, I woke up as the bus came to a halt at a Motorway service for a pit stop. Everyone else had dashed straight off the bus to make use of the toilets. I was the last off, and I must confess, I was a little disorientated as to where I was and very hungover. To make matters worse, all of the windows on the bus were covered by our magnificent UKIP decal, meaning that when the engine was off, the lights were off, and there was pitch darkness.

I staggered from my bunk, found my way to the stairs by touch and very carefully made my way down them in the dark. I worked my way to the door and managed to open it. Suddenly, the pitch darkness of the bus was shattered by what initially felt like blinding sunlight. I was so dazzled that I literally couldn't see anything. I took one step off the bus before finding that the curb next to it was very high. So it was that the first day of the UKIP Brexit door began with me tripping and falling face-first onto the pavement outside a Midlands Motorway services station.

Despite having face-planted the tarmac rather hard, I immediately bounced back up quickly, looking around to see if anyone had noticed. Unfortunately, my eyes still weren't focusing, so I will never know how many people had a good chuckle at my expense. I staggered into the service station and rather too loudly berated my fellow campaigners for having left me on the bus. As I slumped into a chair, one of the team approached me and asked if I wanted a coffee, which was all too obvious considering the state I was in. As my mouth was as parched and dry as the bottom of a birdcage, I decided I needed caffeine and a lot of liquid. I asked for a large Frappuccino, the ice-cold coffee that chain cafes and service stations seem to excel in. My friend came back quite quickly with a large cup, which I immediately swigged deeply from. Unfortunately, he had misheard what I had said and bought me a large scolding hot Cappuccino. No sooner had I begun thirstily emptying the liquid into my throat than I felt a burning sensation from the extremely hot liquid and spat it out all over the table. It's fair to say our first day on the road was not a great experience for me.

As the days went by, the tour became a fantastic success. Every town and city we visited seemed absolutely full of cheering Brexit supporters, and I began to think this referendum was going to be a slam dunk and a huge victory. This all changed at the end of a great day of campaigning in Worcester. We resumed our places in the coach and turned our phones back on to post pictures of our campaigning on social media. It was only then that we learnt the news of the murder of Jo Cox MP.

The murder of Jo Cox was absolutely awful. Nobody should be murdered because of their political views or party, least of all a bright young woman with such a great future. We were all stunned and horrified. Disappointingly, the media spin on the incident made what should have been a tragedy we could all share our concerns and sympathy for into a political incident. The narrative was that the person who had committed the murder had done it as some kind of pro-Brexit terror attack and that we were somehow to blame for winding up. This was puzzling as the police had categorised him as a mentally ill individual acting alone.

The Brexit campaign was halted for several days just as we felt the momentum was with us, and when we restarted, the atmosphere had changed.

Brexit supporters were not so publicly vociferous, and several people actually approached us in the street, blaming us for the murder. As ludicrous as this is, it shows the influence the media can have on shaping opinions and instilling myths into the public consciousness.

Nevertheless, we continued campaigning and working hard. Yes, we also played hard, but that was at the end of days of leafletting and canvassing people in the streets. If you have ever done that kind of work, you will appreciate just how important it is to be able to wind down at the end of a tough day.

When we finally arrived in the North West, the support and the general excitement were bubbling again. We had a fantastic day in the beautiful town of Chester, which we also learned has more than its fair share of beautiful ladies. We rolled up outside a large pub in Blackpool, and a crowd of several hundred people cheered and waved as pro-Brexit speeches from Margot Parker MEP and myself were very well received.

We rolled into the Bolton area, and our overnight stop was at the Queens pub in Bradley Fold with its UKIP-supporting gaffer Sean Hornby, our host for the evening. Sean is a great guy and a very effective local politician, as well as being a classic good old-fashioned pub landlord. We disembarked, and a fantastic night ensued. Huge amounts of beer were consumed, and the locals all made us feel very welcome. Even when a few of us retired back to the bus for a breather, Sean kept the beers flowing.

We were joined on this leg of the journey by Paul Nuttall. Ever the good sport, Paul must have downed well over ten pints during the evening and was the life and soul of the party.

The next day, we rolled into Bolton and prepared for a day of campaigning. We were all the worse for wear, particularly Paul. We had to react pretty quickly when a BBC team, complete with a camera crew, approached us and asked for an interview with MEP Nuttall. We searched around in our belongings and managed to find a pair of sunglasses to hide his bright red eyes and propped Paul against the bus for his interview, which, much to his credit, he managed to get through without any obvious slurring.

Not all of our receptions were so warm. Our stop in Manchester city centre was distinctly uncomfortable, with plenty of abuse being thrown at us and a few eggs hitting our bus as we left. Liverpool city centre was equally as tough a crowd, but with great credit to the volunteers on the bus, we stuck at it and worked each area very hard.

By the end of the bus tour, we were all exhausted, and I have to admit, after such a long period of time of being inhabited by hard-living males, the bus did not smell too pretty either. It had been a phenomenal experience, but I think we were all very relieved when it ended, and we survived.

The Day of the Brexit Vote

Despite the bus tour having been over some time before the actual referendum was held, our local West Midlands team had continued campaigning nonstop, and I had been there with them much of the time.

Occasionally, I had to break off from the street campaigning to take part in hustings. I was involved in quite a few hustings, although I was very disappointed that arch Euromaniac Anna Soubry pulled out from one because she refused to share a stage with me. It was a rather odd approach to democracy to refuse to debate an opponent, but I took it as a compliment. After all, maybe it might have been a personal thing, and she was worried she may not have been able to resist my devastating charm and good luck. Just to show I've learned my lesson that people don't always appreciate the way I'm saying things, let me just point out that I just made a joke. Isn't it sad that we live in a time when you have to explain yourself in such minute detail, but sadly, that's the world we live in?

I did take part in a very civilised debate against Phillip Dunne MP in a church hall in Ludlow. Phillip is a classic upper-class Tory who represented a classic Tory area. When I arrived, I was looked at by the assembled crowd with a mixture of what appeared to be fascination and fear. I was under the distinct impression they thought I might well be inclined to desecrate the church and make untoward approaches to the ladies of the local women's guild. Funnily enough, this gave me a huge advantage as I was able to take Phillipe by surprise when it turned out that I could actually stand on my hind legs, form coherent sentences, and cope with the basic formalities of good manners. I won the debate; everyone knew that I won the debate, even though many of them seemed desperately embarrassed to be agreeing with me. To Phillipe's immense credit, he shook my hand afterwards and commended me on a very polite and reasonable debate. He did spoil it a little by saying I was the first UKIP person he had ever met who was not totally rude and unpleasant, but nonetheless, I couldn't help but rather like and respect him.

I took part in a TV debate where the panels were split into teams of relatively well-known political figures in the West Midlands area. I can't remember the Remainer team, but the Leave team was me, Lord Digby Jones and Gisella Stewart MP. Ms Stewart was notable in the campaign for being a Labour MP supporting Brexit, but when I met her briefly before the hustings, it was quite clear she would have been very much at home amongst the rinse Tories at a village fete. Before we began, she actually took me on one side and said words to the effect that she didn't want me spoiling it by ranting like a typical UKIP madman. I was not particularly impressed and essentially told her to mind her own business. I couldn't help but smile during the actual debate when, a few minutes in, it wasn't me who went onto a rant and got angry but the esteemed Lord Digby Jones. Funnily enough, Ms Stewart hadn't bothered to give him the pre-match lecture.

After many months of campaigning, the day of the referendum came; I must admit that having started the campaign full of confidence, I was not expecting a victory. The sheer volume of pro-EU propaganda pushed out by the state, the establishment parties, the media, and even President Barrack Obama meant that the pro-independence side was massive underdogs.

I opened my MEP office in Sedgley to campaigners from all around the West Midlands region. I bought several kegs of beer that had been locally brewed at the fantastic Sarah Hughes brewery and bought a huge amount of Indian food from the restaurant conveniently placed next door. We had two TVs in the office, and we settled in for the evening. The first indications were not promising, and for some reason, Nigel appeared on TV, effectively conceding defeat. I phoned everyone I could in his entourage to warn him not to make any more announcements until he had received the results from the Midlands and the North, but nobody would put me through to him or pass on a message. After all, what did I know? I had only spent the last few months non-stop campaigning in these areas.

I was feeling dispirited and walked around to the Indian restaurant to buy more snacks for the team. When the restaurant owner saw me, he asked why I looked so down, and I explained that I didn't think we had won. He then did something that will stay with me forever. He said, "Do not be dispirited, my friend. Inshallah, we will be free tonight" Then he showed me a huge chain of texts from the local Muslim community, all strongly supporting the vote for freedom. Rather heartened, I headed back to the office with food provisions and watched the TV for a while. I then decided to sit alone for a bit of time in a side office. It was only when I heard people literally screaming with a mixture of joy and shock that I ran back to where the TV was and witnessed the historic moment when the people of Sunderland declared their vote for freedom.

The rest of the night was a blur for me. The activists were in a wild frenzy of excitement, and I was working my way very quickly through the beer. Music was being played in the upstairs offices, and people were dancing in another room; I'm pretty sure they were doing more intimate things. It was turning into a fantastic party. As the party was in full swing, the BBC turned up outside wanting to do a live interview. I quickly grabbed some of the more sober team members there and got them to delay the reporters while I cleared a space in the back office for an interview. To my consternation, I could not find my press officer anywhere, but I proceeded anyway. Just as the BBC were about to enter, I noticed my press officer passed out in the very office we were about to do the interview. We very quickly picked up as many "Vote Leave" correx boards as we could find and covered him over, with the last one being placed over his as the cameraman entered. It was a close shave, but we got away with it, and I somehow managed to do a relatively serious interview despite being in a state of mild drunken hysteria. The next day I had to go to Dudley town centre to be interviewed by national TV. To my immense pride, Dudley had delivered one of the biggest leave votes in the country, and it was only appropriate to speak from there. I just about managed to get through the interview. I had been awake either campaigning or doing interviews for over forty-eight hours. As soon as the camera stopped rolling, I headed off home and collapsed into a deep and very happy sleep. Little did I know that things in politics would never be that good for me again.

MEP Missions:
Somaliland

A part of an MEP's role is to visit other countries either on missions to learn more about a certain political situation or to work to encourage international trade. Occasionally, we went on missions that were about Human Rights issues.

Some of these missions are extremely pleasant, with MEPs staying in five-star accommodation and attending glamorous conferences filled with influential businessmen and important political figures. Of course, being a UKIP MEP, I didn't get invited on those missions as they were all snapped up by the established Tory and Labour groups.

Bill in the Horn of Africa

I was invited to visit Somaliland in 2018. It was towards the end of my term, and I realised that my involvement in the Brexit battles was pretty much at an end, so I could pull away from that particular battle for a while. I felt that after all of the horrible media coverage and dreadful damage to my personal reputation, it may be a good thing to try and secure a legacy of having done at least one good thing that absolutely nobody could say was anything but a noble act. So, with this positive intention, I accepted the invitation to visit Somaliland.

For those who aren't aware of Somaliland, it is a small, unrecognised state adjacent to Somalia in the horn of Africa. A product of the civil war in 1991, the nation covers the area that was once known as British Somaliland. Its capital city is Hargeisa.

The government of Somaliland were keen to invite foreign politicians to visit in the hope of winning international recognition and, therefore, opening up legitimate opportunities for trade and aid. This seemed a very worthwhile visit to make and an interesting subject to look into.

The visit became even more important when I was made aware that a man born in Somaliland but holding British citizenship was in jail there for a crime and holding a potentially heavy sentence. His crime was to stand outside a police station and read a poem protesting against police brutality. There didn't appear to be any official British contact to try to get him released or even see how he was. It seemed to me to be an ideal opportunity to do two good things in one visit. If I could persuade the authorities to treat him humanely, I could argue that the state was more reasonable than it had previously appeared and make the case for greater international engagement. The plan seems simple, but the events turned out to be very far from that.

The journey to Somaliland is not an easy one. It entails flying to Ethiopia and then swapping at Addis Ababa airport for the connecting flight. The flight from Ethiopia to Somaliland was not a comfortable one. The aircraft seemed rather old and rickety, and as we flew over seemingly endless barren lands, we seemed low enough for me to see the occasional roaming local quite clearly. As it turned out, an aircraft flying that route crashed not many months later, so my fears were clearly quite well-founded.

On landing in Somaliland, we arrived at an airport that was unlike anything I had ever witnessed. It was very small, and as VIPs, we were escorted into the so-called luxury area, which reminded me very much of one of the buildings you see in films about distant outposts of the British Empire, normally under siege by the natives. On thinking about it, I think the building actually was a leftover of the Empire; it certainly seemed old and shabby enough.

We were greeted by a significant contingent of troops. These troops looked hot, short-tempered, and generally had their hands far too close to their guns for my liking. We were loaded into an ancient Land Rover with two armed guards, sat in the back, and driven to our hotel.

On the journey to the hotel, I became fully aware of the problem facing the people of this benighted land in vivid detail. In fact, everything was vivid due to the incredible brightness of the searing sun. It was the kind of bright sunlight I had never experienced anywhere else, and I was glad that I had been advised to bring sunglasses, which managed to take a little of the glare off. Of course, accompanying such powerful sunlight was searing, relentless heat, which to this particular Englishman used to the grey and wet West Midlands was almost unbearable. Sadly, the weather was the least of the concerns facing these struggling people.

As we entered the city and rode towards our hotel, we were aware that the roads were extremely bumpy. After a while, it became clear that the roads had not been properly repaired from the shelling during the war. The centre of the city is marked by the wreckage of a MIG Jet fighter standing on a plinth, another grim reminder of the war. As we proceeded, we saw the living conditions of the locals, and it was horrifying. Many of the buildings were still in ruins, and the people had created shelter by gathering rubble and wreckage to take shelter as best they could. We passed a market, the centrepiece of which was made up of pallets and pallets of bank notes, a clear sign of the crippling hyperinflation and the loss of confidence in their currency. We were relieved when the hotel came into view, especially as we were apparently staying in the very best hotel in the country.

On arriving at the hotel, we were greeted by armed guards who checked our paperwork; then, our driver had to navigate his way through the barriers which were in place to stop suicide bomb attacks by people ramming the building with vehicles. The hotel itself was far from pretty, and as Somaliland is a strict Muslim country, there was, of course, no bar. I was assured I had the best room, which was nice to know, but I pride myself on not being too precious about where I stayed and was just happy to have somewhere to go and rest. On entering the room, I had to ask myself if this was the best room and what the hell the rest was like. It was a very small room with a rock-hard bed, a barely functioning tiny shower, but with the most important thing of all, a huge ancient but still functioning air conditioning unit.

Each morning started with the same blistering sun and heat. I made a point of getting up to have a little stroll before heading off to the day's business. Breakfast was provided, but I limited myself to cups of coffee as I wasn't at all comfortable that the food would sit well with my stomach during the busy days ahead. As an unintended bonus, I lost 8 pounds in weight during the week I was there due to no alcohol and barely any food, so that was a good thing, at least.

The morning was also notable for the seemingly endless and incredibly loud broadcast of the call to prayer across the whole city, plus other broadcasts in Arabic, which I presumed were of a religious nature. Somaliland is run as a strictly Islamic state. The women are all completely covered when out in public, and alcohol is strictly prohibited. Well, it is strictly prohibited for the people, but those in high positions can still access it, as I witnessed.

The only intoxicant that appears to be allowed is something called Khat. This is a leaf that can be chewed, sprinkled on food, or smoked. The vast majority of its use in Somaliland seemed to be by chewing. The effect of Khat is similar to Cocaine in some ways. When you take it, the effects can include increased blood pressure, a feeling of being more energetic and a faster heart rate. Amongst the negative effects are the potential for mood swings and violent behaviour, which probably explains a great deal. Khat was as normal here as a cup of tea. Our hosts bought a batch of the leaves, which we shared with our armed guards on reflection that was possibly a little risky as they always had their hands far too close to the trigger on their automatic weapons, in my opinion, and the last thing we wanted was for them to be hyped up. I tried a leaf; the effect was almost instant. Despite my sunglasses, I felt as if I could see everything with greater clarity than ever before, and my awareness and alertness of everything around me was heightened dramatically. Some of the other members of our group had significantly more than one leaf with the effect that when we got back to the hotel, they found themselves running around outside the hotel in the searing heat until they came down from it and passed out in their rooms.

Before we got down to the serious diplomatic business of the visit, we were taken on a cultural visit. We were driven a distance outside of the city and parked up in a desert wasteland. From there, accompanied by our always nervous armed guards, we climbed up into the mountains for half an hour. It was gruelling and extremely hot, especially in a suit and tie, but it was truly worth it. We entered a site that was perhaps the most interesting archaeological area I have ever seen. The caves carved into the mountain walls were decorated with paintings that dated back several thousand years. The caves themselves supposedly led to ancient tunnels, which, if followed to a conclusion, would take you all the way to Egypt, a prehistoric trade route. Sadly, nobody had properly investigated this due to the fact that the locals were absolutely convinced that the caves and tunnels were inhabited by the Jinn. Jinn are creatures from Arabic folklore that were believed to have the capacity to change into human or animal form, as well as disguising themselves as inanimate objects such as stones or trees. The belief in and fear of the Jinn was still alive and well with my hosts, and I was certainly not bold enough to put it to the test by entering these huge dark caves.

While at this site we saw something which had the appearance of a huge seat carved into the mountain. We were reliably informed this was the throne of the Monkey King. We approached it, and sure enough, there were droppings all around it, which my hosts informed me were from the monkeys. I was sceptical but reasoned that I had never seen monkey droppings before, so why not? The story became a little more meaningful as we drove back to the city. We noticed our driver slowing for an obstruction in the road. When we got closer, I witnessed perhaps the strangest thing I have ever seen. A troop of rather large monkeys was walking down the road out of the city, presumably heading back to the caves and their king's throne. At the lead was a monkey significantly larger than the rest with a long growth of beard. If there is such a thing as the monkey king, I believe we saw him there and then. Apparently, it was quite a regular feature for the monkeys to enter town and steal food. It was totally surreal; they were acting like a human gang of marauders. Charles Darwin would certainly have been impressed at this demonstration of how similar we are to our distant relatives.

Monkeys were not the only unusual visitors to the city. One of the few things Somaliland has a plentiful supply of is Camels. In fact, Camels are their biggest export. I witnessed firsthand how plentiful the supply of camels was, seeing several of them quite casually strolling down city centre streets while I was there.

The serious business of the visit involved a series of meetings with government officials. It became clear that the governance of the country was split between high-level representatives of different clans, and there was no real consistency to any of it. I became frustrated and told our guide I had to meet with someone who could make a difference, or the whole trip would have been a waste of time.

Sure enough, the next day, we met with the judge and his assistant, who was dealing with the upcoming trial of the British citizen we were interested in talking to. I stressed to them the importance of being seen to be fair and how beneficial it would be to be seen to be helpful. The whole conversation was based on my somewhat overstating of the importance of being British and the potential impact we could have regarding aid from the EU. I left the meeting feeling hopeful that we may have left our mark.

We certainly had left our mark. The next day, we were told that the judge had recommended the prisoner be released. This would have been great, but the trial had not started yet, so it was, therefore, understandably quite suspicious to the authorities.

We were summoned to the jail where the prisoner was being held, and mysteriously, we were left with a driver, but our armed guards were no longer on duty. This was a pretty clear warning sign that we might have a problem. These warning signs became significantly more direct as the day went on.

When we arrived at the jail, we were ushered in through the back gate. My impression of the building was that it was very similar to a French Foreign Legion fort of the kind Beau Jest may have been familiar with, but I'm sure it was a little more modern than that. We were ushered into a room and asked to sit at a large table. The member of staff I had travelled with, as well as a Polish Human rights advocate, sat at the bottom end of the table, and I was placed near the top. The room we were in was ringed by at least half a dozen armed guards. The heat was overwhelming, and the atmosphere was so tense that our guide appeared ready to put his hands up and beg for mercy.

To my surprise, the judge and his assistant we had met with previously were the first to enter the room. I nodded and smiled at them, only to see them look away quickly after having given the slightest of shakes of their head. It was apparent that they did not want to admit to having spoken with me. This in itself was ringing alarm bells in my head. These alarm bells turned to sirens when the Governor walked in.

A huge man in military uniform with a row of medals across his chest, the governor carried an air of aggression with him that had his fellow countrymen cowering as he entered. He walked in and sat at the seat next to me, stating, rather than asking, "You are the Englishman" I confirmed that I was not only English but stated with as much of an air of importance as possible that I was also a member of the European Parliament. He looked at me with a fearsome expression on his face that I can well imagine was a look many people may have witnessed before having violence inflicted on them and then launched into a tirade of abuse. I cannot remember what he said word for word, but the general gist of it was that Britain no longer had an empire, who did I think I was and in fairly florid terms that he didn't appreciate me being there.

When he paused for breath, I looked around the room. My two colleagues understandably looked absolutely petrified. Our local guide appeared to be sitting so low in his chair that he was under the table, and the soldiers ringing the room looked very tense. I decided I had to make a decision very quickly about how to deal with this situation. The first and most appealing option was to basically beg forgiveness and see if he would let us out. It is important to keep in mind that we were on a mission unsanctioned by the British government, and if we had disappeared, it would not necessarily have been a very high priority for them to find out where we were. It was at this point that the years of going through life at a tough school and then working with Psychopaths in the Steel industry served me well; I was used to dealing with bullies, and although this guy was the most dangerous bully I had ever dealt with

I knew what I needed to do.

Summoning every ounce of courage, I had and using an immense amount of what my dad has always referred to as "Salesman's Bull Shit", I fired myself up, leaned forward so that we were effectively locking antlers and started shouting back. My counter volley took him by surprise. One of the key skills of being a salesman is to listen to what people are saying, as they will always give away what they are worried about or what they want. His relentless ranting about the British Empire led me to believe he was actually quite worried, maybe from some distant folk memory, that a troop of red-coated British Expeditionary soldiers may be on their way. I focussed on persuading him that I was a very important British politician and that I was not used to be being spoken to so disrespectfully. Then, I offered him a way out. I told him that while I was in the country, it was very important to treat a British subject with respect but that I would not be there forever, and if there was any further inconvenience caused after I left, I wouldn't be in a position to say or do anything. There was a brief pause, which genuinely seemed to last for hours as I stopped speaking, and we stared directly at each other, looking for signs of weakness. To my eternal relief, after this brief pause, he burst out in uproarious laughter, shook my hand and slapped me on the back, saying words to the effect that he rather liked me after all. At that moment, I felt a relief so immense that my eyes didn't focus clearly, and I thought for one second I was going to ruin it by fainting. For the avoidance of doubt, I'm not a brave man, but I know when cornered, you have to stand your ground. I felt like I had just rolled the dice and won against heavy odds.

The prisoner was brought in. He was a large and handsome young man with armed guards on either side of him. It was totally apparent he hadn't been treated well, and although no bruises were showing, he walked quite gingerly and carefully. The governor smiled and said, "Here he is. Ask him how he has been treated" The very last thing I was going to do was put this young man at further risk of physical harm by putting him in that situation. Instead, I shook his hand and told him who I was. I mentioned that we were discussing his case and managed to get a photograph taken with him. I felt the photograph may be useful at a later point if anything happened to him to pinpoint when he was last seen in one piece.

It appeared that my discussions with the Governor had gone even better than I had hoped. Not only did we get out of his office alive and our armed guards restored, but I later found that the brave young man I had met had indeed been released and was safely back in London.

With our ordeal nearly at an end, we decided to have a meal at the hotel the day before departure. Without going into too much detail, within an hour, all of us suffered from the most extremely upset stomachs I have ever witnessed. I have heard of projectile vomiting before, but never until this point had I experienced projectile defecation.

The journey back became an adventure in its own right. When we stopped off in Ethiopia, we had quite a long gap between flights. Fortunately, the airport there is quite modern; we possibly have to thank Geldoff and co for that, so we decided to have plenty to eat and drink after a week of abstinence and upset stomachs.

Inevitably, this meant we needed the toilet. The conveniences were quite hard to find in such a large airport, and each journey was quite a mission. As I sat drinking coffee with one of my colleagues, another member of our party returned with quite an excited look on his face. He told us in a rather jolly tone that he had just been in the most exquisite and fancy toilet he had ever been to. Intrigued, we followed his instructions as to where he had relieved himself, and there was indeed a toilet sign, but to our horror, we realised that the structure in front of that sign was the Islamic Ablution room where Muslims ceremonially wash before prayer. This was far from a humorous situation. Obviously, it was mortifying to think that one of us had made such a grave faux pas, but even more concerningly than that, we were concerned he would be dragged from the airport and subjected to some form of extremely severe punishment for such an act of blasphemy.

We formed a nest with our cases against a wall and got our colleague to sit low so that he was barely visible behind them while the rest of us sat in front of him to obscure the view even more. When our flight was called, we literally ran to the exit. I only started to relax when the place was in the air, and we were on our way back to the West.

My week in Somaliland was literally the equivalent in my mind of having been to Hell and back. Easily the most awful and frightening place I have ever witnessed, I made a pledge never to return. My sincere hope and prayer is that one day, the international community will find a way to open up the country enough to provide aid. I had suffered in this dreadful place for a week but was lucky enough to be able to leave the people who live there do not have that option.

MEP Missions:
Morocco

My other mission to Africa was very different.

I was invited to the Western Sahara area of Morocco, which was another controversial and disputed region suffering from the involvement of international politics.

The region is subject to an ongoing conflict and dispute between the Kingdom of Morrocco and the Polisario Front, which is backed by Algeria and Libya. The problem, as with much of the developing world, stems from the end of the European Empires and the breakup of the territories they once possessed. This time, it was the Spanish who had left things in a mess.

Morocco is a monarchy, which suggests an outdated and archaic approach, but nothing could be further from the truth. King Mohammed is, by the standards of the region, a forward-thinking moderniser.

The modernising approach in Morocco is opposed by the terrorists of the Polisario, who have a great deal in common with other Muslim extremist terrorist groups that we have all become unfortunately aware of in recent years. They have a liking for beheading people who cross their paths and are not predisposed to civilised negotiation.

The issue first came to my attention whilst at the EU parliament. A group representing the kingdom of Morocco asked to meet with me. This was not unusual, as we were continually lobbied by various groups, but this meeting was different. The Moroccans wanted support in increasing their export trade, particularly in the fishing sector. Their exports were severely hampered by EU measures that were totally counter to the principles of free trade and were officially about sustainability quotas but, to my mind, were more about protectionism. I found myself in full agreement with their aims and started a very informative and constructive dialogue.

This was one of the few areas of policy that I vehemently disagreed with Nigel on. He was in support of the EU protectionist measures ostensibly because of his concern for the natural environment and the sustainability of fish stocks. It may be contrary to his public image, but Nigel really does passionately care about these issues and has spoken in the parliament many times on related subjects. I equally passionately felt that he was wrong on this particular issue. I believed his much-loved artisanal fishing idea was simply another word for inefficient and outdated industrial practices. It is also one of my strongest beliefs that if people want to improve themselves through hard work and free trade, they deserve support rather than fanciful and romantic notions of traditional fishing techniques preserving natural resources. The kingdom of Morocco has huge resources in the sea just off its coast; they have every right to seek to make use of those resources just as two hundred years ago, the UK used its natural resources, leading to more wealth and eventually better living standards for all.

Over a period of time, our relationship with Morocco grew so strong that I was invited to visit the Western Sahara area. It was a visit that was as positive and hopeful as any trip I had ever been on.

I travelled with a member of staff, and we were treated to a brilliantly organised programme highlighting the steps being taken in the region. Our hotel was on the coast and was a wonder of architecture. Almost entirely built using sustainable materials and powered by solar panels, it was an example of the strictly modern and environmentally friendly approach to developing the area.

Tourism is an area the Moroccans are looking to develop in the area. They have opened up to outside investment, most notably to a huge hotel complex being funded by international superstar Celine Dion. The sea is ideal for water sports, and the scenery is quite beautiful. The sun sets remarkably quickly and reveals an amazingly clear night sky with more stars visible than I have ever seen.

We were taken to a meeting with local dignitaries at a new hotel on the coast. They displayed an amazing array of seafood for the banquet. The cost of such a meal in Europe would probably be hundreds of pounds each, but such is the plentiful bounty of the sea in this area that the cost was more like pennies. It was clearly visible the Moroccan fishing industry was not so much a hidden gem as one deliberately stifled.

We were taken to a fish processing plant where we saw literally every part of the fish being used with amazing efficiency. Even what would normally be classed as waste products was turned into Protein packs. As you can imagine, the fish factory was not the most pleasant environment, but I couldn't help but laugh at our flamboyant guide, who walked through it clad in a pure white set of protective clothes and carrying himself with the air of visiting royalty, which I have a suspicion he probably was.

Later in the trip, we were driven out into the Sahara Desert in a four-by-four vehicle. Our local guides were amazing navigators finding their way across the endless desert landscape. Our destination was the camp of a woman who was a senior figure to the locals, and we were to pay our respects. We arrived at an encampment which could have been straight out of the set of Laurence of Arabia. A handful of white tents near a small oasis was home to this royal lady. We entered her tent and were welcomed warmly. A group of pillows and rugs lined the edge of the tent, and we were directed to sit down.

Once in the tent, we were given traditional garb to wear, and we happily agreed. It felt very much like real frontier diplomacy. The talks went well, but I was beginning to feel the effects of the intense heat and the lack of air. This was made worse by the fact that the incense burners in the tent were making the air very thick indeed, but I soldiered on.

When the food arrived, it was another challenge to my rookie diplomacy talents. First of all, we were invited to snack on dates, which, when I reached for seemed to be moving, but actually, it was the flies covering them. Determined to make a courteous impression, I waved them away and ate a few of the very sweet and sticky dates. Next, we were offered traditional bowls full of liquid to drink. It was my first experience with camel milk, and I must confess it was not a happy one. I haven't drunk it since, and I do not know if cauliflower milk is supposed to taste like sour yoghurt, but that was the flavour that overwhelmed my taste buds. Still, I smiled and drank it all down. Worryingly, this was not the end of the culinary delights; the main course was yet to come.

The main course was a huge plate of rice that sat atop a glistening piece of meat that the server proudly informed me was the finest cut of a camel. The camel meat was very juicy; indeed, the grease from it was saturating all the way through the mountain of rice. It was served in such a way that we should all help ourselves and eat together. I subtly picked away at the bottom of the pile of rice, maintaining a full plate but trying to limit the amount of grease. Unfortunately, my host noticed this and thought I was being polite, allowing everyone else to have my share of the meat, so they reached over, took my plate and loaded it with meat. The meat itself was, of course, edible but not particularly enjoyable. The best description I can conjure is to compare it to the greasiest, undercooked piece of lamb possible.

My staff member had noticed my discomfort and was quietly chuckling. With a sense of humour, this was particularly noted, for he decided to compound my situation by asking that more incense be burnt. This ensured that the air was so thick you could cut it with a knife. Adding that to my efforts to keep down a meal that was sensationally not to my taste was too much. I just couldn't breathe, so I had to get out and bolt out of the tent to try to breathe some fresh air. Of course, this being the Sahara desert in the heat of the afternoon, as soon as I got out Of the tent, I was met with a burning sunlight that was quite hard to bear, but at least I could breathe. Eventually, I resumed my position in the tent, and we finished our meeting, which, despite everything, ended very positively, and I was sure we had made a good impression.

When we left the tent, we were treated to something that was quite remarkable and very hard to explain. Out in the arid desert, there were two circular-shaped pools, each about the size of a paddling pool you might buy for the kids to play in the back garden with. When we approached the pools, our host took off his shoes and socks and sat dipping his feet into the water, beckoning us to do the same. When we did so, the relief of the cool water was wonderful, and it took us a while to realise that the pools were full of fish. The fish had a habit of nibbling away at the hard skin on a weary travellers' feet. To my disappointment, they gave my feet a wide birth, although, after a full day sweating in the Sahara sun, I don't really blame them. My colleague, on the other hand, had his feet swarmed over by the fish, which he was rather enjoying until a somewhat larger one came along and took a painful nip at his toe, which prompted him to squeal and rapidly retreat from the water. You know what they say about karma being a bitch well, that was a very enjoyable example.

The next day, we were given the great honour of being invited to a luncheon banquet at the palace of the regional Wali. A Wali is a regional governor appointed by the king, and his palace lived up to the splendour of his title. My staff member sat away from me, and I was ushered to the top table of the Wali himself. I shared the table with what I regarded as our competition, a trade delegation from France.

Typically disregarding the niceties and red tape of the EU when it suited them, the French had already got a trade envoy and offices in the area. It was clear that our European friends weren't overly keen on having an Englishman join them. After a cursory greeting, they moved the whole conversation into French, which the Wali was fluent in, but I certainly am not. I decided this was time for the "Stiff upper lip" and smiled along as the conversation progressed. With great credit to the Wali, he recognised I could not contribute and changed to speaking English with me for a while. During that conversation, I emphasised how useful a post-Brexit UK could be to his attempts at developing international trade. I believe the point was effectively made before my French friends interrupted with typically gallic manners and seized back the conversation.

After the opulence of the Walis palace, we were shown the developments in the growing nearby city. Education and medicine were being made available to the people as never before. Significantly, women were being given greater access to educational facilities than they are in many other Muslim countries. I had a fascinating chat with one young lady at a college who told me her aim was to be a politician and represent her people in their quest to improve their lives and raise their standards of living. I was enormously impressed and felt that I was witnessing the beginning of real positive change.

I was introduced to many cultural traditions in Morocco, but the one that has stayed with me as the most impressive and rather wonderful is taking tea. Taking Tea in Morocco is not a case of dropping in a bag of PG Tips and filling your cup with water. It is a ritual in its own right and considered a way of honouring your guests. The woman of the house is usually very well-versed in this ritual and will even sometimes dress in ceremonial garb to do it. The tea is added in leaf form to ornamental vessels and repeatedly strained and poured from one to the other. This takes some time, but the ritualistic style of it is fascinating and somehow enchanting. Not only that, but the finished drink tastes absolutely fantastic.

Perhaps the most amazing thing that the Moroccans are doing is the irrigation of the desert. Water is being directed to large farm units, which are effectively huge glass-covered greenhouses. These fantastic facilities allow the speedy production of vegetables and fruit on a huge scale. It was genuinely a marvel to me to see such efficient and large-scale food production in the Sahara Desert.

One of the most amusing and potentially awkward aspects of my trip to Morocco was the fact that many of the locals simply did not believe I wasn't a Moroccan. On several occasions, I was asked, "Where are you from?" When I replied England, they would follow up with, "But where are you really from, brother?" They were absolutely convinced that my family must have hailed from North Africa. On one occasion, one gentleman went as far as identifying the family clan that I was associated with. I do tan very easily, and in the Saharan sun, I went very brown, but as far as I know, I am not of African descent, although if I were, it would make absolutely no difference to me one way or another. I had to explain this in great detail to several people who suspected I was somehow ashamed of my African or Arabic heritage. On a couple of occasions, it became quite awkward until I offered the olive branch of saying maybe they were right, but I just didn't know, to which they assured me they were definitely right with an air of absolute confidence. This is part of what prompted me some time later to have an ancestry DNA test. The result was nothing but English and North European, somewhat to my disappointment, as the idea of an exotic ancestry was quite intriguing.

When I left Morocco, I was left with an image of what a modern developing state can be like. Yes, democracy is limited, but it is growing. The King and his representatives are putting a great deal of effort and work into developing the economy and the standard of living of his people. Importantly, they have no time for Islamic extremism or terrorism and are a valuable bulwark against potential terrorist threats sponsored and supported by their neighbours. This is the kind of nation that the UK should be reaching out to and creating a strong alliance with. They are also an example of how free trade and enterprise can help a nation grow and improve the lot of its people.

MEP Missions:
The United Nations in New York

I was honoured and delighted to be invited by the Moroccan government to testify on their behalf at the United Nations in New York.

As the Western Sahara is officially a disputed area, the UN tends to have a hearing and discussion on the matter every year or two. The Moroccans bring a delegation, as do the Polisario and their Algerian allies.

I was booked to speak on the second day of the debate. On entering the United Nations building, I was surprised to find that the part that I was in was actually no grander than the EU parliament. In fact, if anything, it was less splendid. I took my place and donned my headphones to listen to the various contributions to the hearing. The Polisario delegation could not have done more harm to their case if they had tried. Speaker after speaker came forward, with each one getting progressively angrier and making thinly veiled threats of war if they didn't get their own way. It was quite chilling to see the other side of the argument and to understand what kind of hate was waiting to take the place of the progressive changes that the Moroccans were making.

I contributed my testimony, speaking honestly about the wonderful positive developments I had seen in the area under Moroccan rule. It was an easy assignment, but I did find myself wondering just how many Comprehensive School kids from Wolverhampton had ever gotten to speak at the UN, even if it was only a few minutes. I must admit to feeling rather proud of myself.

Although there was no resolution to the issue after the UN hearing, it was clear that the Moroccan delegation had won the day. Our Moroccan contact was so happy that on spotting a group of South American women who had obviously been attending a different hearing, he dashed over to them, kissed the hand of the most beautiful amongst them, and informed her that he would happily pay a hundred camels for a night out with her. Fortunately, she took it in the good humour it was meant in, and much laughter ensued.

When we arrived back at our hotel, the rest of the delegation treated me as a star. I was taken on one side by a very important female delegation member. She was a senior member of a very important family, and when she spoke, everyone listened and almost bowed in deference. She told me she had something very important to discuss, so of course, I followed her to a more private table. When seated, she very seriously asked me if I was married, to which I replied that I was divorced. She then proceeded to tell me that with the way I looked, which could easily pass for someone of Moroccan heritage, she could easily arrange a very beneficial marriage for me if I chose to settle in her homeland. I was, for one of the very few times in my life, stunned into silence; she pushed her case further during the pause by telling me that, unlike the women in the UK, who she considered to be unhealthy, think she could get me a very strong and healthy Moroccan bride with plenty of meat on her bones. The kind of woman she could set me up with would give me plenty of children, and if nobody suitable was available, she would even consider taking me for herself. Now, this was, of course, extremely flattering, but not one part of it was at all tempting to me. It took all of my accumulated sales and negotiation skills to back away from the situation, leaving it so that I would be in touch when our business at the UN was over and stating quite honestly that I was extremely flattered.

As for New York itself, I'm sorry to say I hated it. Massively overcrowded with people and overshadowed by buildings that were so huge that they left me feeling like a puny ant. I found being there deeply unpleasant. I did manage to walk around Central Park and found it hugely impressive. I also visited the spot where John Lennon was murdered and had to concede it was a deeply moving experience. This was countered by the fact that everything was horribly expensive and the people, as in every big city, were far from friendly.

Having said that, there was one brilliantly spontaneous moment that I will always remember with a smile. On one of the evenings of our stay, I joined a colleague on a walk a few blocks to where he had located a bar specialising in expensive Cigars and high-quality Whiskey. The place was fantastic, and I'm pretty certain that if we had not mentioned we were on a political mission with business at the UN, they might not have welcomed us in so warmly, but we did, and they did.

After a truly splendid few hours, I sat in very comfortable armchairs, savouring some wonderfully aromatic Cigars and drinking the whiskey recommended to us that would suit the cigars. I felt on top of the world. I was disappointed when it was time to leave, but the place was Hellishly expensive, and my money was far from infinite.

As we left, a huge stretch limousine rolled up outside the bar. It deposited a couple of extremely wealthy-looking individuals and parked by the sidewalk. Having had a few drinks and being in a jovial mood, we approached the huge vehicle and admired it loudly, speculating about how much it cost and wondering what it was like inside. Much to our surprise, the driver wound down his window and called us over. As we approached him, we recognised that he was in full chauffeur uniform, including a cap. He engaged us in conversation, and we found him to be a friendly and humorous guy. After a while, he asked if we wanted a ride, to which I very quickly told him that as much as we would love to, we were a little short of money and certainly couldn't afford a journey in this kind of opulence. He hesitated for a while, then asked where we were staying. When he realised it was only a few blocks away, he told us not to worry, it was not a problem, just jump in and enjoy the journey back.

For a moment, I was hesitant, thinking that this was far too good to be true and wondering if we were about to be rather ostentatiously kidnapped, but I had a few drinks, so I threw caution to the wind and went for it. The inside of the Limousine was absolutely amazing. Everything about it reeked of wealth and privilege. We settled in for the ride, and to top the event off, the driver put some Frank Sinatra on the sound system. The journey back was a little longer than it should have been, as he took us around a couple of times, but it was a fantastic way to round off a great evening. I was very honoured and proud to have spoken at the UN, but I was delighted to leave the Big Apple.

MEP Missions:
Crimea

My most controversial mission, and the one with the most lasting consequences, was the trip to Crimea.

I was approached by one of the many "fixers" in the parliament and invited to visit and speak at an International Economic Conference being held in Yalta. Incidentally, the term "fixer" probably sounds more sinister than it really is. These guys are simply lobbyists for hire who seek to put people together or find people of note to attend significant conferences or events.

The conference was clearly a major event, and it was being held in a part of the world that, even back in 2018, was in the international spotlight. Brussels was absolutely crawling with people lobbying for the Ukrainian government, hoping to get support for EU action in their serious ongoing territorial dispute with Russia over Crimea. I'm sure the Russians had their representatives going around as well, but they were significantly less obvious.

I agreed to go and was told I could take a team with me. It seemed to me that this was far too good an opportunity to miss for several reasons. Primarily, if there was a conference where global investors and governments were discussing opportunities for investment, I sure as heck wanted to be there to argue the case for investing in the West Midlands. I believe in free markets and international trade. If there was a chance to bring investment and jobs to my area, I was going to go there and fight for it.

The other important reason for wanting to attend was I wanted to see the truth of what was going on in Russia. I had heard nothing but constant sabre-rattling in the EU, with many of the representatives seeming to be one step from foaming at the mouth in their desire to confront Putin. I felt that this was an interesting opportunity to really understand the mood of the Russians. I reasoned that if they were inviting people from all around the world to an economic and trade conference, they either wanted to do business, in which case war wasn't on their minds; after all, who bombs their customers? Alternatively, they were inviting us all there to send a message and display just how far and powerful their reach was. By the end of the week, I was in absolutely no doubt as to which of these options was the truth.

After arriving in Yalta after a long journey, which had involved a connecting flight in Moscow and then a bus journey lasting several hours, we arrived at our accommodation. We were staying at the same place where the conference was being held, and it was a spectacular location.

The weather was very temperate, the scenery was beautiful, and the hotel was the absolute image of opulence.

There was a busy schedule of meetings and work for the coming days. My first duties were to be interviewed by the Russian media. Despite the fact that there were representatives and businessmen from all over the world there, including the USA and other European countries, there was a particular interest in the English as just a few weeks earlier, the assassination attempt on Sergei and Yulia Skripal had happened in Salisbury, and Novichok poison was liberally and obviously spread around the area.

Tensions between the UK and Russia had risen significantly as a result of the incident in Salisbury, and the Russian media wanted to talk to a British politician about it. This was a time when I was glad that I had learned so many lessons in speaking carefully and using diplomacy during my time in politics. I would really have struggled to cope with the situation a few years earlier. My message was consistently that the event needed to be thoroughly investigated and the culprits brought to justice. It was too early to throw accusations, and the best interests of the British and Russian people were best served by trading with each other rather than hostility. It was a reasonable position to take at the time as the evidence making it totally clear that this was a political assassination attempt sponsored by the Kremlin was not confirmed at this stage. I was also acutely aware that I didn't want to say anything publicly that would fan the flames of an already tense situation.

The next stage of the trip was to visit the site of the famous Yalta conference held at the end of the Second World War. I sat at the same table where Churchill, Roosevelt and Stalin had convened their legendary meeting. I made a speech in which I focussed on the benefits of international trade and the futility of reverting back to Cold War Politics. The general idea was to let our nations have a friendly relationship and make money, not war.

I must have given the impression, with my efforts at being diplomatic, that I was rather soft on foreign policy issues. Nothing could be further from the truth; I am the definition of a "Hawk" in terms of defence of the realm, but I prefer hostilities to be a last resort. The Russians are famous for seeking to curry favour or gain Blackmail information by the use of the "Honey trap". This entails getting a femme fatale to approach the typical balding, overweight middle-aged politician, a description I suited to perfection and seducing them. Once under the spell of the femme fatale, they are either blackmailed to do the Kremlin's bidding or, under the spell of a Russian beauty, spill whatever secrets they may have. Unfortunately for our hosts, I was impervious to Blackmail as my image was already that of a womaniser, and I genuinely had no information or secrets to spill. As a UKIP MEP, you were as far from the inner circle of state secrets as Wolverhampton is from Sydney.

This did not stop them from trying, though. During the course of the visit, a strikingly attractive young woman kept cropping up in my vicinity. One day, she was one of the organisers; the next day, she was supposed to be a journalist, and one evening, she was dressed as a waitress. After a few days, she waited for a point in the evening when I was suitably relaxed from having a significant amount of Vodka to approach me. She and another very attractive lady came and sat with me and struck up a conversation. They were charming, flattering, sexy and way too obvious. After chatting with them for about twenty minutes, I put my hand up to pause the conversation. Then, much to the concern of the colleague sitting within earshot, I spoke honestly; it was not at all diplomatic. I remember the words very clearly, and I meant them, but in hindsight, it was probably straight talking taken way too far.

Solemnly, I said, "Ladies, I have enjoyed your company, but I know exactly what you are here for. Please do me a favour and pass this message back to the people in charge. If it turns out that Russia has hostile intentions towards the UK, I will be strongly in favour of bombing you all back into the Stone Age" The message was obviously clearly received, and they retreated, maintaining as much dignity as they could.

It became apparent during the visit that my team's and my efforts to attract investment and interest in the West Midlands were a crushing failure. To be brutally honest, we were very small fish in this particular pond. However, it was extremely informative.

As each session of the conference took place, it became increasingly obvious that what we were witnessing was Russia building a network of allies across the world in an attempt to rival the influence of the USA. The cast of nations represented was very reminiscent of the scene in the Mel Gibson classic comedy "Blazing Saddles", where Hedley Lamar gathers all of the worst and most vile people from history together in a united front for the final set piece battle. Syrians, Zimbabweans, North Koreans and a who's who of rogue pariah states were there. Each of them was being presented with awards of huge amounts of money from Russian investors and the state. They would all make snivelling speeches praising "Mother Russia" for its support and protection. I actually had to sit on a panel with a representative of Zimbabwe who used his speaking time to criticise the "Vile British Imperialists" It was extraordinarily hard to limit my remarks to a politely stated rejection of his characterisation of our great nation.

Each evening, our entertainment would be prefaced with videos of Russian armed forces on parade and in action, accompanied by martial music. It felt very much like I was witnessing the build-up to war.

One of the most interesting parts of the trip was when we were allowed to go out into the local town, see the sights and visit the local market. In fairness, there were no signs of any official presence or military in the town. When we spoke to the locals, they were just like ordinary people everywhere in as much as they didn't really care about politics. However, similarly to ordinary people everywhere, their views were shaped by media propaganda. I was astonished to be continually asked why Britain wanted war with Russia and whether I was frightened of what my government would do to me when I returned. The everyday folk of the area were genuinely expecting to be under attack from the UK imminently. I tried to assure them that the UK is not a nation that launches unprovoked attacks, but they simply didn't believe me. They believed what was beamed into their TVs every night.

The disconnection from the truth of the people of Crimea in regard to the intentions of the UK towards them made me wonder a very serious question. If they can be so misguided based on their TV news, I wonder how far from the truth the news that we are allowed to see in the UK is. I suspect that people all over the world are given versions of reality some distance from the truth by media organisations with their insidious agendas.

The trip was not without its light-hearted or humorous moments. One evening, we were due to be entertained by a ballet troop. Being a philistine on such matters, I cannot recall the name of the ballet, but I was assured that they were the Bess Knees when it came to women balancing on their toes accompanied by classical music. The performance was about to start when I received a text from one of the members of our group that was rather perplexing. It was a request to send one of our female colleagues to the toilets to meet him. Now, I'm no prude, but neither am I a pimp, and I sent him a message back telling him to ask her himself. He duly messaged her, saying, "Please come urgently" Intrigued by the message, the lady duly headed off to see what it was all about. I felt pretty confident that if he had anything of a romantic nature in mind, he would probably get a sharp slap, so I left them to it. A few minutes later, they returned together. Apparently, our male colleague had misread the toilets sign and found himself in a cubicle attending to a call of nature when the whole area outside was taken up by the ladies of the ballet, who proceeded to disrobe and prepare for their performance. He had been sat with his legs drawn up so nobody could see he was there desperately googling the Russian for "I am not a pervert" Fortunately, our female colleague managed to get him out of there without incident.

On another occasion, we finished our day by going to the hotel disco area. As with the rest of the complex, it was absolutely spectacular. We were escorted to a private room where buffet food and bottles of vodka awaited us; as an aside, it's important to note that the vodka in Russia has very little in common with the Vodka we are used to in the UK. It is much smoother and easier to drink without a mixer; in fact, a mixer would spoil the flavour. The particular bottles of vodka we were treated to in this private room were even better. The flavour and smoothness were exceptional. The food was delicious, and the whole experience was incredibly pleasant. Sadly, it was interrupted by panicking members of staff who very quickly moved us to a different area. Apparently, they had put us in the wrong room. The room was reserved for the president of the region, who was renowned for being a hard man, and his nickname was "The Goblin". We were only too happy to move and not be held responsible for consuming the feast laid out for the Goblin.

On the final day of our stay, we were out at a meeting when we received frantic messages from a member of staff. He had stayed behind due to an upset stomach, which I suspected was more of a hangover. The hotel staff were trying to move our belongings out of the rooms, and he was trying his best to act as a one-man picket line, arguing that we still had one night left and needed the rooms. We returned to sort out the issue. It was clear that a classic misunderstanding had taken place. Due to many of the other delegates having left, they were trying to move us to the presidential suite on the top floor and were baffled as to why an angry Englishman was trying to block their efforts. We ended up staying the last night in the Presidential suite, and I can honestly say that the rooms were bigger than the whole of the apartment I currently live in and far better furnished. It was a generous gesture to us on the last night of our stay.

The drama was not quite over. The journey back saw our party split into two groups, leaving the hotel at different times and catching a different connecting flight to Moscow before heading home.

I was in the first part of the group, and we arrived on time at Moscow airport. We decided to have a walk around outside the airport just to catch a brief glimpse of Moscow. To be fair, most areas around airports are not exactly pretty, but this was seriously grim. Barbed wire fences, grey foreboding skies and rows of buildings that looked as if they were straight out of a Le Carre spy novel. We decided to head back inside and wait near the boarding gate.

Time went by, and the second part of our party had not yet arrived. As the clock moved closer to boarding time, I became extremely worried. Our phone networks were not working in Moscow, so we had no way of contacting our colleagues, and the time was rapidly approaching for us to leave.

I decided that I had to take one for the team and told the colleague I was with that he better board the plane and I would stay behind to try to be here to find a solution if our other team members missed the flight. Strangely enough, he made no objection, picked up his bags and began walking quickly towards the departure desk. I was just coming up with a plan of basically waiving my Euro Parliament ID in enough official-looking people's faces until I found someone who could speak English when they arrived. They were literally sprinting across the concourse to get to us on time. When we finally embarked on the aircraft, we were the last people to get on, and it set off very shortly afterwards.

Even then, the drama was not quite over. When we landed back in the UK, we were informed that a special security team would be waiting to greet certain passengers on their arrival. On hearing that, all of the memories of Russian civilians and journalists at the conference came flooding back to me as they had commented on whether I was frightened about what my government would do to me when I returned. At the time, I had glibly assured them that we don't do that sort of thing in Britain, but as I left the aircraft, I was not so sure. I told one of my colleagues to take a photograph of me and record the date and time so that they could report exactly what time I had been taken. It was one of the most wonderfully relieving moments of my life when we walked straight past the security team, and they headed for someone else. We didn't look back to learn more; we just got out of there as soon as we could.

MEP Missions:
Washington DC. The Swamp

I'm sure we have all heard the term "Drain the swamp" many times when American politicians and commentators talk about Washington, DC. Naively, I had always thought it was just an insulting metaphor for the kind of politics and politicians that operate in the USA, and of course, in one sense, it is, but I never realised that Washington, DC, is literally built on a swamp.

The heat and humidity you experience in DC in the Summer is virtually unbearable. We were literally scampering to get from shade to shaded area in order to stay out of the Sun as much as possible.

Having commented on the unbearable weather, I must be fair and speak about the huge number of positive things about DC. First of all, it is literally the cleanest city I have ever seen. Not only is there very little rubbish lying around, but the buildings seem to gleam in the sunlight. As it befits the nation that has been, for much of the last century, the most powerful nation in the World, the scale and splendour of the architecture are absolutely magnificent. To deal with the tourist guide part, first, here are a few things that just have to be seen.

The Whitehouse is a truly spectacular building. Although I took a brief moment to smile and think that we evil Brits had once burned it down, I couldn't help but be impressed by it. Its palatial façade does not take away from the air of it being a very modern seat of government. Whilst you can approach the gates for a better look, you are always aware of very high-tech and efficient security all around you, quite rightly so.

Not far away from the Whitehouse is the Lincoln Memorial. It truly is a wonder of design the way that the memorial is reflected in the long body of water just in front of it. When you approach the memorial, climbing the steps to the magnificent memorial statue, it really feels like you are touching a part of history. All around the walls are the words of the Gettysburg Address, which is arguably one of the most brilliantly moving speeches ever made. I spent well over an hour reading those immortal words and really drinking in their full meaning, and of course, one sentence in particular should resonate with all of us. "and that government by the people for the people shall not perish from the earth."

Those words bring a tear to my eye when I think of how corrupted and far from that ideal, so-called democratic governments around the world have become.

Anyway, it's down to business. The point of the visit was to speak with American politicians and officials about Brexit and explain the potential benefits our new status could have to our relationship with them.

Whilst It had long been American foreign policy to support the EU and its "ever closer union", a change of president combined with the fact that they must have been deaf and blind not to notice the anti-American sentiment expressed in the Euro Parliament meant that there was an opportunity to help forge a new approach.

Unlike in the UK, it is actually remarkably easy to get access to meet with and speak to most elected American politicians. All you need to do is make appointments with a couple of them who will officially state that you have a legitimate business; then, once you are into the congress building, you can literally walk down corridors, nocking doors, and more often than not, get quite a polite reception.

One of my first ports of call was my friend, Congressman Scott Taylor, from Virginia. We had met previously on my trip to Jerusalem and had got on famously. I was aware from a few chats with Scott in the meantime that he was a fan of the BBC series "Peaky Blinders", so I went armed with gifts. When we entered his office, I presented him with a Peaky Blinder flat cap, and we spent the first few minutes of the meeting listening to his entertaining but not very good attempts at a Peaky Blinder-style West Midlands accent. Scott is a great anglophile and friend of the UK. He is a great man who has served his country with distinction both in uniform and in politics, and I hope that the future holds good things for him.

We also managed to get meetings with representatives of the Trump administration. Obviously, not being Nigel, we could not talk our way into meeting the President himself, but his representatives were truly cut from the same cloth. Plainly and directly, they expressed how shocked they were by the actions of the UK government.

The Trump representatives told us that they had prepared a deliberately generous and supportive trade deal for the UK, and it had been on the table since not long after the Brexit vote, but that the UK Government were stalling on engaging about it. They were surprised that after a vote to leave the EU, Theresa May's government was still determined to adhere as rigidly as possible to EU rules and regulations as it possibly could, thus making a deal with the USA very problematic. To explain this further, it is important to understand that EU trade deals have very little to do with trade. I had sat in on some public sessions when the EU negotiators had discussed their progress in trying to strike a deal with the USA. Most of the conversations had been about workers' rights and environmental standards rather than reducing tariffs and encouraging trade.

The other thing that the Trump representatives could not understand was the UK being reluctant to engage in fracking. They explained in some detail how they were not only becoming energy self-sufficient but also massively reducing costs to the public and businesses. One representative actually laughed and said that within a very short time, the USA would have left the European countries so far behind on energy that there would be literally no comparison between how our economies worked.

I was fortunate to evangelise and be invited to a very important meeting outside of the capitol building but still in the most influential part of DC. I was invited to speak at "Wednesdays with Grover". These Wednesday meetings in DC are a very important fixture in the diary of movers and shakers within the American conservative movement. They are run and hosted by the formidable Grover Norquist. Norquist is the lead of important advocacy groups, including "Americans for Tax Reform" as well as being one of the managers of "the conservative coalition" He has the ear of many senior conservative figures, and his meetings have been attended by such notable figures as legendary journalist Karl Rove, and he has been known to be listened to and respected by figures as senior as George Bush and Newt Gingrich.

I was in with some very big-time people at the Grover meeting. We were all limited to just a few minutes for our speeches, and then we were given the opportunity to network and break away into private meeting areas with other attendees.

I knew I had a short time to speak, so I was determined to make an impact. My speech was about how the UK could be an even more formidable ally in world affairs and trade now that we were an independent state with the opportunity to be free of EU interference. My remarks started with the sentence, "My name is Bill Etheridge. I am from the third most popular party in the UK. We are called UKIP. You may not have heard of us, but just think of Nigel Farage; he is our leader. If you are still unsure of what we are about, the only difference between us and the UK Conservative Party is that we are actually conservatives" This had the desired ice-breaking effect. I rounded off by saying, "There is a new kid on the block. It's a country with the fourth most powerful armed forces in the world, one of the top ten economies and unparalleled diplomatic reach. That new kid is from the UK, and I hope the USA takes the opportunity to work with us." Those words summed up the whole of the mission, and they were very well received. There really was an opportunity for post-Brexit Britain to forge a whole new path. It just needed bigger fish than me in positions of genuine power to want it.

I did have one very nearly disastrous encounter in Washington, DC. I had popped outside of the hotel we were staying in to make a phone call. After finishing the call, I found myself in conversation with a very smartly dressed lady who was clearly a rather important businessperson. She was using a Vape, and I remarked to her that I was not keen on them as they made me feel like my throat was burning. She insisted that I try what was in her Vape and assured me that it would not give me a burning sensation. With her encouragement, I took a deep inhale of the vapour and held it for a little while. The effect was remarkable; whatever was in that Vape certainly was not derived from tobacco or anything that would be legal in the UK, I'm sure. I spent the rest of the afternoon concentrating very hard on trying to avoid either bursting out in fits of laughter or curling up in a corner and going to sleep. The lady certainly knew how to load a Vape!

During our time in Washington, DC, we engaged in a great number of serious meetings and experienced the real feeling of power around the place. One thing that struck us as a little odd was the sheer number of meetings that we had arranged, which unfortunately got cancelled at the last minute. Of course, this could be because these hugely important people had more pressing matters, but it did coincidentally begin to occur almost immediately after UKIP Head office learned that we were there and what we were doing. I am sure the two things are not at all related but having spent most of my time as an MEP having to work extremely hard to avoid every media or public appearance, I was planned to make in the UK being blocked by them, it is hard not to have a sneaking suspicion they may have had a word with a few people. I guess I'll never know.

MEP Missions:
Israel

I have already spoken about my adventure in Jerusalem. It was a genuinely life-changing experience. I had obviously left a good impression on our hosts as I was invited back to visit the Judea Samaria area.

The main purpose of the visit was to speak with university students who were learning about international politics. I found the young Israelis to be refreshingly positive and patriotic about their country. In the UK, we become used to students being cynical about our country and totally obsessed with the perceived evils of our past and the need to make up for all of that by rabidly focussing on reducing carbon emissions in order to save the planet. These young Israeli people were aware of these issues, but their whole outlook was sunnier and forward-looking.

I also made use of the time to be taken out in the area, which yet again falls under the label of a disputed territory. There was a definite trend that most of the places I was invited to go to were too hot to handle for regular politicians, and it certainly helped to make for much more interesting and dangerous missions. I was taken to a family vineyard deep into the disputed territories. As we drove there with our armed guards in our armoured mini bus, we witnessed the Biblical wilderness all around us in all of its majesty. There was hardly any form of life for miles on end; then, you would see a sign for settlements either manned by Israelis or Muslims. I was left with the impression of it being rather like the Wild West, a largely undeveloped wilderness with small roads leading to trading posts and townships.

When we reached the Vinyard, we began the drive up the hill towards the buildings and our hosts. As we drove, we had to pass through several checkpoints and watchtowers manned by volunteers. Obviously, security is a huge issue in the area. When we reached the summit, we were treated to a glass of wine and the story of the vineyard. It is a story that I consider one of the most extraordinary I have ever heard.

The owner of the vineyard had spent many years working for the Israeli government in various engineering roles. When he reached the point that he could have a decent retirement payment, he decided to fulfil his lifelong ambition and look into opening up a vineyard with his friends and family. On reconnoitring the area, he found a group of hills that looked ideal for grape growing. On further investigation, he found that wild grapes were already growing on the slopes in some numbers but that he could not recognise the type. Being rather well-connected, he sent the grapes to the local University for analysis. The results were astonishing. The grapes were of the exact type that had been found in but not used since the Romans had been producing wine in the area. The wine that was produced there had a very strong chance of being of the type that was drunk at "The Last Supper."

Even more extraordinary still, when they further investigated the hillside, they found a large stone-carved relic. When experts came out to it they found that it was actually a wine press dating back some two thousand years.

So, a series of extraordinary events had led this man and his family to a hillside which had originally been used for wine production at around the time of Christ. As I stood atop the hill watching the sunset over the amazing biblical landscape, drinking this wine, I felt very profoundly that I was experiencing something that would have been very similar for people living there thousands of years ago.

Frustratingly, due to political issues, sanctions and boycotts, the wine could not be exported in any great quantity, so the experience was even more unique. A truly once-in-a-lifetime moment. Nobody visiting this particular area of the world can do so, unaware that there are two sides to the story and that my charming Jewish hosts were not the only people in the area with a claim. I had an extremely illuminating meeting that opened my eyes to the situation whilst I was on this trip.

I was taken to an industrial estate. Manufacturing and production were taking place on a significant scale at the site. With my previous experience in manufacturing and Steel, I felt very much at home. The businesses were Israeli-owned, but many of the workers were people who were secretly commuting from the Palestinian Authority area.

The foreman at one of the firms was a Palestinian gentleman who told me a story that showed the true horror of living under the control of terrorist organisations. He and many of his colleagues would secretly leave their property in the Palestinian-controlled areas every day to work at the Israeli companies. They earned significantly more money than was possible in the area they had come from and enjoyed far better working conditions. To me, this was most laudable and was the epitome of Norman Tebbit's advice about how his father "Got on his bike and looked for work". Sadly, though these workers who were only seeking to improve the lives of themselves and their families lived under constant threat of punishment from the Palestinian authorities. On several occasions, men had been dragged from their homes and publicly beaten very badly by the terrorist thugs running the Palestinian area, all for the crime of working with an Israeli company.

Another similar story of how the people living in the zones designated as under Palestinian control were badly let down by their leaders was recounted to me at a nearby university. The local Muslim population had, for generations, made a living as charcoal burners. This is clearly not the healthiest of professions; life expectancy was low, and chronic illness levels were high. The University had devised a technique for charcoal burning that was much safer and more efficient. They had approached the local burners and their leaders, offering them the technology for free as a gesture of goodwill. It was rejected, and threats of violence were made to anyone entertaining further conversations with the Israelis.

The truth of the situation in Judaea Samaria is that not all of the Muslim population are bad guys, and not all of the Jewish population are good guys, but the leaders on both sides are so deeply entrenched that negotiated peace seems impossible.

Was it Covid?

I have some very strong views about the pandemic and how it was handled that I will get on to a little later, but first of all, I present you with another question. Did I have COVID-19 in early 2019, many months before we were told it was supposed to have leapt out of a lab, got into someone's bat soup or whatever the latest media cover story is?

It was coming towards the end of my Brussels term, but I was still continuing to do the job as usual. In other words, work hard, play hard.

One morning, I was sitting in my office, and I felt extremely unwell. At first, I thought it might be a hangover kicking in, but it soon became clear that was not the explanation.

Having consumed as much alcohol as I have over so many years, I am familiar with what a hangover feels like, and this was much different. I was hot and sweating whilst being short of breath and generally feeling very weak. After a while, my Brussels staff realised I wasn't feeling too well, and they approached me to ask how I was.

I confirmed I wasn't well, and they offered to go to the shop to get something to help with the situation. I thought that it was very touching of them to be so caring and give them some money. I was somewhat less touched when they returned with shopping bags full of cleaning products and spray and started disinfecting the area around me. They hadn't brought back so much as a cough sweet.

As the day went on, I began to feel much worse, and despite my lifelong reticence about seeing Doctors, I submitted to the insistent demands of my staff to call the Euro Parliament medics to the office. For readers who do not know me, trust me; I need to be feeling absolutely awful before I even admit to not being on my best form, let alone ask to see a medic.

The medics from the parliament arrived very quickly. After briefly checking my symptoms and temperature, they insisted I go with them to the medical centre. On trying to stand from my chair, I was overcome with dizziness and had to cling to the desk and office walls to stay upright. The medics tried to get me to be wheeled down to the medical centre in a wheelchair, but I was determined that would not happen. In life, and particularly in politics, I do not believe in showing signs of weakness in front of your enemies or indeed anyone if you can help it. The idea of being seen being wheeled to the medical centre looking exhausted and broken past the offices of other UKIP MEPs, most of whom by then had contributed to my back being metaphorically full of knives and even worse past the Federalist MEPs I had been locked in conflict with for years was totally unacceptable to me.

After a very slow journey, staggering my way to the medical centre, I was given the most efficient and quickest check-up I've ever known. The temperature was taken again, a blood sample was taken and instantly analysed, and a diagnosis was given seemingly in the wink of an eye. Credit where it is due; the EU medical staff were absolutely fantastic. They told me that I had a form of Flu that they had never seen before, that it was bad and that I should do everything I could to keep my temperature down but not hesitate to call them again if I felt the hospital was needed.

I spent the rest of the week in the apartment I had rented opposite the parliament by this stage. I stocked up the fridge with a Belgian equivalent of Lucozade and lots of water and then proceeded to try to get well. The next three days were horrendous. My temperature was sky-high, and I had no energy. I couldn't even get into bed and spent most of the time on the couch. I also had to sleep sitting up, as when I lay down, I literally couldn't breathe.

When the time came to get the train back home, I managed to get a car to transport me to the station, and then I slept and sweated all the way back to the UK. On arriving home, I shut myself into my bedroom and spent most of the following week in bed, trying to get my breath back to normal.

At this point, I had never heard of COVID-19, and in hindsight, if I had, I would not have taken a journey crossing Europe and then travelling from London to the West Midlands. I've no doubt Covid obsessives reading this may have me down as a modern-day Typhoid Mary, but in my defence, the medics did not say I shouldn't mix with people for fear of contaminating them, and my office staff did not become ill, so maybe I wasn't patient zero.

My suspicion is that COVID was on the loose way before we were told and that I was an early case of it in Europe. After all, Brussels is a major hub for international travel, with travellers from all over the world either visiting there or getting connecting links.

So, this is one to ponder. Did I have Covid?

Lockdown and a Total Change

When I left the European Parliament for the last time in 2019, my political career was over.

I had no party, having left UKIP. I had joined the Brexit party to support Nigel, only to be totally let down and treated with contempt.

My ideas about local campaigning and building teams of motivated local activists were roundly rejected by the Brexit party. My personal qualities as a politician were also rejected, with them preferring owners of old-school ties rather than political war horses.

I had actually taken the time to rebuild the old UKIP organisation in the West Midlands, bringing key activists and regional leaders online to set up a Brexit party branch structure that was basically ready to go and simply needed the nod to activate.

I was informed by the brain trust around Tice that activists and branches were all very inconvenient and totally unnecessary. Instead of pounding the streets and talking to people, they would win elections through clever use of social media and making use of star performers on TV.

This is obviously utter nonsense and simply showed that the people running this new party had zero experience of how political campaigning is done in the real world. Up to the point of my writing this, they had dismally failed to record polling figures anywhere near those achieved by UKIP in the previous electoral cycle, and I seriously doubt if they ever will

I also had some limited experience dealing with Richard Tice and quite simply did not trust him. In my own personal opinion, he is the most destructive personality ever to be involved with the Eurosceptic movement. As I see it, his own ego does not allow him to work well with others or to unite the splinter parties that were created after the collapse of UKIP. At the same time as his gargantuan ego being an issue, his lack of understanding of how powerful genuine grassroots campaigning and pavement pounding can mean the Reform party is doomed to ultimately fail.

It saddens me that the Reform party is dominated by such an unsuitable figure, as many of the people who have lent their support are very genuine and decent patriotic souls for whom I have a great deal of time. What's that old saying "Lions led by Donkeys".

With no party to work with, I was experienced enough to know that standing as an independent is a costly and difficult ego trip with very little chance of success.

I decided it was time to move on.

I had worked on several exciting business ideas with former colleagues, but all of them were to be scuppered by the pandemic and the lockdowns that accompanied it.

However, I had started one project that I could continue with during the lockdowns. I had decided to set up a charity.

The charity is called Support Futures. The idea is a simple one. I had seen the effect on the physical and mental health of people wandering into boxing gyms looking for mentoring and guidance and decided why not formalise this into a combined physical and mental health training programme.

The paperwork and bureaucracy involved in setting up a charity is huge. I spent a lot of time working on it and a lot of money paying solicitors to help.

Early in March 2020, I organised a fundraising night to help with the set-up costs, hiring boxing legend Frank Bruno to be our star guest. More of this later.

On either side of this event, two things happened that would change my life forever. The afternoon before the night with Frank Bruno, my beloved Uncle Bill died, and a few weeks later, the country entered the first lockdown

The loss of a man who had been such an important part of my life is very difficult to describe, and I am finding this part of the story very hard to tell, but he deserves to be properly mentioned and remembered.

He was not just my mentor in the ways of chatting up women; although we had some awesome times doing that, he was so much more.

He was the man who saw me every day until I was eleven years old. He was the man who had become a mixture of best friend, uncle and trusted confidante over a relationship spanning my whole life.

Uncle Bill managed to combine being the suave man about town with being the ultimate party animal and yet simultaneously a completely reliable pillar of strength. I have been very fortunate to have had such a wonderful family, and Uncle Bill was a major part of all of our lives.

His business exploits were legendary. He was the first person any of us knew who had a mobile phone in his car back in the early 1980s. He had made a fortune selling everything from Steel to Nuclear Fall shelters, and he had repeatedly lost that fortune. The thing was that he always seemed to bounce back stronger; he almost seemed to take on the persona of a superhero at times.

Sadly, in March of 2020, he was admitted to hospital. His health had been declining for many years. He had smoked, drunk and partied himself into being a frail shadow of the handsome, bullishly strong character so many people knew him as.

Totally irrationally, I fully believed he would rally and make another magical comeback. For a while, it looked like I might be right as he stabilised in hospital, but sadly, the day before we were due to host Frank Bruno at our first fundraiser, I received the call telling me I needed to get to the hospital as the end was near.

The hours I spent in that hospital room with my parents and his children, watching his struggle for life gradually fail, haunted me, almost literally, for many months to come. Naively, a Do Not Resuscitate order had been signed in line with wishes he had stated many years earlier. It is my firm opinion that far too many of our hospitals interpret a Do Not Resuscitate order with a "Please Euthanise" request. I watched as he repeatedly fought to get out of bed and try to communicate before a series of nurses came in to "Make him more comfortable" with a series of unidentified jabs.

That day, I saw Superman die, and I realised that eventually, a time will come when we actually all must face the no-win scenario. I was also riddled with overwhelming guilt, feeling that I should have intervened somehow because I knew with absolute certainty he would never have given up on me.

The next day, I had to host and interview Frank Bruno at the Robin 2 venue in Wolverhampton in front of a crowd of around two hundred people. As you may imagine, I really did not feel in the right mood. I motivated it by thinking that the greatest tribute to Uncle Bill would be to go ahead and do the night and not only get through it but sell the hell out of it. The night was a significant financial success, and in my own way, I felt I had paid a very special tribute by actually going ahead and making it a success. Victory in the face of adversity was so much of what his life had been about that I felt it was fitting.

Not long after this traumatic time, the media was filled with hysterical headlines about the growing Pandemic with frankly ludicrous projections about the mass death toll we were about to face. The UK government wilted in the face of the media onslaught and, encouraged by the fact that other supposedly democratic countries had gone down the same route, instituted the first of a seemingly endless stream of lockdowns.

At first, I took the reports of this new plague very seriously. I bought emergency provisions, including oxygen, and stored them with my parents. I would not leave the house without wearing gloves and a mask, and I kept my distance from other people. I felt that it was only sensible to not leave anything to chance, especially with two elderly parents who were and still are very dear to me.

Over a period of time, it became increasingly apparent to me that there was something wrong with the narrative. How were cloth face masks and rubber washing-up gloves actually protecting us from this killer virus? Why were people not collapsing in the streets as we had been shown in the fake news from China, and why were people still allowed to go out and stand in queues to shop as long as they kept a seemingly randomly selected arbitrary distance from each other?

The TV news coverage was becoming increasingly hysterical and obviously some way from reality. Crazed doom-mongers like Piers Morgan appeared to be having a field day.

Then the regular SAGE briefings began, accompanied by constantly upwards ticking death toll and infection figures shown next to the grim-faced scientists and medics. It came to the point where I simply stopped believing what I was being told when I realised that the death figures were based on any mortality reason so long as the person had been diagnosed with COVID within the last twenty-eight days. You could literally die from being hit by a falling Asteroid, but if you had been diagnosed with COVID-19, that was counted as the reason, and it was included in the figures.

This madness, combined with the ever-growing series of restrictions being imposed on our freedoms, gradually started to impact my mental health. I felt constricted and virtually imprisoned like a citizen of a police state.

I could not bear the imposed inactivity. After a life of non-stop twenty-four hours working and partying, suddenly there was nothing. Nowhere to go and nothing to do. It was a new experience and one I struggled to deal with.

I sought to occupy my time by doing the administrative work that is essential for setting up a charity nowadays and combined that with studying for a qualification in hypnotherapy. It helped, but I still felt trapped and deeply unhappy.

It became increasingly more difficult for me to function normally. I couldn't sleep, and my mind was constantly racing. I did a huge amount of outdoor exercise and walking as there is nothing like a government dictate limiting how long I can exercise to motivate me to exercise longer and harder than ever before, and it did help a little.

My nights were haunted by recurring nightmares of being back in that hospital, watching my uncle being slowly euthanised. The scene was the same in the dream every night, and the overwhelming feeling of guilt and failure was so intense when I woke up each day, it was very difficult to cope with.

The combination of what had happened to my uncle and what was happening in our country left me with a feeling of helplessness I just could not come to terms with. I have always believed that if you fight hard enough, you can turn any bad situation into a better one, but this time, I didn't even know how to fight.

It was at this point that I received a phone call that probably saved me from falling into complete depression. Dan Emmerson is a few people's idea of an angel of mercy, but in this case, he really helped me save myself unknowingly.

Dan is a former UKIP man from London. We were aware of each other in our UKIP days, and I think it's fair to say that Dan had made it pretty clear he didn't rate me much. Dan was one of the UKIP members who saw my more socially liberal ideas as making me a bit wet. Imagine that, at the time, the media was literally portraying me as a NAZI. A large portion of my own party thought I was a liberal softie. You really can't please all the people all the time.

The point of me mentioning Dan is that he approached me to be involved in a new project he was working on. He was creating a YouTube channel based around free speech, and very importantly to me, it would cover issues challenging the lockdown narrative. I was to be a guest and occasional host.

Our programmes included panels of, due to the remote locations we were all speaking from, were literally "talking heads" Dan organised all of the technical side, invited the guests and set the topics. As time went by, I became more of a host or chairman for these shows, and I loved it.

Our guests included notable names like the heroic Andrew Bridgeon, who has fought a one-man battle in parliament to try to bring issues around the possibility of excess deaths being caused by the experimental jabs passed off as vaccines against COVID-19. I enjoyed interviewing Andrew; he is hugely intelligent but very blunt and forthright. He is the kind of politician that I hoped I would have been had I made it to Westminster.

Other guests included Laurence Fox, who gave a typically flamboyant and entertaining interview whilst being driven between appointments and finishing his lunchtime sandwiches. Laurence is a man with his heart in the right place and has some very good points. Sadly for him, I believe he lacks the benefit of having experienced political figures and activists around him to advise him. Regardless of this, I have huge respect for the way he has put his principles ahead of his career and lost millions of pounds worth of earnings potential to stand up for his beliefs.

We had a great many entertaining and informative guests, including Anne Widdicombe, who quite rightly told me off for not wearing a tie while I interviewed her. Anne is an eccentric lady with some overly conservative social and moral views, but I found her charming and a real pleasure to speak with.

Godfrey Bloom and Roger Helmer were also regular contributors. As you can imagine, with these two gentlemen involved, there was not a dull moment. Their eloquence and the clarity of their genuinely conservative views made each appearance a real delight.

Our shows began to gather a following, and the viewing figures had real momentum and promise. Frustratingly, it was at this point that we realised just how much censorship was being undertaken by social media platforms. No sooner would our video go live than it would be cut off, or if it did manage to get broadcast live, the recording would be deleted. I felt desperately disappointed for Dan as he had put a huge amount of time, effort and money into the project.

The period of time that the UK and much of the Western world was subject to lockdowns was an unprecedented time in our history. Our freedoms were stolen, our free speech outrageously censored, and there was a historic transfer of money from the poor to the super-rich.

Global corporations increased their fortunes exponentially whilst new multi-million-pound enterprises seem to pop up almost overnight, allegedly due to government patronage and dodgy deals. In the meantime, small businesses and sole traders were forced to close their businesses. Millions of people were bribed to stay at home with money that the government had borrowed, with the responsibility for servicing the future debt falling to future generations of taxpayers.

Of course, there were deaths due to COVID-19, and we could not just ignore it. It is impossible to properly quantify those figures due to the deliberately unreliable way that they were collated, but it is very clear that the elderly and infirm were most at risk. This fact makes the government policy of emptying hospital wards full of untested patients into care homes all the more monstrous than it appeared at the time. This undoubtedly resulted in a significant number of unnecessary deaths. At the same time, the younger and fitter segments of the population were forced to stay at home and were not allowed to go about their business. Most monstrously of all, children who are basically in next to no danger from the virus were stopped from attending schools and then forced to keep a distance from each other and wear masks. The psychological damage and effect on the mental health of all of this will only be seen properly in the years to come.

Studying Hypnotherapy

Much of my time during lockdown and for the first few months after some limited freedoms were restored was taken up studying to get an accredited qualification in Hypnotherapy.

Hypnotherapy is very different from the stage hypnosis techniques we have all heard about, where people end up quacking like a duck or acting in similarly undignified manners after being put under the influence of a stage performer. Hypnotherapy involves a broader understanding of techniques included in Psychotherapy and elements of counselling.

I found the subject interesting and was an affirmed believer in its benefits after having had several appointments with Hypnotherapists in the past, including in the lead-up to my first Boxing match. I knew that if you take a positive approach and keep an open mind as the client it really can work wonders.

The idea is simply to help break the circuit of certain self-destructive habits and behaviours. This is done by accessing the subconscious mind through inducing a very relaxed state in the client.

One of the areas of hypnotherapy that fascinated me was neurolinguistic programming. This approach involves associating certain emotions with powerful words or symbols in order to change a client's behaviours. Obviously, that is a very curtailed description, but you aren't reading this book for a lecture.

By understanding the techniques involved in NLP, I started to understand what was happening to the general public at the time of lockdown and the Pandemic. The government and the media were using very basic NLP methods in order to rewire our subconscious and change our habits and behaviour. The constant repetitive use of certain words coupled with colours that were known to have a powerful impact on the brain was very obvious. The disgusting advertising drive was also where we were urged to look into a pair of very sick-looking eyes and tell them why we hadn't followed orders.

Understanding what was being done helped me to comprehend why so many otherwise rational people were slavishly following utterly absurd rules and sacrificing their freedoms with so much enthusiasm.

Gladly, since the situation has relaxed somewhat, I have been able to use the Hypnotherapy techniques I qualified in for great good. I seem to have a degree of talent in this discipline and have managed to induce a state of hypnosis in dozens of people since qualifying. Just in case any of our friends from the media are reading this, may I stress that on every occasion, it was voluntary on the part of the client, and I am not going around behaving like the snake from The Jungle Book!

Amongst the people I have been able to help are several people seeking help with weight management, a number of people with symptoms of anxiety, a lady who had developed agrophobia during lockdown and a local semi-professional football team. To my delight, the football team won promotion after the sessions with me had helped them dispel any negativity from their approach.

It was one of my ambitions for the charity I set up that it would not be solely dependent on grants and handouts if we could help it. Over the course of 2022 and 2023, I embarked on a significant number of events with guest stars and celebrities with the aim of raising money and awareness of what we are about.

These events have been a huge challenge but also a great opportunity to meet some fantastic people as well as some rather less pleasant characters.

Frank Bruno

Our first event was with Boxing legend Frank Bruno. It was particularly relevant for a charity that works with people on their physical and mental health, as Big Frank has had his share of issues with mental health.

We had a packed room of around two hundred people for the event. The atmosphere was superb. It was clear that despite the passing of the years, people still loved the big man.

Frank himself is still an imposing physical specimen. He obviously still works out hard, and when he shook my hand, he virtually crushed it.

It was clear during the event that Frank had some dramatic ups and downs, but he was very happy to speak openly and honestly about them. His battles with Mike Tyson were definitely fascinating to hear about, and it was striking how he still felt he had let people down by losing. I did mention that losing to Mike Tyson was nothing to be ashamed of, and actually having the guts to go into the ring with him was something to be extremely proud of.

The evening went extremely well. I was left with the impression of a man who had been a proud warrior in the ring. In his more mature years, he was very self-aware and knew the importance of mental health, hence why he speaks about it regularly.

Matt Le Tissier

I first met Matt when he was a guest on one of Dan Emmerson's online shows during lockdown.

To any football fan of a certain age, we remember him as a ridiculously gifted talent on the pitch. One of those once-in-a-generation sportsman who seem to be able to effortlessly break the rules of what we think is actually possible with their awesome skill.

He had also forged a significant career as a pundit on the Sky Soccer Saturday show hosted by the redoubtable Geoff Stelling. This show had been a staple of most football fans on Saturday afternoons for many years.

More important than any of that, though, is the fact that Matt is an exceptionally intelligent, honest and decent man. He had made a stand during the lockdown, pointing out holes in the arguments for the theft of our freedoms, and had moved on from there to be one of the first people raising concerns about the safety of the experimental jabs being rolled out in response to the Pandemic.

Standing up for his right to free speech had cost Matt a hugely lucrative contract with Sky. It had also led to him being labelled a "conspiracy theorist" and "Nutter" by much of the media. Having been a prominent member of a political party written off as "Boggle loons", I could relate to what he had gone through.

We hosted Matt at the Sedgley Working Men's Club in Dudley. The room was absolutely packed with around one hundred and ninety people wedged in. In hindsight, it may have been more financially sensible to charge more than £12 each for the tickets, but part of what we do is to try and make these evenings accessible to ordinary folk, giving them a chance to meet their heroes and allowing us more people to speak to about the charity.

Matt was the perfect guest. He mixed with and chatted with dozens of people before and after the event, posing for dozens of selfies and having time for everyone. The man who had been known to Southampton fans as "Le God" is certainly an approachable and generous person.

During the evening, we spoke at length about his football career, running through some of his most famous goals and discussing many of the great players he had encountered. In the second half of the evening, I took questions from the crowd, with many of them asking about Matt's political views. He answered with such courtesy and thoughtful honesty that I couldn't help thinking he would have made a fantastic political leader.

It also struck me that Matt had lost a very lucrative career in football punditry for expressing his opinions, and yet the highest-paid presenter / Pundit on TV is Gary Lineker. Lineker is far from shy about expressing his opinions, and they are easily classified as left-of-centre and highly political. His colleague Gary Neville openly supports the Labour Party and retains his very lucrative contract on TV. If Matt's opinions cost him his job, it can only be because he is of the Libertarian Right politically. The only conclusion I can reach from this is that free speech is only tolerable in this country as long as you say what the establishment wants you to say.

As you often find with people who are very good at a particular sport, I also learned that Matt had been an exceptional Cricketer and is still a very good tennis player to this day.

A great sportsman and an intelligent and decent man. Matt Le Tissier is a genuinely impressive guy.

Paul Merson

We had another bumper crowd when we hosted Paul Merson.

Paul was another footballer who seemed capable of magic on the pitch, but his life off the field had been very different to Matt Let Tissier's.

Merson was very open about his history of addiction, with gambling being his most notable vice. He has lost huge sums of money gambling and has to go through a great deal of suffering and hardship as a result. In this respect, he was very similar to another of our guests, the legendary Peter Shilton, who spoke with similar brave honesty about his issues with gambling.

Paul Merson and Bill

There were some funny sides to the evening with Paul. He had a huge number of naughty tales that can probably be best described as "laddish" My favourite one was about the occasion that he was sent to a specialist centre for rehabilitation only to find that another guest at the facility was the one, and only Paul Gascoigne. I won't spoil Paul's tales by repeating them all here, but needless to say, his spell in Rehab with Gazza did not achieve the desired effects.

When asked by a member of the audience what he thought about the treatment of Matt Le Tissier, he gave an answer that I think was one of the most sensible and astute things I think I have ever heard. He remarked that Matt was one of the most intelligent people he had ever met, and while he was not in opposition to the comments his colleague had gotten into trouble for, he was also very reliant on keeping his earnings as a pundit. He coined the phrase, "Sometimes it's clever not to be clever" This has stuck with me, and I think it's rather profound. It occurs to me that many of the people who get by in the modern-day world deliberately avoid commenting on controversial issues because they know there will be consequences. This is a very wise approach from Paul, but what does it say about freedom and our democracy?

Meeting Heroes

Our events have afforded me the opportunity to meet several people who were either heroes or influential in my life in my younger years.

The old saying warns us not to meet our heroes for fear of disappointment, but I must say I have found that it is not always true.

One man I was very much looking forward to meeting was Shaun Ryder of Happy Mondays. I have always loved his music and the rebellious approach he has taken to life.

I was very much looking forward to him and was delighted when I agreed on terms with his management company for him to be a guest. Annoyingly, Mr Ryder travels with a road manager.

The Travelling Road manager decided that it was up to him to rip up the terms of what had been agreed and basically ruin the evening. He demanded changes to the timings of the event and dug his heels in, refusing to accept that the paying public would want photographs with the "Madchester" star. This would not have been quite so intolerable had all of the details not been agreed in writing in advance.

The whole event was pretty disastrous, with confusion reigning thanks to the glorified Roadie deciding he was going to take charge of what we could and could not do. I had not expected Shaun Rydder to be an easy guest. After all, he is one of the most anarchic figures in modern music, but it was rendered impossible by the guy who had decided he was going to mother him.

On the other hand, our other guests from the music scene were superb. Bez, Shaun Ryder's notorious bandmate and "Freaky Dancer" in Happy Mondays, was an absolute delight. He turned up with another legend of "Indie" music, Clint Boon of the Inspiral Carpets.

On arrival, Bez was a perfect gentleman. He had time to speak to everyone and was very flexible as to how the evening went. I also fulfilled a lifetime ambition of swigging back a few drinks with him.

Clint conducted the on-stage interview, and he is clearly an accomplished and intelligent performer. They spoke about Happy Mondays and all things to do with the Manchester music scene. During the conversation, Clint revealed that Noel Gallagher of Oasis had worked as a roadie for the Inspiral Carpets. When the time came for Noel to move on to launch his own spectacular but famously fractious career with his brother as the lead of the legendary Oasis, Clint had helped him along his way with contacts and even a sum of cash to help them set up.

We had a brief break, and when the second half of the evening began, it was clear that Bez had liberally partaken in some intoxicating refreshment backstage. I shall not comment on what I believe went on during this interval or what was consumed, as I deliberately made a point of not going there. As an ex-politician, I am fully aware of the benefits and principles of plausible deniability. Let's just say Bez was in even better humour but a little less well-coordinated or capable of remembering what he was saying mid-sentence.

The evening with Bez and Clint was great, and I vividly remember that they both stayed at the venue until absolutely everyone who wanted to speak to them or have a photograph was satisfied.

Our other musical guest was one that I simultaneously looked forward to and dreaded. Jay Aston had been one of the 80s pop superstars and Eurovision winners, Bucks Fizz. Since then, she has had a long career in the industry and is still writing and performing her own songs as well as touring with her old bandmates under the name "The Fizz".

The difficult part of this for me was that, as a young man, Jay had been one of my most idolised crushes. In the world of my teenage crushes, she was only bested by Debbie Harry of Blondie and Susannah Hoffs of the Bangles. She even managed to push Pamela Anderson into fourth place, which, as any teenager of the 80s can agree, is no mean feat. My concern was that at some point while meeting her or, even worse, whilst on stage, I was going to blab out the fact that she had been a poster on my bedroom wall. I can think of a few more embarrassing or downright creepy things to say to someone.

My favourite author, Edgar Allen Poe, wrote a story called "The Imp of the Perverse" In this story, he speaks of "The agent that tempts a person to do things merely because we feel we should not" That whole night, I was definitely haunted by the Imp of the Perverse. It was a constant battle not to almost shout out, "I had a poster of you on my bedroom wall" at the top of my voice. I was so concerned about it that I even abstained from alcohol in order to keep my self-control.

As it turned out, although several decades older and having battled with serious illness, Jay is still a beautiful, stylish and talented lady. My interview with her on stage passed without me making a fool of myself, and she treated the crown to a few of her own songs, which I must admit to being pleasantly surprised by. As a heavy metal fan, I have a cynical view of pop music and singers, but Jay was excellent.

I met a very different kind of hero when I managed to do a deal with David Gower to appear as a guest in Stourbridge. David is one of the greatest cricketers that has ever lived, but more than that, he is an iconic hero stirring memories of the suave and heroic gentlemen cricketers of years gone by.

Whilst the evening was probably not as grand as the kind of evening the great man was used to, he handled the whole evening with the kind of grace and style he used to show whilst elegantly stroking the ball from his bat to the boundary. I'll wager it is the first time that he has been to an event where the food is Pie and Mash, but he ate it and then showed it to the bar waitress, saying, "All gone", very much like a schoolboy showing the matron he had finished his dinner.

The evening was perhaps the most enjoyable I have hosted. I must confess I am wildly biased in this, as cricket is my true love in life. David was sparklingly witty and dealt with questions from the crowd with aplomb.

He told some wonderful stories, including the all-time classic about him renting a flight in a Biplane and buzzing low over a cricket ground whilst England were playing a match. His cavalier style was refreshing and entertaining to listen to, with many tales of rather naughty behaviour being concluded with the catchphrase, "It wasn't well received by the powers that be".

He also told a wonderful story about the great Shane Warne. David had been asked by a journalist if he thought the Ashes contest was a clash between cultures, to which he had replied with a typical offhand, "How can it be a clash of cultures when only one of the countries involved has one?" It had been a light-hearted quip, but our Aussie cousins had not appreciated it. In fact, it was fair to say it had not been "Well received."

David and Shane Warne had always got along really well, and as most people who encountered the great "Warnie" testified, not only was he the greatest spin bowler in history but a really nice guy. However, the first time they met after the Gower witticism about culture, an angry Warnie could be seen striding along the outfield of the cricket pitch, shouting his displeasure. Apparently, the Australian was hurling out a very large number of expletives and was very angry. On getting face-to-face with Gower, the Australian explained how angry he was about the comment that Australia had no culture and then proceeded to continue swearing. The response from the suave England captain was a classic as he simply waited until the end of a particularly long stream of expletives before saying very casually, "Point proved, I believe."

Aside from meeting David Gower, there has only ever been one meeting or event with a star where I have felt nervous or starstruck. This does not mean that I am blasé or arrogant, but don't forget during my time in politics, I had been in the company of Prime Ministers, the Pope, the Queen and various rather grand figures, so it will take quite a lot to phase me now.

Having said that, I will admit that I was very nervous when I met Kenny Hibbitt and John Richards. I attended my first Wolves match at the age of four years old back in 1974 and, over the following decades, was a very regular frequenter of the Molineux stadium, home of the mighty Wolverhampton Wanderers. Much of the early part of my life was spent absolutely idolising Hibbitt, the no-nonsense goal-scoring midfielder, and Richards, the dynamic Striker.

Wolves and the Black Country

When they agreed to do a charity event with us, I was almost overwhelmed with excitement. I recalled a time back in 1980 when my infant school team had won a regional rounders trophy, and we had been awarded our medals by John Richards at the Civic Hall in Wolverhampton. I had been so shy and nervous that I had not dared to look at the great striker as he awarded me my medal. I realised all these years later, not much had changed.

I was delighted when I got to know them and then other famous Wolves stars from the 1970s and later. They were real gentlemen and genuinely delighted to be meeting the fans. They gave the impression of almost being surprised that anyone still remembered them, let alone the hero worship that many fans of my age still harbour.

Listening to the tales told by these veteran football heroes, it was obvious that they had played in much tougher and far less well-renumerated times. The link between them and the fans was still strong because they had lived a life that the fans could relate to, and they had never felt themselves to be better than the thousands of locals who spent their hard-earned money every weekend to support them. It is a sad reality that youngsters of the kind age I was when I first attended a match will never get a chance to meet their heroes in later life as the modern player in the premiership is far more likely to retire in a mansion in sunnier climes than still available to share memories and a pint with their fan's years later.

Most of my engagement with retired footballers has been positive and enjoyable. They hark back to a time when football was still the game of the working man, and in many cases, after retirement, they have had to take jobs in the real world as the pre-Premier league wage levels were not even remotely comparable to the modern-day star.

To Boldly Meet the Greatest Hero in the Galaxy

Although it was not at an event that I organised, I must just tell you about the time I met the greatest hero in the galaxy. Well, I met him twice, actually, so this is an amalgamation of those stories, but I think they will give the right impression of the great man.

I have met James Tiberius Kirk, or as he prefers to be known, the actor William Shatner twice. I am an unashamed Trekkie and attend conventions whenever I can. Yes, I even go part of the way towards fancy dress as well, occasionally donning the Gold Starfleet Command uniform top as worn in the series by Kirk.

Star Trek is arguably the most influential adventure story ever told across multiple series and films. Many people who have gone on to be real-life astronauts have been influenced by the intrepid crew of the Enterprise and their adventures. The series has also had an effect on modern technology; if you doubt me, look at your mobile phone and then watch an episode of the original Star Trek series to see their communicators.

Gene Rodenberry's concept of a ship filled with people of all ethnicities and nations exploring the galaxy was a unique and revolutionary one when it first came out in the 1960s. It was groundbreaking in terms of Race relations. It not only featured American TV's first interracial kiss when Kirk kissed Uhura but when the actress playing Uhura, Nichelle Nicholls, wanted to leave the show, she was persuaded not to by none other than Doctor Martin Luther King.

I know it sounds corny or maybe a little crazy, but I have always based my approach to life on some of the principles of Star Trek and, more specifically, the intrepid Captain Kirk. According to Star Trek law, a young James Kirk had been asked to face a simulation at the academy called the Kobayashi Maru test. To cut a long story short, the aim of the test was to see how a cadet dealt with a situation where the only outcome was certain failure and death. After failing the test several times, the young Kirk broke into the computer program and changed it so there was a chance of victory. It led to the legendary phrases "I don't believe in a no-win scenario" and "there are always possibilities" being uttered. This has influenced my approach to life since I was a very young child watching the programme for the first time. No matter what the odds or how hopeless the situation looked, I always believed there was a way to win, just like my hero, James T Kirk.

With all of this in mind, you can imagine how thrilled I was to get the opportunity to meet William Shatner at a Trek convention. Despite being over ninety years old, Mr Shatner is still remarkably vigorous. He has something of Kirk's air of authority about him, or maybe he was in character for his adoring fans; either way, he was very impressive.

On one occasion, the queue to shake his hand was spiralling out of control, and the stewards in attendance were beginning to panic. Unhesitatingly, he left his spot in the photo area and walked up the line, ushering people into a more orderly queue and advising the stewards of where to stand. He paused for a brief word with some of the fans who had been becoming a little disgruntled and effectively defused the whole situation.

I only spent brief moments with Mr Shatner, but the experience was truly invigorating. Let's not forget that as well as helping to create an iconic character in Star Trek, he has also had a career in TV and film going back some seventy years. His longevity is absolutely miraculous.

The Mad World of Professional Darts

We have engaged in several darts events as part of our fundraising effort. The positive point with darts is that if you get it right, you can attract a huge crowd. The negative points include that you have to put together a bill including current top players, or nobody will attend, and the current players demand huge sums of money.

Other negative points about organising darts events include the fact that the industry is awash with money and therefore awash with con men and some players who act like spoilt babies if they don't get their every desire catered for

One particular con man was an agent who tried to charge us big money for the players he managed and set a date that he knew very well was within a few days of a show they were doing not more than five miles away. It was his intention to ruin our efforts even before we got underway, as his pal organising the other event was keen on the competition.

Another con man was a faded, almost constantly drunk former star player who talked his way into us arranging a number of events with him, then tried to demand cancellation fees when, with several weeks' notice, we had to cancel the events as literally nobody wanted to buy a ticket to come and see him. Keep in mind no contract had been signed, quite possibly because he wanted payment in cash, which I can only speculate might have been an attempt at tax avoidance.

On other occasions, I have had to confront players and explain to them that their role was to entertain the crowd rather than sit and get drunk whilst being waited on. This is not the behaviour of all of them or anywhere near half of them, but a significant proportion of them suffer from serious delusions of grandeur.

Players

On each of these occasions, I have been forced to behave in a way I desperately wanted to leave behind. I have tried very hard to be pleasant and reasonable in my business dealings as it is one of my biggest hopes to leave the image of a nasty political war horse behind. However, when the occasion required it, I reverted back to character and left people in no doubt that they were dealing with someone whose most notable talent was the ability to win battles and drink his opponent's tears.

I have made some great friends in the world of darts, including Jamie Caven, without whom we could never have made the contacts to get any shows underway, Steve (The Bronzed Adonis) Beaton and the brilliant Mervyn King, amongst others.

They have all been hugely supportive and helpful. I have to give a particular credit to Mervyn. For many years, he has been the pantomime villain for darts fans due to his stoic demeanour and no-nonsense approach. I can honestly say no public image can be further from the truth, with his catchphrase being "Get me a pint of cider or I'm going home" Merv has a classic dry sense of humour and is a joy to know. He is also the only one of our sports guests who has actually taken the time to come along and see our charity coaching sessions in action.

For those who haven't been to a darts exhibition, they can go one of two ways. They can be an immaculately organised but rather sterile event, or they can be a boozy, wild, free-for-all. No prizes for guessing how my events turned out.

I'm pretty sure all of the paying customers had great times, but for those of us doing the volunteer organising and general work, they were extremely demanding trials of strength and patience. On one occasion in Shrewsbury, we were short of money to cover our costs on the night. It meant that after five hours of constant walking up and down stairs and making sure everything was running smoothly, I had to literally sprint up a hill into the town to withdraw more money from a cashpoint. For a man of my size and years sprinting up hills isn't a great idea at the best of times, and I lived to regret it when I developed crippling cramps in both legs on the way back down the hill. I somehow managed to limp my way to the venue and resolve all outstanding issues. The whole event had been nine hours nonstop hard work, and I was delighted to get to my bed, which was in a room above a pub at about 1 am. I wasn't quite so delighted when a choir of drunken rugby lads started singing their full repertoire outside the window with a five or six-song set starting and ending with rousing versions of Jerusalem. Posh people are an odd lot when they are drunk.

On several occasions, I have worked with Darts legend Adrian Lewis. Despite not being at the heady levels he was at a few years ago, Adrian is still massively popular. He is also, according to some people, very similar looking to me. This has been a source of great fun when I have been approached by drunken darts fans asking for autographs or a quick game, particularly as I am probably the world's worst darts thrower. Adrian is a tough character who has had his share of showdowns on the oche, and there have been times when we have had our moments of disagreement, but he has always been a man I can have a straight conversation with, and I very much respect him for that.

The biggest darts star we have dealt with is the brilliant Gary Anderson. A tough, gruff Scotsman, Gary has been and still is one of the world's greatest players. Despite his warlike reputation, I found him to be an absolute pleasure to work with. We are of a similar age, and I've always felt we have a great deal in common in the way we approach work and life. On one occasion, after a darts event in Shropshire, I received a frantic call from Gary's agent saying he had lost his phone that night. I engaged in a thorough sweep of the area with no joy, even travelling back the following day. Fortunately, it had been found and handed in at a nearby pub, and the clientele were honest enough to let us know. Whenever I speak to Gary, we laugh about that frantic search, and it's a memory that will stay with me for a long while as it is no easy task to literally walk the length of an entire small town searching in gutters and any other likely area for a lost phone.

The darts events have been a huge team effort, as has the charity overall. I have been very lucky to have a group of friends who throw their weight into supporting what we do. It really can be a mammoth undertaking, but at times, it reminds me a little of the good old days of UKIP in as much as it is ordinary working-class people coming together to give their all to try and make a difference.

So, there you have it. I have tried my best to give you an honest history of how this Rhino crashed through the looking glass.

I would never have dreamed as a young man that I would be writing of this kind of experience as I approach my fifty-fourth year. I have certainly proved the Star Trek line that "There are always possibilities" but probably failed to prove that there is "No such thing as a no-win scenario."

I still hold very strong political views. I sincerely believe that the world is heading into a new era where freedom is no longer going to be allowed in the way we have recognised it in the past. Advances in technology mean surveillance and monitoring techniques will make sure Big Brother always has his eye on us. Even more disturbingly, the drive towards Digital IDs will mean that all of our personal information will be more available than ever before, whilst the efforts to eradicate cash and replace it with digital currency render us more susceptible to financial control than at any time in our history.

Governments have seen that with the right fearmongering and control tactics, people will give up freedoms that took centuries to achieve in the blink of an eye. Indeed, modern thinking appears to consider freedom as more dangerous than valuable. After all, the followers of the Green cult and its somewhat strange figurehead, Greta Thunberg, believe that free markets and people making their own decisions are a massive contributory factor to global warming and mass extinction events. These Green-based views are becoming more mainstream all the time with the backing of huge global corporations who can see very obvious opportunities for profit and control as a result.

Freedom of speech and opinion is gradually being outlawed for fear it may cause offence. The days when the ideas expressed in Voltaire's famous quote, "I may not agree with what you have to say, but I will defend to the death your right to say it", seem long past. Now we have nebulous laws covering Hate speech and other rather ill-defined legal reasons to stop people saying what they think.

Free market economics seems to have been abandoned not only in practise but as an idea to argue for. The political debate now appears to be about how much the state should grow, how high the tax burden should be and which protectionist block to join with. Nobody is effectively or publicly espousing the arguments that free peoples and free markets lead to better living standards and growth for us all.

With the certain knowledge that I am in a very small minority of people who share my political views and that there is definitely no political party that is either on the same page as me in terms of ideology or that would actually want this old trouble-make anyway it's clear that there is no prospect of me ever returning to party politics.

This is a real shame in that after the intense volume of experience I have gained over those wild years between 2010 and 2020; I would probably be a far better and more effective politician now than I was then. One of the advantages of having now emerged from the looking glass is that I can appreciate and understand this and move on.

My career is now all about running and funding the Support Futures Charity. It is a way that I can make a difference and help people to help themselves. I always regretted not having more time to spend on constituency work when I was an elected politician, so in a way, I am making up for lost time now. It is also immensely satisfying to help people work on their mental and physical health to get to a point where they can see how huge their own potential is. I know first-hand that there are still archaic class barriers in the UK. Many of the people we see during our work with the charity are immensely talented but simply don't believe that the system will give them a chance. The often feel condemned to living a life on benefits never having the self-belief to reach higher. Our work helps them get to a healthier point in mind and body, which allows them to take a more positive approach. It's an absolute joy to see the results.

As regards wild nights of drunken adventures and womanising, I can safely say they are things of the past. Please don't misunderstand me when I say this; it doesn't mean that I don't like a few beers or a pretty woman anymore, but they are no longer the motivating or dominant factors in my life.

The long periods of enforced inactivity during lockdown led to a large amount of contemplation, leading to more self-awareness. I look back on the person in the adventures documented in this book and hardly recognise him. Time and experience really do change a person, and we can only hope it's for the better.

Only recently, I was spoken to by a woman who said she had followed my exploits from afar and found me very attractive. I was rather flattered and asked her why; her response, with no attempt at an insult or humour, was that she found it exciting to know someone who corresponded with the textbook definition of a psychopath!

Maybe I have behaved and projected myself in a manner that may suggest a somewhat unusual state of mind over the years. During the writing of this book, the thought occurred to me more than once that these weren't the actions of someone who was in a particularly stable frame of mind.

I am very fortunate to still have my wonderful parents, who, despite being of a rather mature vintage now, are still very important parts of my life and still have the ability to absolutely thrash me at card games and board games, including Scrabble, when we get together.

I also have a son, James, who was nineteen years old at the time of writing. A big, strong, handsome and bright lad, he is a credit to his mother, who brought him up while I was off the scene living the life that you have read about. One of the great advantages of living a life outside of politics is that I can now enjoy more time with him. As for his mother, Nikki is yet another of the women who I did not treat fairly in my younger years, but unlike many of the others, she has remained a good and valued friend.

As this book has made very clear, I have led a life full of incidents, adventures and mistakes. I've been partying at historic events and met exceptional and famous people. It hasn't always gone to plan, and in many cases, it's been totally out of control.

Life is for the living, and I have lived mine to the maximum. Hopefully, the mark I have left has been more positive than negative, and you have enjoyed being part of the adventure while reading this book.

I have now emerged from the Looking Glass, and my plan is to live a far calmer and more relaxed life. That is certainly the plan but let's face it, there are always possibilities.

THE BRUGES GROUP

The Bruges Group is an independent all-party think tank. Set up in 1989, its founding purpose was to resist the encroachments of the European Union on our democratic self-government. The Bruges Group spearheaded the intellectual battle to win a vote to leave the European Union and against the emergence of a centralised EU state. With personal freedom at its core, its formation was inspired by the speech of Margaret Thatcher in Bruges in September 1988 where the Prime Minister stated, "We have not successfully rolled back the frontiers of the State in Britain only to see them re-imposed at a European level."

We now face a more insidious and profound challenge to our liberties – the rising tide of intolerance. The Bruges Group challenges false and damaging orthodoxies that suppress debate and incite enmity. It will continue to direct Britain's role in the world, act as a voice for the Union, and promote our historic liberty, democracy, transparency, and rights. It spearheads the resistance to attacks on free speech and provides a voice for those who value our freedoms and way of life.

WHO WE ARE

Founder President:
The Rt Hon. The Baroness Thatcher
of Kesteven LG, OM, FRS

Vice-President:
The Rt Hon. Lord Lamont of Lerwick

Chairman:
Barry Legg

Director:
Robert Oulds MA, FRSA

Washington D.C. Representative:
John O'Sullivan CBE

Founder Chairman:
Lord Harris of High Cross

Former Chairmen:
Dr Brian Hindley, Dr Martin Holmes
& Professor Kenneth Minogue

Academic Advisory Council:
Professor Tim Congdon
Dr Richard Howarth
Professor Patrick Minford
Andrew Roberts
Martin Howe, KC
John O'Sullivan, CBE

Sponsors and Patrons:
E P Gardner Dryden
Gilling-Smith
Lord Kalms
David Caldow
Andrew Cook
Lord Howard
Brian Kingham
Lord Pearson of Rannoch
Eddie Addison
Ian Butler
Thomas Griffin
Lord Young of Graffham
Michael Fisher
Oliver Marriott
Hon. Sir Rocco Forte
Graham Hale
Michael Freeman
Richard E.L. Smith

MEETINGS

The Bruges Group holds regular high–profile public meetings, seminars, debates and conferences. These enable influential speakers to contribute to the European debate. Speakers are selected purely by the contribution they can make to enhance the debate.

For further information about the Bruges Group, to attend our meetings, or join and receive our publications, please see the membership form at the end of this paper. Alternatively, you can visit our website www.brugesgroup.com or contact us at info@brugesgroup.com.

Contact us
For more information about the Bruges Group please contact:
Robert Oulds, Director
The Bruges Group, 246 Linen Hall, 162-168 Regent Street, London W1B 5TB
Tel: +44 (0)20 7287 4414 Email: info@brugesgroup.com

www.brugesgroup.com